D0428607

IN THE ARENA

IN THE ARENA

A Memoir of the 20th Century

Caspar W. Weinberger

with GRETCHEN ROBERTS

For Emily Pike – with my great appreciation for all you did for our Party + our State

Cap

Since 1947
REGNERY PUBLISHING, INC.
An Eagle Publishing Company • Washington, DC

Copyright © 2001 by Caspar W. Weinberger and Gretchen Roberts

All rights reserved. No part of this publication may be reproduced or transmitted in any form or by any means electronic or mechanical, including photocopy, recording, or any information storage and retrieval system now known or to be invented, without permission in writing from the publisher, except by a reviewer who wishes to quote brief passages in connection with a review written for inclusion in a magazine, newspaper, or broadcast.

Weinberger, Caspar W.
    In the arena : a memoir of the twentieth century / Caspar W. Weinberger, with Gretchen Roberts.
        p. cm.
    Includes bibliographical references and index.
    ISBN 0-89526-166-9
        1. Weinberger, Caspar W. 2. Cabinet officers—United States—Biography. 3. United States. Dept. of Defense—Officials and employees—Biography. 4. United States—Politics and government—1945–1989. 5. United States—Foreign relations—1945–1989. 6. United States—Military relations. 7. Weinberger, Caspar W.—Friends and associates—Anecdotes. I. Roberts, Gretchen. II. Title.

        E840.8.W44 A3 2001
        973.927′092—dc21
        [B]
                                                                    2001048334

Published in the United States by
Regnery Publishing, Inc.
An Eagle Publishing Company
One Massachusetts Avenue, NW
Washington, DC 20001
www.regnery.com

Distributed to the trade by
National Book Network
4720-A Boston Way
Lanham, MD 20706

Printed on acid-free paper
Manufactured in the United States of America

10 9 8 7 6 5 4 3 2

Book design by Sun Young Park
Set in Berkeley

Books are available in quantity for promotional or premium use. Write to Director of Special Sales, Regnery Publishing, Inc., One Massachusetts Avenue, NW, Washington, DC 20001 for information on discounts and terms or call (202) 216-0600.

DEDICATION

Eleven years ago I dedicated my first book, *Fighting for Peace: Seven Critical Years in the Pentagon*, to my wife in these words:

"And then there is Jane, my wife, who was there at the beginning when we were both in the army, and who was at the next beginning running my first campaign for the California legislature, and who is always a constant source of the support and inspiration we all need, and a constant example of the courage we all should have—and it is to her I dedicate this book."

The past decade has only reinforced the feelings and opinions I expressed then.

Jane has continued all her activities: her writing and publishing many books, her gardening, the organization and management of our homes, her splendid entertaining, and the good she does for so many people in all walks of life. She is still very much the constant source of support and inspiration we all need, and still a constant example of the courage we all should have.

It is to her I repeat these words, and to her I dedicate my autobiography.

Contents

PREFACE

"My God, you're going to live forever!" Katharine Hepburn's mother exclaimed when she read my palm at her home in 1936, after being exposed to the conservative views of a very young Harvard student—views quite repugnant to her liberal soul.

I have indeed lived a very long time since that summer day, though not quite forever, and I have known numerous joys and challenges and many extraordinary people.

Since I always prefer reading first-person accounts of events to second- or thirdhand versions, I decided to set down on paper my own recollections while my memory still serves me reasonably well. Experiences always seem to me much more vivid when told by someone who was actually there, and I am fortunate to have been a participant in a number of exciting activities, particularly within government. I hope that in this memoir, I have succeeded in conveying a real sense of what it was like to tramp through the jungles of New Guinea in wartime; to feel for the first time the electricity that Ronald

Reagan brought to any gathering he attended; to struggle with congressional committees over funds; to help plan military actions; and to struggle with other members of the administration over policies such as Strategic Defense and support of the British in the Falklands, as well as the daily combination of minutiae and great issues that are the staple of holding an office.

It is my hope that this book will be more practical and compelling than academic in tone. Policy issues are certainly examined, but in the context of my own experience rather than from a theoretical standpoint.

Undoubtedly, there will be people who remember things differently than I do, or who disagree with some of what I have written in these pages, but my purpose here is only to record some of the history I saw, as *I* remember it.

Unlike my first book, *Fighting for Peace*, which focused primarily on my years at the Pentagon, this book covers a much longer time span—more than three-quarters of a century—from my childhood in San Francisco to the present. This volume is organized, for the most part, chronologically.

A common thread throughout the story of my life is my abiding interest in politics and the workings of government. Since I was very young, I have been fascinated both by the ideals upon which our country was founded and by how our democracy generally works. As early as 1924, I followed the national party conventions closely, and, at the age of fifteen, I asked a congressman to send me the *Congressional Record*, which I read avidly and daily. By the time I was in high school, I rewrote my school's student constitution, modeling it after the U.S. Constitution, and many of my school papers reflected my strong opinions, even then, about the virtues of a market economy and the inherent evils of repression and big government.

I became more outspoken with my conservative views by the time I was in college at Harvard, and expressed them, no doubt at tiresome length, both in classes and in editorials for the daily *Harvard Crimson*. My first direct (though quite limited) participation in national politics came during this time, when I served as an usher at the 1936 Republican convention. In 1938, my last year in college, and the next three years of law school, my interest in domestic politics was completely superseded by deep interest in, anxiety about, and incessant discussion of the war.

It came as no surprise to anyone who had to listen to me then that I enlisted in the infantry almost as soon as I had finished law school in 1941. Indeed it was only my father's strong and logical persuasion that kept me in law school. My desire to serve my country and her allies in World War II was very strong indeed, and was fueled by Winston Churchill's eloquent and inspirational rallying cries against appeasing Germany. I considered my participation in the war effort not merely a duty, but a privilege—an opportunity to further a noble cause in which I believed passionately.

I felt that same exhilaration of being a part of something larger than myself, being a part of history, throughout my civilian career in government. A few years after the war was over, I embarked on my political career—first as an assemblyman in the California legislature, then in the ranks of the California Republican Party, and later, as a cabinet member in the administrations of Governor Reagan, President Nixon, President Ford, and President Reagan. My service in these various capacities was periodically interrupted by my return to work in the private sector (which, admittedly, had its financial advantages), but I always found public service far more rewarding and satisfying. Each post brought exciting new challenges and a sense of honor that I felt could not be matched outside of government. And yet, paradoxically perhaps, I always wanted government to be small and nonintrusive.

In the process of writing this book, I have drawn on the extensive collection of personal papers in the Library of Congress (it seems I

saved nearly everything!), and on the recollections of a great many
people who have been subjected to me or whose lives intersected
mine over the years, to help spark my memory. As I tried to call up my
own reminiscences, I often found myself thinking of John Buchan's
autobiography and particularly its title, *Memory, Hold the Door*.

As anyone who read the introduction of my first book knows,
Theodore Roosevelt is a great hero of mine, and his words best
summed up my wish to be in the arena, and not in the stands with
the timid souls:

> Service is rendered...by the man who...is actually in the
> arena, whose face is marred by dust and sweat and blood; who
> strives valiantly; who errs, and comes short again and again,
> because there is no effort without error and shortcomings; but who
> does actually strive to do the deeds; who knows the great enthusi-
> asms, the great devotions; who spends himself in a worthy cause;
> who at the best knows in the end the triumph of high achievement
> and who, at the worst, if he fails, at least fails while daring greatly,
> so that his place shall never be with those cold and timid souls who
> know neither victory nor defeat.

I originally thought that the title *In the Arena* best expressed my
belief that one should be down on the playing field, taking an active
part in great events.

However, shortly after my publisher accepted the title and began
the long task of entering it into all the various systems in the book-
selling network, I found that Charlton Heston had already used that
title, as indeed had Richard Nixon some years before.

I told my publisher I wanted to change it and call the book *And
Not to Yield*, from *Ulysses*, a favorite Tennyson poem:

One equal temper of heroic hearts,

Made weak by time and fate, but strong in will

To strive, to seek, to find, and not to yield.

But apparently, mechanically, it is virtually impossible to change a title once it is selected and initially advertised.

So with my apologies to my friend Charlton Heston, whom I have greatly admired for many years, we will have to continue our joint use of the same title.

When I give speeches, I always try to include a question period, because that way I am reasonably sure that at least one person in the audience is interested in what I am saying. Unfortunately, there is no such opportunity when writing a book, so I can only hope that what is of interest to me is also interesting to the reader. So without more, let us begin.

IN THE ARENA

PROLOGUE

*T*he air in Washington was crisp and cold on January 20, 1981, and a gray blanket of clouds stretched to the horizon. For the first time, a presidential inauguration ceremony was taking place on the West Front of the Capitol, at the request of President-elect Ronald Reagan. West, after all, is the direction of California, indeed, of America. Thousands of people covered the lawn that sloped down from the inaugural platform built out over the west steps of the Capitol. Stands were also banked steeply up behind the platform, where sat, shoulder to shoulder, members of the outgoing Carter administration and the incoming Reagan appointees. President Carter looked gaunt and weary—a defeated man in more ways than one.

But when President-elect Reagan took the inaugural oath, his voice infused the air with his characteristic confidence and sparkling vigor, lifting the pall and almost literally parting the clouds. As I had witnessed many times before, Reagan effortlessly summoned brightness; a golden stream of sunlight broke through the dark sky, first shining only on him, then showering everyone present. It was as if he carried the sun in his breast pocket everywhere he went, warming everyone around him with the hope and faith and optimism that were as much a part of him as his modest smile.

After concluding the oath of office by adding, "So help me God," the new president began his inaugural address. As he spoke, I began to reflect on how I came to be there, sitting behind a new president as his secretary-designate of defense.

> The orderly transfer of authority as called for in the Constitution routinely takes place, as it has for almost two centuries, and few of us stop to think how unique we really are. In the eyes of the world, this every-four-year ceremony we accept as normal is nothing less than a miracle.

My mind drifted back to nights in San Francisco, over fifty years earlier, when my father would sit between my brother's and my beds and weave for us the exciting story of the Constitution. He made it come alive for us, telling us how the document was drafted, the points of debate, how agreement finally was reached, and how close we had come to the whole convention's dissolving in disagreement— an outcome that would have left us simply a group of separate, small, impotent states. And now, here I was, watching, and indeed part of, this quadrennial miracle. It was the latter that I found most difficult to realize. For to a far greater degree than in previous inaugurations, I felt the sudden transfer from spectator to being part of the cere- mony itself. I suppose I felt the sudden onrush of responsibility.

The president had turned to the problem of inflation—the cruelest tax—which had been gripping the country for at least half a decade. When he said, "Ending inflation means freeing all Americans from the terror of runaway living costs," I thought back to my days at the Office of Management and Budget (OMB), under President Richard

Nixon. We believed that a large part of the inflation problem was caused by runaway government expenditures. I recalled many days, and nights, when we struggled to roll back spending—paring departmental budget requests and eliminating ineffective, redundant, or unnecessary programs—only to be overruled by Congress (and sometimes by the president). Particularly, I had a brief recollection of the time when, as director of OMB, I had pointed out to President Nixon that a proposal to increase Social Security benefits was not justified because we had recently increased them beyond what even inflation required. "But, Cap, it is an election year." The tone of that message precluded any idea of an appeal I might have had in mind.

I also remembered President Reagan's unprecedented feat when he had been governor and I was director of finance: the state's constitutional requirement for a balanced budget had forced him to ask for a tax increase, but, thereafter, we were so successful in cutting state spending that he was able to return the substantial resulting surplus to the taxpayers of California. "If government is running a surplus, taxes are too high," he said then. "Government is not in the business of earning income." He had been willing to defy the conventional wisdom and make cuts where needed despite the presumed popularity of many programs. He understood that government had its place, but that place was primarily protecting and not burdening the American people.

I again focused on his inaugural speech as he was saying, "It's not my intention to do away with government. It is rather to make it work—work with us, not over us; to stand by our side, not ride on our back." I knew that if anyone could tame inflation and slow the cost and growth of government, Reagan could.

President Reagan did indeed make us feel good about ourselves, and he knew that when Americans regained pride and self-confidence, there was no limit to what we could do. His words and this deep belief could bring out the best in people.

With all the creative energy at our command, let us begin an era
of national renewal. Let us renew our determination, our courage,
and our strength. And let us renew our faith and our hope.

Then he spoke of everyday American heroes who exemplify these
very qualities and who, together, make up our national character. I
thought about some of my own heroes—Theodore Roosevelt and
Winston Churchill—leaders who inspired by their example and who
rallied nations to their highest callings. But those were not the kind
of heroes President Reagan was speaking of that day. He was speaking of people like my mother and father, who quietly enabled their
sons to be educated at Harvard. And not only was I able to attend
Harvard for four years of undergraduate study and three years of law
school, but my parents also made it possible for me to make those
long train trips across the country four times a year so that I could
spend Christmases and summers at home. All of this during the
Great Depression.

Then, I heard the president repeat what he had many times discussed with me: how vital it was that we rebuild our military strength
and credibility as an ally. As he spoke, a scene from my training in
the army during World War II flashed across my mind. We had been
so unprepared for war, and so lacking in basic war materiel, that we
had to train with World War I–era rifles, or even wooden replicas of
them, and blocks of wood labeled "hand grenade" in white paint.

We will again be the exemplar of freedom and a beacon of hope
for those who do not now have freedom. . . . As for the enemies of
freedom, those who are potential adversaries, they will be
reminded that peace is the highest aspiration of the American people. We will negotiate for it, sacrifice for it; we will not surrender
for it, now or ever.

Our forbearance should never be misunderstood. Our reluctance for conflict should not be misjudged as a failure of will. When action is required to preserve our national security, we will act. We will maintain sufficient strength to prevail if need be, knowing that if we do so we have the best chance of never having to use that strength.

Above all, we must realize that no arsenal or no weapon in the arsenals of the world is so formidable as the will and moral courage of free men and women.

The cadences in that matchless voice rolled on, and I could almost feel the eagerness of the crowd's response. What he was saying was what Americans had been waiting to hear. The president was pointing the way for what we desperately needed to do at the Pentagon— the effort that he intended me to lead as his secretary of defense. The vast responsibility with which I was entrusted swept over me again. I still was not sure why the president had chosen me, but I felt a renewed determination to do what he and I knew the country— indeed the world—most needed.

At that moment, President Reagan read from the diary of Martin Treptow, a World War I infantryman:

My Pledge:

America must win this war. Therefore I will work, I will save, I will sacrifice, I will endure, I will fight cheerfully and do my utmost, as if the issue of the whole struggle depended on me alone.

I knew again that kinship I always felt for the infantry and the pride that I had served in it so long ago.

But as daunting as our task may have been in 1981, President Reagan's imperishable optimism and confidence made it all seem possible if we only worked at it hard enough. He had always had the

---

ability to imbue his audience with the same spirit he had, an ability that was evident from the first time I saw his smile light up the room at a political rally in California years earlier. As he concluded his inaugural address, he lifted us all to that higher plane:

> The crisis we are facing today... requires... our best effort and our willingness to believe in ourselves and to believe in our capacity to perform great deeds, to believe that together with God's help we can and will resolve the problems which now confront us.

Filled with this exhilarating hope (tempered by vague reservations about my ability to do all of this), I took one more look out over our beautiful capital city, with its gleaming monuments to the great people who ensured the beginning and the continuity of our republic, and I recalled the last line of Arthur Hugh Clough's poem that Winston Churchill quoted when World War II looked its darkest: "But westward, look, the land is bright."

For me, the West represented much of my own personal history and the forces in my life that had brought me to this day. My abiding interest in government had been formed in my San Francisco childhood, and grew continuously, there and during my years in the East at Harvard, and through my army service in the South Pacific, and up and down California as a legislator and state finance director. I always knew I wanted to serve in government, and had already served in the army and at the federal level under Presidents Nixon and Ford. But I never imagined I would serve as the secretary of defense, at such a critical time in our history.

From the inaugural platform, we moved back into the Capitol, where the Congressional Inaugural Committee gave the traditional luncheon in honor of the new president and vice president in one of the large caucus rooms. It was there that President Reagan received word, and was able to announce, that the fifty-two American hostages who had been held for over a year in Iran were on their way home.* I believe this came about largely because the captors knew full well that President Reagan would not stand idly by while American citizens were held by kidnappers. To others, it was evident that Iran had great contempt for former president Carter.†

Whatever the reason, the hostages' release was an auspicious beginning for the Reagan administration and was particularly welcome after the president's uplifting inaugural speech. But later, as I rode down Capitol Hill and along Pennsylvania Avenue to the inaugural reviewing stand in front of the White House, and during the long afternoon parade that followed, my thoughts were not about the pageantry but about the tasks ahead—and where it all began.

---

* One of the most moving events I experienced as secretary of defense was on January 27, 1981, when I had the great privilege of helping to welcome the hostages home. I flew by helicopter with Vice President Bush, Al Haig, Howard Baker, and Tip O'Neill to Andrews Air Force Base in Maryland and formed part of a receiving line on the tarmac to greet them. As stirring as it was for *us*, their emotion far exceeded anything we could have been feeling, and it was expressed differently in each person. Some shouted for joy. Some kissed the ground. Some wept openly. Some still wore the mask of weary stoicism.

They had undoubtedly changed because of their ordeal, but they were coming home to a changed country as well. There was new hope, new confidence, new patriotism, ushered in by Ronald Reagan, and I think they could feel it from the moment they stepped off the plane.

The compassion of the American people was also apparent as we all rode in a bus motorcade to the White House for an official welcoming ceremony with the president. Lining the route were thousands of countrymen waving flags and holding signs, an overwhelming outpouring for the freed hostages.

On the South Lawn of the White House, along with families, friends, government officials, a military honor guard, and surviving members of the attempted rescue mission, they met their new president face-to-face—the man whose resolve and strength of character, I believe, were the catalysts for the hostages' release.

† Peter Goldman illustrated this well in the February 2, 1981, *Newsweek*: "Teheran, having helped in [Carter's] ruin, piled on a final insult by holding the freedom flight on the ground until just after the rite of succession and so depriving Carter of a bow and a bit of refracted glory."

Chapter 1

A California Childhood

his memoir begins during the First World War. Nineteen-seventeen was the year the United States reluctantly joined the three-year-old "war to end all wars" in Europe. German submarine attacks on British and American merchant and passenger ships finally convinced President Wilson that we could no longer ignore events an ocean away. He was well aware of the strong isolationist sentiment in this country, and for that reason, and also because of the vague hope (which he called "idealism") that events in Europe would make it unnecessary to decide, he had hesitated and displayed the indecisiveness and weakness that so enraged Theodore Roosevelt. Particularly galling to TR and those who thought Germany was wholly to blame was Wilson's insistence on America's fighting as an "associated power," not a full ally of Great Britain and France.

That same year also saw the birth of the world's first Communist state—the USSR.

San Francisco in 1917 was settling into maturity after the bawdy opiate of the Gold Rush and the devastating 1906 earthquake and fire that had shattered all the illusions of invincibility with which San Franciscans cloaked their idea of their city.

But the Panama-Pacific Exposition in 1915, with all of its fantastic buildings and ethereal lights, was San Francisco's declaration to the world that it not only had survived but had triumphed over even such devastation as the earthquake and fire had wrought.

Indeed, Californians have always possessed indomitable optimism and a pioneer spirit—as did my father, who moved to San Francisco in the early teens of the century, because he felt that Colorado was getting too crowded!

So, when I was born in my parents' San Francisco home in 1917, I, by right of birth, was naturally endowed with this generally sunny, optimistic nature.

I was named Caspar, after a great friend of my mother's from Denver, Mrs. Stanley Caspar, who became my godmother.

It was my father who first called me Cap. There was a novel about San Francisco shipping life at that time called *Cappy Rix*. The Cappy Rix character in the book was a skipper of one of the ships, and for some reason, my father started calling me Cappy, and then Cap. Later, in grammar school, I was often teased about my unusual name. I told my tormentors they were just jealous because they did not have a unique name, but that did not seem to deter them. Finally a small fight settled the matter. Maybe this was the beginning of a feeling that occasionally confrontation is better than compromise.

My father's father, Nathan Weinberger, emigrated from what was then Bohemia in the late 1800s and opened a general store—a small forerunner of the department store—in the small mining town of Idaho Springs, Colorado, a few miles from Denver. My father, Herman, was born there. He supported himself while he was in high school by working nights as an operator at the town's telephone exchange. He was always fascinated by, and good at—then and later—working with all things electrical. In the town telephone office he rigged up a system that would ring a bell and wake him up whenever a call came in. That way, he got at least *some* sleep on a bunk that he had also constructed. The telephone and electricity were the high technology of that time. Today my father would have been a skilled and fascinated user of computers, the Internet, and cyberspace. In retrospect, I have wondered why my father chose the law rather than some scientific or technological pursuit as his lifework.

In 1904 my father went to the University of Colorado in Boulder. To help put himself through college, he ran a successful boardinghouse for students, ordering the food and hiring the cooks. He also edited the *Coloradoan*, the class album, and ran the school newspaper, the *Silver and Gold*. In addition, he was involved and successful in debate contests. My father, in a quiet but determined way, was always striving. He completed the university's A.B. and LL.B. programs in six years instead of seven by taking his last year of college and his first year of law school in the same year.

During one summer in law school, he served as a clerk to the Judicial Committee of the Colorado legislature. After graduation, he practiced law with a partner for a couple of years in Boulder, and at the same time he was appointed general manager of student activities at the university. It was during that time that he met my mother, Cerise Carpenter Hampson, who was a young, talented violin artist and teacher from Denver.

Shortly thereafter, my father went to California to practice law. He soon found a job as a very junior attorney and manager of the office boys at the San Francisco law firm of Chickering & Gregory. He lived in a boardinghouse and walked downtown (more than twenty blocks) every day to the firm's offices in the Merchants Exchange Building at California and Montgomery Streets, in the heart of San Francisco's financial district.

Some of his friends and classmates told him and me later that he would have undoubtedly become governor of Colorado had he stayed and followed the well-recognized paths to political success there. Indeed, many years later, when a not-too-brilliant classmate *was* elected governor, my father expressed this thought himself—but not with much regret.

In January 1913 he returned briefly to Denver to marry my mother and bring her to San Francisco, where they rented a small house on Tenth Avenue in the Sunset, an older, moderately priced area of San Francisco. My father continued as an associate at Chickering & Gregory, but left in 1918 to open his own law office (in the same building), where he practiced for the rest of his life.

My father felt responsible for all his family members, no matter how distant. I, on the other hand, did not. It seemed to me that some relative of his was always showing up, and it was my father's instinct and practice to entertain them, with dinners at home or long drives around the city. My father was very proud of San Francisco and always showed it off to visitors with a slightly proprietary air. I cared little for those visits by relatives, frequently pointing out that they were relatives only by an "accident of birth." I particularly disliked it when they smoked long, evil-smelling cigars in our car. I fear I was just not nice about family.

But perhaps a couple of them deserve mention. Of my father's two brothers and three sisters, two stand out in my mind. Bella was deaf, and quite a remarkable lady—she learned to read lips and taught school in New York City. I visited her there a few times when I was attending Harvard and was always amazed at her ability to read lips and at her courage. Another sister, Luella, married a man named Harry McNeil. They lived in Sheboygan, Wisconsin, and had a son, Don, who later hosted a famous radio program, which some mid-westerners might remember: *Don McNeil's Breakfast Club.*

My mother was an only child, the daughter of Charles Marshall Hampson and the former Lillian Louise Carpenter of Denver. Charles, whom I always called Charlie, was a successful mining engineer who patented a few of his inventions, including a railroad turntable. His wife, my grandmother, always called "Mumsie," was an active newspaper reporter and writer for Denver's *Rocky Mountain News*. She was a spirited, modern lady for her time and drove to her various assignments in Denver's first electric auto.

My mother's inclinations were more musical, and when she was very young she learned to play the violin. In fact, at the tender age of fourteen, at her own request, she went to Leipzig, Germany, to study violin. Mumsie accompanied her to Baltimore, and from there she set out alone on a transatlantic ship, not knowing German or the family with whom she was to stay. But she spent a very fulfilling year or two there, studying under a pupil of the renowned violinist Leopold Auer.

After returning to the States, she gave some concerts and taught violin, both in Denver and at the Grand Island College Conservatory of Music in Grand Island, Nebraska, before she married my father and moved to California. After that she gave up her career, played the violin less and less, and concentrated entirely on homemaking and raising her children.

Mother was close to her parents, and shortly after I was born, they moved to San Francisco as well. They were frequently at our home, and some of my earliest memories are of sitting on my grandfather Charlie's lap at our house. He had a wonderful Charles Evans Hughes–type beard and moustache, and altogether was a most impressive figure. At that late stage of his life, after retirement from all his engineering activities, he started selling life insurance door-to-door and office-to-office—something at which he excelled and which he apparently genuinely enjoyed. He studied the whole insurance business thoroughly, leaving several old texts on the subject in our library. He was a patient, devoted grandfather, and I have only the happiest memories of him.

My older brother, Peter, was born on Halloween Day in 1914. He was more outgoing and venturesome by far than I, as well as much more handsome and athletic. We didn't do very many of the same things, especially as we got older. By the time he was in high school, he had largely broken away from home—always going out with his friends (and, I'm sure, even with *girls*—creatures who terrified me at the time). I still did not see Peter much when later we roomed together at Harvard. He did his own thing, and I was still very shy and quite overwhelmed with the volume and difficulty of my studies and, later, with my virtually full-time preoccupation with the *Harvard Crimson*. But although he and I were quite different, he was a wonderful brother. I recall how vigorously he worked for me when I ran for office years later, walking the San Francisco precincts and putting in many hours campaigning in my behalf.

On religious matters, many people assumed that I was brought up in the Jewish faith, but I was not, and neither was my father. Two or three generations back, in Bohemia, there had apparently been some kind of quarrel in his family over various factions in the Jewish synagogues, which left my father—and his father as well—with a feeling of indifference toward virtually any church. I do not think my father knew any of the details of the argument (at least he never talked of it), but he was completely inactive in religion throughout his life, although supportive of my mother's attachment to the Episcopal Church.

My mother's family had been Quakers. She, however, became an active Episcopalian, playing violin in many church services before she was married. Mother taught us the Lord's Prayer, the Ten Commandments, and various other basic tenets, and we occasionally went to a nonsectarian Sunday school, and that was about the extent of our involvement in religious matters. The secular aspects of all holidays—

Christmas, Easter, etc.—were special occasions and cause for major celebration.

During college and World War II, I gradually became more active in religion, occasionally attending the college chapel services in the morning and on Sundays going to Christ Church, the Episcopal church across the street from Harvard Yard. Occasionally I went to informal church meetings in the evening at the home of the Reverend Kinsolving, our Episcopal minister. He urged me to go into the ministry after graduation, but I never considered it, although my faith and belief were and are unshaken and my trust in God has been an enormous influence and comfort all my life.

I did attend services as regularly as I could while I was overseas during the war. (I suppose I felt I needed all the help I could get.) Then, when I returned to San Francisco in 1945, I became actively affiliated with St. Luke's Episcopal Church of the diocese of California, and remained so for many years. I was elected to the vestry of St. Luke's and later became chancellor and then treasurer of the diocese, and was a delegate to various church conventions.

It was in 1918, when I was not even a year old, that my father moved our family into a larger, shingled house he bought in the new Forest Hill area of San Francisco, only a couple of blocks from the Twin Peaks Tunnel streetcar station. Forest Hill was a wooded and up-to-then undeveloped part of the city, with a great deal of open space around it. From the outskirts of our little enclave, rolling sand dunes ran west toward the ocean—literally to the edge of the continent. Then northward, along the beach, one came to Golden Gate Park, where I remember with fondness several happy boyhood afternoons with my family, picnicking and riding the beautiful old carousel. Farther north was, by the 1920s, Playland, an oceanfront amusement park correctly called the "Coney Island of the West."

Ours was the end house of the first four new homes on Merced Avenue, and my father also bought the lot on either side of the house—one for a garden and the other for baseball, football, and occasionally tennis. It was a modest house, but it seemed like a castle to me, with six or seven rooms, a half basement, and a storage attic. It was one of the only homes in the area with a freestanding garage. There was also a porte cochere (which I, for years, thought was spelled "porker sheer") and a flight of stairs from the driveway up to the front door.

Soon after we moved in, my parents enclosed the big back porch, which became the bedroom my brother and I shared when I got a little older. I remember the conversion fascinated me, and I was frequently out on the old porch—undoubtedly very much in the way—as it was being made over. About this time, there was a worldwide influenza epidemic that struck our family as the construction was going on. It must have been a terrible time for my parents, but I remember no complaints.

We never moved from our comfortable home. The house stayed in the family until around 1970.

I was often at home because I had frequent mastoid infections. Whenever I got the flu (which was a regular occurrence), it would always settle in the ear. Doctors made house calls then, and Dr. Gelston made many visits to our home. Without anesthetics or antibiotics, the doctor would lance my eardrums with a needle and tell me to stay still for several hours while it drained. Many days in bed followed, because you had to have a 98.6 temperature for three days before you were allowed up.

The only diversions I had were reading and conducting mock battles with my toy tin soldiers, placing them strategically in the trenches and hilltops of the sheets. The battlefield was large, as my parents often let me appropriate their bed for these long periods of recuperation. (Where *they* slept all that time, I don't know, but I do not recall being very concerned about that at the time.) In any case, of course, I had no inkling then that later in my life I would be responsible for the deployment and safety of *real* troops.

At the age of six, I spent an interminably long month in the children's hospital with a staph infection that required a mastoid operation. My mother spent hours reading to me and providing solace. She must have gone home occasionally and helped with Peter, but my memory is that she was always at the hospital. One night when the operation started bleeding, my father was hastily summoned to the hospital to donate blood for a transfusion. Even after the mastoid operation and the long hospital stay, ear trouble persisted throughout my childhood.

Earlier that same year, 1923, my mother had become ill. Both of her parents had recently died, and not long after that, Mother suffered a nervous breakdown, or what I suppose today would be called depression. She stayed in bed in a darkened room for a number of weeks, which was probably the worst thing for her to do. (I have never liked dark rooms since then.) My father hired an in-home nurse and a couple of ladies to help with the housework, the cooking, and looking after Peter and me.

Mother made a full recovery but tended to stay at home. She was shy and retiring, never really interested in outside activities, and preferred taking care of my brother and me to anything else. Only reluctantly did she agree to go with my father on a business trip to Los Angeles not long after her recovery (Dad felt that she needed a change of scene). I still have a letter she wrote to me during that trip, and it was clear that she could hardly stand to be away: "I miss my little boys every second—more than words can tell, and I would start right back tonight if Daddy would not mind, but he would be so disappointed."

My immediate family was close-knit, and our home was always warm and secure. I was very fond of both my mother and father, and they clearly felt the same way toward me and Peter (and were careful not to favor one of us over the other). It seems to be rather fashionable now to dwell on unhappy childhoods or insensitive parents. I can claim neither. I had a happy home and loving parents.

My brother and I did not get an allowance; instead, my father devised a "point" system by which we would earn points for doing certain tasks around the house—cutting the lawn, helping with the dishes, and so forth. Conversely, we would lose points for "conduct unbecoming." Once we reached a certain number of points, we would get a baseball mitt, or some other thing we really wanted. The system worked well.

I do not remember getting into any trouble as a child; my brother and I probably received occasional paddlings, but certainly nothing particularly traumatizing. In fact, I suspect that I escaped such punishment more often than Peter, simply because I was so ill and weak so much of the time. (There were a *few* advantages to being sick.)

One incident I do recall, however, occurred one day when I was about five. I don't remember exactly what prompted it—I was probably being a particularly obnoxious little brother—but Peter picked me up and threw me over a hedge, breaking my arm in the process. It certainly would not have done me any good to get into a physical fight with him (he was obviously much stronger than I), but I'm sure he suffered dire consequences. Incidentally, my arm recovered completely.

Most of the time, though, Peter and I got along well, and we shared a few activities. We both started piano lessons at a very young age and continued until we went to college. As was the case with many children, we were basically forced into it, but now that I am older, I am glad we were. It gave me a lasting appreciation of music.

In piano, as in athletics, Peter was much better than I; he had better technique (and could play "The Minute Waltz" in fifty seconds or so), though I was said to have a nice touch. Our teacher, Melba Brookshier, was an "older" lady (she was probably all of twenty-five), and she sometimes played duets with us and occasionally with my mother, who had begun to play the violin again. I enjoyed the lessons, but not practicing, and recitals were occasions of terror. However, my first experience with public speaking occurred at these recitals, where I read short biographical sketches I had written about some of the composers.

Both Peter and I much preferred baseball. We played "indoor" baseball—that is, with a larger, slightly softer ball than the regulation "hardball"—but the game was of course played outdoors, usually on the lawn right next to our house. Peter and I, and a very good friend of ours, George Kristovich (who later became a schoolteacher and coach), formed a neighborhood league. Our team was known as the Merchants, and the rival team was the Robins. I was usually the pitcher and also the manager. (I guess the idea was that if I couldn't play very well, at least I could do that!) We meticulously kept track of our scores, batting averages, and every other imaginable detail of our games—it was all very serious business, and along with many other childhood items, I kept these records for years.

We also spent quite some time working on our electric trains, which my father had helped us set up in the basement of the house. We had an extensive array of train-related paraphernalia: not only a variety of cars, which usually came as Christmas gifts, but also all of the accessories—tunnels, villages, signals, and so forth. We even wrote up a charter for "The Weinberger Railroad Lines" and elected my father president; I was vice president and general manager, and Peter was consulting engineer.

Dad was deeply involved in this hobby—he knew all about things mechanical and electrical, and I know he had as much fun as we did. I remember one Christmas day, very early on, when a terrible storm blew a tree over, which consequently knocked down the main power line near our house. My father wanted so much to get the new trains hooked up and operational that he went outside in the pouring rain and tried to piece together the power line himself. He was not successful (and, fortunately, not injured either). Finally, late that night, the power company came out and fixed it, but not in time for us to try out our gifts on Christmas. Fixing the power line was vital for another reason. We had one of the few electric ranges in the city and there could be no Christmas dinner until the electricity was restored.

Another favorite activity that filled a good bit of my childhood was reading. I suppose this came partially because I spent a lot of time ill in bed, but it was also because my parents read a great deal to me and to Peter when we were quite young. My father even made up a long bedtime story, told over many nights, about the Constitutional Convention. This would not normally hold the attention of youngsters, but he told it so dramatically that it came alive for us and was, I believe, one of the foundation stones on which my lifelong interest in government was built.

My mother introduced me to Hugh Lofting's Doctor Dolittle books, which I enjoyed greatly and read to my own children many years later. I was also very fond of *My Book House*, a six-volume anthology of children's stories, which included "Hans Brinker (or, The Silver Skates)" and "The Nuremberg Stove." They were very handsome books, beautifully bound, and I remember that my parents bought the set from a door-to-door salesman, something practically unheard of today.

Peter also read to me early on—tales of King Arthur and histories of England and our Revolution—and even helped teach me to read. This led to my lifelong interest in English history and, indeed, all things English.

When I got a little older, I spent quite a lot of time at the Mechanics' Institute Library in downtown San Francisco. The Mechanics' Institute was founded in 1855, originally to provide "schooling for indigent mechanics." The library was, at first, only a small part of it, but after the University of California and the state school system were founded, the Mechanics' Institute concentrated less on giving classes and more on building up its library. By the time I started using it, the institute had become, and still is, entirely a private library, and a very good one. I liked it because it had open stacks and allowed you to browse, as in a bookstore, whereas at the public library you had to fill out a form and wait forever for someone to bring a book out.

I was a rapid reader, so I was able to absorb a great many books; I usually checked out three or four books at a time. I had a catholic, eclectic taste. I read many mysteries by Edgar Wallace, Sax Rohmer, and others, as well as history, particularly English history, biography, archaeology. And books about dogs, thanks to Albert Payson Terhune's Sunnybank Lad books. It was because of Terhune's stories that we eventually got a collie. (Before our collie, we had a cocker spaniel named Buster, and even before he, or I, came along, my father had a fox terrier named Judge. Judge was so jealous when my brother was born that my father had to give the dog away.)

My greatest interest, however, was politics, an early passion largely engendered by my father. I had one of my first brushes with a political figure in 1923, when my family was vacationing at Brookdale Lodge near Santa Cruz. We were having dinner one evening in a beautifully rustic dining room, through which a small creek ran, when I spotted one of California's U.S. senators, Samuel Shortridge. Being a reasonably good campaigner, Shortridge noticed the enormous interest with which I was watching him, and he came over to our table and introduced himself. My father was very pleased, and I was quite astonished, at the age of six, to have shaken the hand of a United States senator!

I followed the 1924 national party conventions as closely as I could from the newspaper, and I listened intently to the 1928 and 1932 conventions on our Atwater Kent radio. I was enthralled— particularly by the 1924 Democratic convention, because it took 103 ballots to determine the nominee.

In the election of 1930, the mayor of San Francisco, James Rolph Jr., was running for governor of California. Being from northern California, he wasn't given much chance of winning, but my father knew him and thought he was a good man, so we (Dad let me pull the lever in the voting booth) gave him a "courtesy" vote—and he won.

When Herbert Hoover was running for president in 1928, Dad took me to a campaign rally. I remember that as Hoover shook hands with people, he would sort of pull them through, to discourage them from standing and talking. He was not a very cheerful-looking man, and with his high, stiff collar and rather frozen expression, he seemed interested in getting the reception line over with rather than in meeting the people. Still, I was a strong Hoover supporter and was awed to see him in person.

On Election Day 1932, President Hoover came home to vote, and I went with my classmates to see him in front of City Hall. He knew that he had probably been defeated. He looked more tired, discouraged, and depressed than I had seen anyone look.

That same year I wrote to our congressman and was placed on his list to receive the *Congressional Record*. It always came about a week late, but I read each issue cover to cover. Through it, I gained a reasonably good knowledge of congressional procedure, though the *Record* was, and is, a highly sanitized document: congressmen and senators still take out everything they don't want in and add anything they wish they'd said had they thought of it at the time—all of this under the rubric of "revising and extending their remarks." So it was not an entirely faithful record, but it interested me nonetheless. I also used to save any letters that a congressman wrote back, because of the letterhead of the U.S. Congress on them; I was intrigued by all such governmental trappings.

The whole mechanism of democratic elections—conventions, campaigning, returns, counting of the votes—fascinated me. I put together scrapbooks of newspaper clippings about conventions, elections, and political events. I considered assembling these scrapbooks an absolute priority. I worked very diligently on them, meticulously pasting in articles, and even sent away for postelection copies of newspapers around the country, because our own had very little news about elections in other states.

I found that my burgeoning political views and preferences were increasingly those of the Republican Party. When my political consciousness was first beginning to take shape, Calvin Coolidge was president, having succeeded to that post after President Harding's death,* and then winning it in his own right in 1924. Coolidge's laissez-faire, probusiness policies and his cuts in taxes and federal expenditures seemed reasonable and proper to me (and my father) as instinctively the right course to follow, even before I had formally learned about economics. I knew that business was good for my father and for his clients, and that the country was enjoying unprecedented prosperity. All of that convinced me that the Republicans were doing something right.

President Franklin Roosevelt's tremendous expansion of the federal government in the Depression-wracked 1930s only solidified my views that the best government was the least government. Many credit FDR and his alphabet soup of programs with bringing the

---

* I have particularly vivid memories of President Harding's death in August of 1923. He had fallen ill on his way back from an official trip to Alaska and so stopped over in San Francisco. The balcony outside his rooms at the Palace Hotel on Market Street was hung with U.S. flags and bunting.

Then there were headlines that his condition had worsened, and one afternoon when I picked up our phone to call my father, the operator, instead of the usual "Number, please," said, "The president is dead." That was my first encounter with the mystical aura that surrounds the presidency. Later, the newspapers devoted their full front page to pictures of the president with, in huge type, the words "President Is Dead" superimposed over the picture. The flags on the balcony at the Palace Hotel were changed to heavy black draperies. All of this filled an impressionable six-year-old with awe and excitement.

country out of the Depression; I believe that that, if anything, made things worse. New Deal spending was almost entirely financed by taxation—which left people with even less to spend—which meant less consumer demand—which meant less supply was needed—which meant companies were not hiring—which meant there was widespread unemployment—which left people with less money to spend—and so went the vicious circle.

I felt quite strongly in 1932 (and have ever since) that expanding the power of the federal government was not the answer. Nor was strangling individuals and businesses with the noose of regulation. I was particularly troubled by the Soviets' "master plans" and successive "five-year plans," which I felt was the kind of system that completely foreclosed all opportunity for the individual to flourish. I feared that the more the New Deal developed, the more we would become like the Soviets—the more power the government had, the less power there would be for each individual to chart his own course and rise as far and as fast as his abilities could take him.

As it was, I believe it was only our entrance into, and massive mobilization for, the Second World War that brought some improvement in our economy. But long before Pearl Harbor, millions of Americans were suffering; virtually no one was untouched by the Depression.

During the building of the Golden Gate Bridge in San Francisco, I remember lines of desperate, out-of-work, able-bodied men who would wait, day after day, for one of the construction workers to fall or injure himself so they could take his place.

Those years were very difficult times for my father as well. In such economic straits, it was generally felt that, while food and utilities had to be paid for, doctors and lawyers didn't, so Dad lost quite a bit of regular income. It was especially hard for him since he had a one-man law practice, but even in the worst times, he never let on or even discussed finances. We always lived comfortably, though not lavishly by any means, and Dad never gave any indication that we did not have enough money for whatever we needed. The subject simply never came up. I learned only later what a great strain it had been for him to pay the bills.

I followed big news stories avidly. One that I particularly remember was a major effort to get flu anti-toxins to Alaska during an epidemic. I tracked their progress by air and then dogsled. I can still see the big headline: "Anti-toxin Reaches Nome."

Air travel was in its nascent stages, and its development was thrilling to witness. Each new achievement was a cause for national celebration. I remember, when I was very young, my parents went out to see Colonel Maugham land on the old Crissy Field in the San Francisco Presidio, after the first dawn-to-dusk flight across the United States. He had left from New York in the early morning, in a biplane, and arrived in San Francisco shortly after sunset. Of course he made many stops along the way, but it was still considered a tremendous feat.

Then, in 1927, Charles Lindbergh made his historic solo, nonstop flight across the Atlantic. As in many cities around the country, a huge parade was held in his honor in San Francisco. There were no stands along the parade route, which made it difficult to see anything unless you were in the front row. So my father rented a small room at the old Federal Hotel on Market Street, and my family crowded in there to watch the parade. My father had one of the first Bell & Howell home movie cameras. He later edited his home movies and showed them for years. Lindbergh was an authentic American hero and could do no wrong—until his isolationist views before World War II meant he was in opposition to the Allies.

In 1932 the Lindbergh baby's kidnapping made constant head-lines. Americans became familiar with H. Norman Schwarzkopf, head of the New Jersey Police Department, who gave innumerable press conferences regarding the investigation. Little did I know that many years later, I would interview his son and then approve his appointment to head the U.S. Central Command, in which capacity he led our forces in the Gulf War.

Prohibition, which was in effect for most of my childhood, didn't bother my father. He had seen the effects of drunkenness in Idaho Springs—the miners, who worked six days a week, would get paid on Saturdays and then go out and destroy themselves with liquor. They had to be dragged back to work on Monday mornings. So my father was essentially a teetotaler, but he wasn't fanatical about it. In fact, in 1932, when the repeal of Prohibition was in the works, my brother was very anxious to try a can of 3.2 percent beer (the first thing legalized). Dad went down to Marshall's Pharmacy to get one for him. I had a taste of it, but I did not like it—it was sour and bitter, and didn't taste anything like chocolate! I much preferred wine, which I tried many years later. It was not a question of principle or prejudice, but simply that I never liked the taste of most alcohol.

My first experience with school was dreadful. Starting in the early 1920s, my family often spent the summers at a garden apartment, the Kingscote, on the Stanford campus, about thirty miles south of San Francisco, and one summer my parents thought it would be a good idea to send Peter and me to the Palo Alto Military Academy.

I do not remember the classes, but I most vividly recall the marching. We had to wear terribly hot, scratchy, World War I–era uniforms and march in formation out on a dusty field in the blazing sun. I also remember that everyone was required to eat at the same time, and to eat the same thing, which was something absolutely ghastly and always included rice pudding. In short, there was little room for individuality or individual development at the military academy. After only about a month, my parents decided the whole experience was counterproductive and mercifully took us out of the school. It was fortunate, as it later turned out, that this brief experience did not adversely affect my view of the military in general.

After we returned to San Francisco at the end of that summer (1925), Peter began attending Commodore Sloat, a public grammar school, and a home tutor, Miss Dorothy Rector, was engaged to provide my instruction. Since I had been ill so much, it was thought that I needed to gain my strength back before entering school, and by that time, I would need to be prepared to enter the fourth or fifth grade. Miss Rector came to the house for four or five hours a day. I remember her as a nice young lady and a good teacher, and I enjoyed preparing for schoolwork.

In 1926 my parents sent me to the Frederic Burk School. It was a progressive school that allowed each student to advance at his own pace in various subjects. This was the so-called Dewey system, then a very advanced idea. This school was chosen mostly so that I would not fall behind when I was absent with frequent illness, as I would have in a traditional school. It was a good system, and classes were small, so every child received individual attention and encouragement.

The school was part of the laboratory of the San Francisco State Teachers' College, and all of my instructors were in training for their teaching careers. My favorite teacher was Miss Violette Kindt, and we kept in touch by letter for quite a while after I started high school.

One other faculty member that I recall was Miss Spozio, the principal. She was a formidable and imposing woman. If you were sent to Miss Spozio, you were in deep trouble, and I was exceedingly relieved that I never had to make a trip to her office. Years later, I met a lady commissar in Tashkent, in the Soviet Union, who reminded me strongly of Miss Spozio.

I basically enjoyed grammar school. I made decent grades and was class treasurer and editor of the school newspaper.

It would have been most logical for me to go on to Lowell High School, which was considered the "academic" high school; most pupils who were planning to go on to college went to Lowell. But my brother was already attending Polytechnic High School, and he had impressed on me, and I fully agreed, that "real men" went to Poly. So in 1930 I started high school there.

Polytechnic was oriented more toward manual and mechanical training, at neither of which I was very good, but they did have all of the normal courses. I especially enjoyed English and all kinds of history, and of course I was particularly interested in anything that had to do with government and politics. Many of my school papers reflected my strong opinions, even then, about the virtues of democracy and the inherent evils of Communist repression and New Deal economics. In a number of my essays, I warned against "the Soviet Menace," economic planning, and the views espoused by Professor Rexford Tugwell, a radical, early "Brain Trust" adviser of President Franklin Roosevelt. Indeed, my writing then, and now, shows a certain consistency (or perhaps more properly, a lack of growth).

I was extremely shy as a child, a trait I no doubt developed from my mother, and which, I am sure, was exacerbated by the fact that I started school so late. But at Poly, I took part in a number of extracurricular activities, which brought me out of my shell somewhat.

When it came to girls, however, I was still incredibly timid. It's not that I wasn't interested; I certainly was, but I never felt I could advance the cause myself. I was always afraid I'd be bothering the girl. (I didn't realize until much later that many of them actually *like* to be bothered.) If a girl showed interest in me and took the initiative, then that was fine, but not many of them did, so I would mostly just admire them from afar and pine for better days.

I was much more comfortable with other endeavors. I joined the Drama Club and worked mostly behind the scenes—if you lacked talent, you were put in charge of the lights. But I did have a small part in a mystery play called *The Thirteenth Chair*. My big line was, "It's no use—he's dead." (Why I so clearly remember that particular bit of trivia, while I've forgotten so many other things, I don't know.)

In my senior year, I was elected president of the student body. I had run on a platform promising to establish a new constitution. With the help of my father and my faculty adviser, Miss Polly Hatch, I drafted a constitution that provided for a legislative body similar to the U.S. Congress, a student court, and other institutions borrowed from federal government models. I felt that this would be a good way to learn about the American government, but primarily I wanted to carry out my campaign promise to establish such a constitution. It took me several months and at least ten drafts to get it completed, but it was eventually voted on and ratified.

By my senior year, I knew that I wanted to be involved in government in some way. My graduation speech was on "The Honorable Profession of Politics." I know that many thought it a rather strange title, but the idea came to me after reading results of a poll that showed about 70 percent of parents did not want their children to have anything to do with politics. I told the audience I firmly believed that while politics can indeed be a dirty profession—just as dirty as we let it become—politics can also be an honorable profession—just as clean and honorable as we want it to be. We can make and keep it honorable by our own participation. The choice is ours.

After I graduated from Polytechnic in December 1933, I took a few more courses there during the spring semester, including economics, Pacific relations, and California history to nourish my insatiable interest in government affairs (and to fill up the time until the college years began). I also made extensive use of Stanford's library during our summers on the Stanford campus, a trip we made almost every year of my childhood. One summer there, I drifted into the back of some classes on American politics and political parties. Professor Barclay was the instructor, and these classes further fueled my interest in all of these matters.

My father had a client from England who had encouraged both Peter and me to think about a Rhodes Scholarship and applying to Oxford. Being a confirmed Anglophile even then, I found that a very attractive idea, but I soon learned that I had to attend an American college first. It seemed to me, from what I had heard and read, that Harvard was the best college in the United States, and I have always wanted to go to the top. Inquiries about Harvard led me to the Harvard Club of San Francisco, which annually awarded the William Thomas Scholarship. This was the only scholarship at that time named for a living person, and Mr. Thomas, an elderly San Francisco attorney, personally selected the winner. After an enjoyable interview with him, he announced that I was his choice to be that year's recipient.

Needless to say, I was delighted, and I set about meeting Harvard's entrance requirements. Fortunately, I was able to do that without much difficulty because Harvard exempted from all college entrance examinations those applicants who were in the highest seventh of their high school if their school was in an area not served by the College Entrance Board Examination. San Francisco and I both fit these exemptions.

So now my course was set. I had not the slightest doubt then—or since—that Harvard was indeed the finest university in the land.

CHAPTER 2

THE FINEST UNIVERSITY

*M*y whole family—Mother, Dad, Peter, and I— loaded our newly acquired one-year-old Cadillac (with twelve cylinders—at that time Cadillac made the only twelve- and sixteen-cylinder engines) on a late summer day in 1934 and set out for Cambridge, Massachusetts. (After attending Stanford for a year, and the University of California at Berkeley for one semester, Peter transferred to Harvard when I received my scholarship.) It was a long trip, and the longest time my father had ever been away from his law practice.

For me, the highlight of the trip was our stop in Washington, D.C. Being such an avid student of government, it was wonderful actually to see and set foot in our capital city—the place I had read so much about. Indeed, in our spare time on the drive across country I had read my *Washington Standard Guide* and paid fifty cents for the paperback 1932 edition of *The Challenge to Liberty* by Herbert Hoover—his first attack on the New Deal of his successor.

We stayed at a hotel near Union Station in full view of the Capitol, which, lighted at night, seemed to me to be the most beautiful sight I had ever seen. Although Congress was not in session, we visited the empty House and Senate chambers. My imagination supplied the vision of the members whose words (or an approximation thereof) I had been reading in the *Congressional Record*. A passage of fevered prose that I had scribbled down from what I think was a Washington guidebook perhaps summed up my impressions best:

> Here transpire daily events that will leave their impress on the future, and one cannot look upon the scenes where the future destiny of the nation is being formed without feeling that he has touched the very pulse of the government and felt its living throb.

After nearly a month on the road, we came to Boston, with all of its history, crossed the gleaming Charles River, and journeyed into Harvard. The grand, redbrick buildings, standing like stately, wise old men, deeply impressed me. I saw the Harvard Yard bustling with eager, young, confident students and was assailed by doubts. How could I ever acquire such assurance, such a sense of belonging as most of those students seemed to exude? They seemed a world apart, until I found many as uncertain, but few as shy, as I was. Many of all types became my good friends, but early on, I felt out of place and unsure of everything except my political opinions. I expressed these quite didactically, and I am sure quite irritatingly.

My mother took an apartment on Prescott Street, one block over from the Harvard Union. She was a worrier, unhappy at our separation, and decided she would stay until Christmas to "get us started" while my father hurried home to his law practice. He would return to spend Christmas with us at Harvard, and then my parents would return together to San Francisco.

Peter and I shared a room in the Union, a building just behind the Yard, in which were located the dining hall and a few meeting rooms for freshmen. There were only five or six large residence rooms on the top floor, a library and language rooms on the second floor, and the dining hall on the first floor. I remember being impressed, even then, with the way the West Point cadets, who came for the Harvard-Army football games, would file into the dining hall. With impeccably straight posture, they were quite a contrast to their slumped and sloppy Harvard hosts who followed.

My brother continued to be much more outgoing than I, so although we roomed together, we really did not see much of each other. While he often went out with friends, I was quite overwhelmed with work and often in Stillman Infirmary because of chicken pox, measles, and recurring ear infections. I really had led quite a sheltered life up until then, so admittedly, it was helpful that Mother was nearby. My father came back to Cambridge as planned for that first Christmas. We celebrated the holidays in Mother's small apartment, with a tree and wreaths—everything as much like Christmas at 60 Merced as possible.

After my parents left, I set aside time nearly every other day, usually around 5 P.M., to write letters home. (Fortunately, I was a fairly proficient typist, so I spared them the eyestrain of trying to decipher my awful handwriting.) My parents wrote to me almost as often. Whenever I returned to Cambridge from a summer or Christmas vacation, my first stop would be the Western Union office in Harvard Square to wire them that I had arrived safely.

The cross-country trips were a financial strain for my father, as indeed were my college years, coming at the depth of the Depression. But somehow my parents always made it possible for me to come home for summers and Christmas. The four-day, three-night train trip seemed interminable, but I was always grateful to be able to do it. It helped considerably that I had won the scholarship that covered my first year's tuition—the princely sum of four hundred dollars. That was a major turning point in my being able to attend Harvard, though my father called it a "loss leader," meaning, "they got you into the store with what looked like a bargain, but then all the other prices went up." I did not hear the expression again until I was at the Federal Trade Commission and discovered it was an unfair trade practice.

Once I was at Harvard, I watched my expenses closely and sent my father a regular accounting. As in the earlier years of the Depression, however, my parents always made it work with a minimum of strain on Peter and me, and I remember more than one instance when, boarding the train to return to Harvard at the end of a summer or Christmas at home, I discovered that Mother had deposited a dollar bill or two in my jacket pocket. I tried to tell her in subsequent letters that that had been entirely unnecessary—if much appreciated. A dollar in those days could buy a subway ticket into Boston and back, a haircut, a couple of football programs, or a few greeting cards, with change left over.

I also tried to earn a little income of my own. For a couple of summers when I was home from Harvard, I wrote editorials for the *Argonaut*, a fairly conservative, business-oriented, and now long-defunct weekly San Francisco magazine. I covered local issues and events, such as the deportation case of longshoremen labor union leader Harry Bridges, and other industrial disputes, but occasionally I would cut loose against the big government agenda of President Roosevelt or the appeasement policy of Neville Chamberlain.

At Harvard, I wrote a regular column for the *Argonaut*, entitled "Along the Atlantic Seaboard," providing Californians with a window on "how the other coast lived." I reported on local politics, weather, sports, the arts, and other goings-on throughout New England and the East. My experience with the *Argonaut* perhaps kept alive my latent interest in journalism, already fueled by work on the *Harvard Crimson* (of which more later). And I have to admit, an added attraction was the reasonably regular income (ten dollars a column as I recall it).

When I first started college, I had no specific plans for the future. I suppose there was an unspoken assumption that I would go to law school, though, frankly, I wasn't all that enthusiastic about it. As was the case with many college students, I rather drifted from one idea to another. The thought of being a doctor appealed to me, since I had been ill so much as a child, but the science courses were not congenial. A few highly cynical newspapermen with whom I interviewed shortly before graduation talked me out of a journalism career. "This is the worst profession in the world," the editor of the old *New York Sun* told me (he was a college friend of my father).

I majored ("concentrated" in Harvard's usage) in American government but found my courses lifeless and taught with a liberal bias. Indeed, I was often the lone conservative in class. I did, however, greatly enjoy English history and literature courses, and by my third year, I wished I had started out on that track instead. Of course, at that point it was entirely too late to start over, and Harvard did not offer "minors."

The class workload was extremely heavy. I was quite ill-prepared for it, coming from a relatively easy, carefree existence at San Francisco's Poly High. Another problem was Harvard's language requirement. To graduate, students had to have a reading knowledge of an ancient and a modern language. I did well enough with Latin, since I had studied the basics of it in high school. For a modern language, I chose a double course in German, largely because my mother had studied violin in that country. After prodigious efforts, I passed with the only two C's of my college career, but I was happier to have those two C's than any of the higher grades I received later, because they met the required reading knowledge of a foreign language and relieved me of the need for further language courses. But I now regret that I never mastered a foreign language, and I think it is a great mistake that our public schools do not require foreign language instruction starting in elementary school. When I was in the California legislature, I secured passage of a bill requiring teaching of a foreign language by or before the sixth grade. Sadly, the teachers' union forced its repeal only a few years later because "there were not enough qualified teachers." I suggested we use educational television, but it turned out that that was precisely what the teachers' unions most feared.

Harvard also had an athletic requirement for graduation, which included swimming fifty yards. Because of my chronic ear infections, I had never learned how to swim. After two years of trying, followed by several successive ear infections, I was granted a waiver. I still cannot swim, which was later a great worry to my wife and the Secret Service detail whenever I would take my motorboat out alone in Maine. It was also inconvenient to me as an army lieutenant leading troops across various shallow (I hoped) jungle streams in New Guinea.

With all of Harvard's other requirements, however, I did reasonably well. My professors were of course well known and respected in their areas of expertise, and many were the world's authorities. The great majority of them were considerably more liberally inclined than I; some were genuine New Dealers, and most favored expansion of federal government power.

As war clouds gathered over Europe, many were, if not isolationists, at least far more interested in domestic matters. This bias was apparent even in the thesis topic I was given. The last of my tutors,[*] Professor E. Pendleton Herring, pressed me to write my senior thesis on the Farm Credit Administration (FCA), then recently created as

---

[*] Every student had a "tutor," usually a tenured professor, to guide him in his class selection, supervise his class work, and help with his thesis. For many, the work with a tutor was more important than classroom work.

part of Roosevelt's New Deal. (Theses were required if one wanted to graduate with honors.) I, of course, would have preferred to write on political parties or conventions or other aspects of politics, but I let myself be persuaded to write about the FCA. I am sure that from an educational viewpoint it was a suitable subject, for I knew absolutely nothing about farms or credit policy—but I did not know a great deal more even after writing the thesis.

As a freshman, I joined the Union Debating Society; I had heard many of my father's stories of his work on debating teams at the University of Colorado. I also felt that debating might help me overcome some of my shyness, which it did. It may have even fostered my interest in law. I stayed busy in politics, too. At election time, I worked with newly formed college committees for local Republican candidates. I was elected treasurer of the student council, which was fun but not terribly challenging, since student government at Harvard was neither very strong nor considered very important. My work there consisted mostly of evaluating scholarship applications, recommending courses to new students, and keeping track of the council's limited finances. The best part was working with my classmate Francis Keppel, who was the president of the council. He was a brilliant, thoroughly charming New Yorker who had an exuberance and enthusiasm comparatively rare among my classmates. He had wide-ranging interests, studied sculpture in Rome after graduation, and later was appointed dean of the Graduate School of Education—one of the youngest deans in Harvard's history. I was a guest in his parents' homes in New York City and in Peekskill, and it was always a delight to be with him and see his quick and brilliant intellect in action.

The most fun of all, next to the *Crimson*, was the Signet Society, a literary club to which I was elected in my junior year. The society often held readings and concerts, and it housed a wonderful library in the Dunster Street clubhouse (into which, I recall, entry was gained by pressing on a loose board alongside the front door). The Signet also served excellent food; I often went there for lunch and enjoyed the food as much as I did the conversation.

Initiation into the Signet involved hazing which, by today's standards, would seem quite mild. Great quantities of alcohol would be consumed (though not by me), while the candidates were required to read aloud amusing poems or stories they had written themselves, and then be questioned by a boisterous audience. I wrote a short poem, the topic of which I have now forgotten, but which was well received—primarily, I believe, because of the inebriation of the audience.

Initiation also included the tradition of giving each new member a rose, which the member was then to send back to the Signet upon publication of his first book, at the time of his first concert, or on the occasion of his first literary, artistic, or musical achievement, whatever it might be. The rose would then be framed and kept at the Signet Society house. The roses of several accomplished members, including T. S. Eliot, are on display. Regrettably, I lost track of my rose and so was not able to carry out this tradition when, in 1990, my first book, *Fighting for Peace*, was published.

My fondest memories of my years at Harvard are of the many long hours I spent at the *Harvard Crimson*—"Cambridge's Biggest [and only] Breakfast Table Daily."

In April of my freshman year, I, quite audaciously for me, tried out for the news board of the *Crimson*. There were four boards: editorial, photographic, news, and business. Forty or fifty people competed for a spot on one of these boards; ultimately only two or three new candidates were elected to each board from the two or three competitions held every year.

As a news candidate, I was given various assignments, which included everything from doing menial tasks to covering football games to getting interviews. We were also encouraged to develop and write stories of our own and not just carry out assignments.

Interview subjects were not specified, but I was able to talk with and write about quite a motley, if small, cast of characters, including the eldest son of one of my great heroes, Theodore Roosevelt.* TR Jr., in Boston for one of his speaking tours, was extremely friendly, eager to put me at ease, and most helpful. He gave me good quotes and never seemed to worry about what I might write about him.

My big triumph (at least in *my* mind), however, was to "get" Tallulah Bankhead. It happened that she was in Boston, starring in *The Little Foxes*, and simply by calling the theater I was able to get an appointment with her in her dressing room after a performance. I had not been able to get a ticket for the play, and the *Crimson* did not provide one, but after she expressed some initial disappointment that I had not seen the play, Miss Bankhead was very helpful and answered all my questions. (It was not until December 6, 1941, that I actually saw her in the play in San Francisco, the night before Pearl Harbor, of which more later.) I was quite flattered that she called me "darling," in her broad Alabama accent—until I later learned that she called *everybody* "darling." In any case, I considered the interview quite a triumph.

But I think it was another coup that got me on the board. British Labour Party economist Harold Laski (not one of my heroes) was

---

* Theodore Roosevelt had been a hero of mine since boyhood. I believe it was my father's strong admiration for TR that started me on this track. My father had seen and heard Roosevelt when he came to Denver, probably in 1910 or 1911, and was most surprised that he had quite a high voice that without any public address system could be heard two or three blocks away. I admired greatly the fact that Roosevelt had willed himself to change from a sickly boy into a man of enormous physical vitality and strength. I also was greatly attracted by TR's writing and other abilities, his early entry into active politics, his war record in the Spanish-American War, and his extraordinarily rapid rise to state and national fame. All of these early impressions were recalled and heightened when, much later, I reviewed the excellent eight-volume collection of TR's letters, and still later when I read Edmund Morris's biography, of which alas only the first volume has been completed. I greatly regret that Morris's biography of Ronald Reagan fell far short of his work on TR.

giving lectures in Boston, but he absolutely refused to be interviewed—and was very unpleasant about refusing. So I went to one of
his lectures, and during the question period I managed to ask him
three questions before he realized he was being interviewed. I wrote
it up as if it were an actual interview, and I have a feeling that helped
greatly in earning me a slot on the news board.

Once on the staff, from the beginning of my sophomore year, I spent
almost all of my spare time at the *Crimson*. I usually had classes, sometimes three in a row, in the mornings on Mondays, Wednesdays, and
Fridays, and then my day at the *Crimson* would begin around two in
the afternoon. The printing deadline was 2 A.M., so despite the late
start, it was indeed a full-time job. There were always numerous varied
tasks to be done: developing and writing stories, editing issues, making
up dummy pages, helping to run the next competitions, and proof-
reading. I learned to read type from the galley proofs upside-down
(inverted so that it would print correctly from the Linotype machine),
and I also became quite good at helping repair the ancient printing
press, which broke down periodically—inevitably around 1:30 A.M.

On one occasion, members of the *Lampoon* staff raided our office
and shut down the press. It took quite a long time to counterattack
and oust them, so it was not until 5 A.M. that the paper rolled off the
press and was folded. We then had to deliver it ourselves, completing
the task about 8 A.M. Although that *Lampoon* raid did not succeed, it
was considered essential to retaliate and harass the *Lampoon*. We used
to stage frequent raids back and forth, and once the *Crimson* even
managed to steal the metal ibis from the top of the *Lampoon*'s quaint
building. (I understand that the bird has been bolted down since.)
Then there were the hoax issues of the *Crimson* put out by the
Lampoon, and vice versa. (The *Advocate*, Harvard's other publication,
considered itself to be intellectually above such pranks.)

In those days, the *Crimson* could not afford to subscribe directly to
the wire services, so every night, usually around 11 P.M., one of my

duties was to take the subway into Boston to pick up the United Press International dispatches from a kind *Boston Herald*. These nightly outings gave me quick familiarity with snow and extreme cold, weather I had not encountered before moving to New England.

The "Red Ink Sheets," the first proofs of the paper, were a source of great anxiety and occasional embarrassment. These resembled freshman themes returned with the professor's comments; the major difference was that the "Red Inks" were required reading for all and replete with the managing editor's comments and criticisms written in red ink, rarely tactfully expressed. The most intolerable error involved infinitives: they were *not* to be split. Factual errors were corrected with scorn; I am sure this improved our writing and accuracy, although usually only after the error had appeared.

Many of the *Crimson's* editorials in those years were very biased (for which I would like to claim some credit). We tried to keep the news pages free of political prejudice, but in one example I remember, we ran a picture of Alf Landon after he was defeated by Franklin Roosevelt in the 1936 presidential election, along with the cutline "Landon Beats Lemke!" William Lemke, a former North Dakota senator, was a third-party candidate. We did not mention FDR's victory until later in the story.

We also did a rather provocative editorial entitled "Are You Mice or Men?" complaining with tongue in cheek that the present crop of students was too weak and meek to have any riots, as they had in the old days. This, of course, caused the deans great anguish and, predictably, produced a riot by students the next night.

I worked my way up to the positions of assistant managing editor and managing editor and was elected president at the end of my junior year. Up until that time, there had always been two managing editors and two presidents from each class per school year. But I felt that that system did not really allow sufficient time to learn how to do the jobs right, so when I was president, we secured the members' consent to have only one president and managing editor a year. However, this did not apply until the next year, so only halfway through my senior year, my term was over and I relinquished the chair to my classmate Morris Earle. Although I did not recognize it at the time, this may have been one of the first examples (besides my constitutional work at Poly High) of my penchant for reorganizing existing systems, which I was called upon to do, and did, a number of times later in life. As for the *Crimson*, I believe my one-president-a-year policy continues to this day.

I made a few other, more minor changes during my term as president. We improved the sports coverage, added more photos, and, in a move that perhaps stemmed from my own sedentary inclinations, installed a copy chute to the basement so editors would not have to walk downstairs every time something was ready to be printed.

As president, I took an active interest in editorial policy. Although I wrote only a few editorials myself, I did try to "improve" some of them with my own biases, particularly those on national and international issues. It was on my watch that, for the first time in a long time, the paper made a small profit, which we distributed among the staff in the form of a dividend.

In addition to the daily paper, the *Crimson* revived publication of *The Confidential Guide to Harvard Courses*, which had been discontinued some years earlier. The guide, largely compiled through student opinion surveys, assessed the courses offered at Harvard and particularly the quality of teaching. It was really the only criticism and evaluation available and was designed to help students choose what courses to take. We did try to be fair, but, not surprisingly, it was viewed with some disdain by the faculty, except those favorably mentioned. It was, however, very popular with students. Its publication was another example of the complete freedom we enjoyed as students.

All of these activities, in addition to heavy class work, left little time for a social life. Most of my time was spent studying at Widener

Library or in my room at Dunster House, or working at the *Crimson*. As a result, most of my friends were from the *Crimson*: J. Sinclair Armstrong, a close friend who became my daughter's godfather; his roommate, Morris Earle, now my son's godfather; Shippen Goodhue; and Cleveland ("Clip") Amory, who became a professional writer with several well-received books to his credit.

Ellsworth Grant and Tom Calhoun were also good friends from the *Crimson*, and right after our spring exams in 1936 we drove up to Fenwick, Connecticut, to see the boat races and visit Ellsworth's fiancée, Marion, a younger sister of Katharine Hepburn. Many years later, Tom wrote an entertaining article about me on that trip for the *Hartford Courant*, but I'm afraid that the way I remember it is not quite as glamorous or prescient as his version.

We stayed at the Hepburns' rambling old house on the water. Katharine was there for part of the time (with her former husband, which I thought a rather strange arrangement). Her mother, Mrs. Hepburn, was a vigorous, earthy woman who had all kinds of views and ideas that for the time were very liberal and advanced. She was particularly vocal on birth control and women's rights and the more liberal parts of the New Deal. At dinner one night, she listened to me defend, in a rather halting and shy way, some of my conservative beliefs, and finally she grabbed my hand and said, "Let me see your palm! Where *do* you get all this?!" She studied it for quite a while, and then, with great irritation, pronounced, "My God, you're going to live forever!" This made me even more ill-at-ease, but I do not recall that she made any other predictions, as Tom Calhoun reports it, about any great power or military responsibilities I might have in the future. I probably would not have believed her anyway!

Three other men in my class who went on to gain prominence, but whom I did not know well during college, were the Pulitzer Prize–winning biographer Arthur Schlesinger Jr., the prolific correspondent, historian, and China expert Theodore H. White, and Wiley

Mayne, a skilled and talented attorney and a congressman from Iowa during the same time that I served in the Nixon administration.

I never knew him well, but John F. Kennedy, class of 1940, was on the *Crimson* business board. I saw him only a few times but remember him as a thin, gangly youth. His older brother, Joe Kennedy Jr., later killed tragically in the war, I knew much better. Joe was a vigorous, enthusiastic man, as quick to defend the New Deal and the Democrats as I was to attack them during several meals we had together in Dunster House. He was an easy man to argue with, and likeable and friendly. I am sure he would have made at least as popular a president as his brother. In fact, all the rumors were that his father was even then grooming him for that office. Joe had a strange (to me) accent. It was a combination of Boston street twang and pure eastern preparatory school. I never could imitate it. I often wondered how *I* sounded to him!

In my junior year, I got to know Clip Amory's younger sister, Leonore, or "Leo," as we called her. She was still in prep school at the Milton Academy Girls School, and I saw her frequently at her parents' home. I most enjoyed the casual weekends we spent at her family's home in Milton, Massachusetts, not far from Cambridge. I generally felt awkward around girls, but I was more comfortable with Leo, perhaps partially because she was relaxed and very bright and knew how to play baseball. (In fact, one of the main reasons I returned to Harvard for law school was to be close to her.)

Her family was always extremely nice to me and seemed to welcome me at their home, but I am sure they never considered a serious relationship between their daughter and me. Indeed, the first, almost automatic Boston response to any matters of that type was, "Who are his people?" In any event, nothing came of it.

Boston and its surroundings had a completely different feel from San Francisco. Of course, it is much older, staid, and smugly proud— a perfectly pressed dinner jacket to San Francisco's well-worn favorite sweater. More attention was paid to social strata and who one's "people" were—an environment I had not directly experienced before. After a few years in Boston, I began to understand and be much amused by the fact that "Lowells speak only to Cabots, and Cabots speak only to God." I amused at least myself by wondering aloud whom Godfrey Lowell Cabot, a most illustrious Brahmin, could possibly talk to.

After freshman year in the Union, students were assigned to one of the houses, massive brick residence halls along the Charles River. I was assigned to Dunster House, and during my sophomore year I again shared a room with Peter. Later I had fine, large quarters to myself for my junior and senior years. This last suite overlooked the courtyard and, beyond its gate, I had a view of the Charles. Dunster House sits in a residential neighborhood, surrounded mostly by private old homes, and is a good ten-minute walk from the Yard and Harvard Square.

The university tried to get a cross section of students in each house, but Dunster, at that time, seemed to have a preponderance of students studying government or economics, and while this encouraged study groups, I preferred to study alone until I entered law school.

The houses were like full-service apartments. Each house had its own library; Dunster's was long and narrow, with rich, dark paneling and plenty of deep, comfortable chairs and couches to sink into. The rooms were homey, and some suites had fireplaces. There were maids (or "biddies" as they were disparagingly called in those politically incorrect days) who cleaned the rooms and were generally nice old Irish ladies. They told me I was one of the neatest residents, a distinction I was proud of but kept to myself. Meals were served in the beautiful paneled dining hall on the first floor by waitresses and student help. The dining hall, consciously modeled after the Oxford and Cambridge colleges, had many paintings of old Harvard and New England figures, including, of course, Henry Dunster, the first president of Harvard. I generally ate breakfast and dinner there (and lunch at the Signet Society),* and I considered the food at Dunster mediocre at best. When I was later in the army, I was ashamed that I had criticized Harvard's food. Army meals made such an impression on me that when I became secretary of defense more than forty years later, I made improving the food, particularly the MREs (Meals Ready to Eat), a priority.

In the summer of 1936 I had my first real, though very limited, taste of participatory politics. I was an usher (along with my good friend, Bruce Griswold, with whose family we stayed) at that year's Republican National Convention in Cleveland. The convention was sparsely attended and I had little to do, being assigned to a section of seats at the very top of the arena. I was also included, though, in a small dinner given by Nelson Rockefeller. Nelson's brother David was on the *Crimson*'s business board, and he has been a much admired friend and Maine neighbor for years.

At the convention, former president Herbert Hoover's appearance brought the crowd to its feet, and his address was far more politically appealing than the rather scholarly talks he had made in his losing campaign four years earlier. The delegates rallied in support of Alf Landon, the venerable governor of Kansas and one of the few GOP victors in 1934. He easily won the nomination. I was convinced that all that enthusiasm was going to translate itself into votes. So confident was I that when I rode back to Harvard afterward with classmate Ben Welles, I bet him (too much) that Landon would defeat Roosevelt. Unfortunately—for my pocketbook, as well as for the nation, in my opinion—I lost the bet. I have never bet on anything since.

---

* In major contrast to most any place today—*especially* colleges—in those days, one could not even get into the dining hall without having a tie on. Indeed, the standard attire of the day for college men included a tie and sports jacket.

My undergraduate years at Harvard were crucial ones for my personal development. It was during that time that I seemed to come out of my shell and gain confidence in myself. I also had a real opportunity to expand my knowledge in many fields. As daunted and out of place as I had felt when I first came to Harvard in 1934, in four years' time I found that I could measure up to the high intellectual standards of the Ivy League and, more important, get closer to my own aspirations, which were even higher.

At the end of my undergraduate career, I ranked third out of 127 men in the government department, and sixth out of 355 in the whole division of history, government, and economics.

On a glorious, bright, early summer day in 1938, I graduated magna cum laude at ceremonies in Harvard Yard. My emotions that afternoon were mixed. Obviously, pride was the predominant feeling, but it was mingled with disappointment that my parents had not been able to afford the trip east to share it.

After the ceremony, I walked back to Dunster House, leaving the Yard through Dexter Gate at the head of Plympton Street. I paused for a moment to read again the inscription above it, which had fixed itself in my memory the first time I saw it back in 1934. It has been an inspiration to me ever since. On the street side it reads, "Enter to Grow in Wisdom," and on the Yard side is engraved, "Depart to Serve Better Thy Country and Thy Kind." It seemed to me then, and now, a good beacon to have before one.

My graduation also brought a degree of uncertainty. I had been awarded the Lionel de Jersey Harvard Studentship, which would have given me a year of relaxed study in Cambridge, England, with residence in John Harvard's old rooms at Emmanuel College, Cambridge. Instead, I entered law school, both mindful of my father's hopes and for other reasons. This was 1938. I have made many mistakes since, but turning down that chance to go to England before the war was one of the stupidest things I have ever done.

If I thought the undergraduate coursework was strenuous, law school was about threefold as difficult, as anyone who has done both well knows. There seemed to be barely enough hours in a day to do all the studying necessary to keep up with the classes.

I never decided what area of law I wanted to practice, but I quite enjoyed classes that strongly emphasized English history, such as real property law and the history of the common law.

The faculty was distinguished, but the *manner* of teaching had a great impact on how much was actually learned. I particularly remember George K. Gardner, professor of contract law, who delighted in being an absolute sphinx and carrying the Socratic method well beyond suitable limits. He only asked questions and would never give the answers, even at the end of the hour, an approach I found maddening. Others, such as Professor Warren Seavey, were far more effective for young students. They would use Socratic questions until about ten minutes before the hour and then clarify and explain the answers to which the questions had been leading.

Professor Edward Warren, known as "Bull" Warren for the vigor and animation with which he taught, was one of the best known and most respected law professors at Harvard. Unfortunately, my own experience with him was cut short when he became ill and retired during my freshman year. Luckily, the professor who replaced him, James Casner, was an extraordinary teacher.

Probably the most useful and helpful component of my law school education was the moot court work, done outside of class. This work, done under the title of the annual Ames Competition, was not compulsory, but everybody took part, as it provided the only real opportunity to go beyond theory into practice. You were elected to a law club—mine was the "Pow Wow"—which then worked as a team, writing briefs and preparing and giving oral arguments for the moot appellate court presentations, which were the heart of the competition. This was a lot of extra work but well worth it. The whole experience was quite realistic, especially once you reached the finals. At that stage, the judges who heard the cases were actual justices from the Massachusetts Supreme Judicial Court or the U.S. Court of Appeals or occasionally even the U.S. Supreme Court. They rendered decisions in our cases immediately after our presentations. The judges also wrote critiques and opinions, which inevitably helped us to improve our preparation and performance the next time around.

In the summer of 1940, I had an additional opportunity for real-world experience, working in the New York law firm of Simpson, Thatcher, Bartlett, a position arranged for me by my father. My useful but unexciting duties focused on researching state laws regulating the issuance of stock by corporations.

More enjoyable was acting as a proctor for undergraduate freshmen in Matthews Hall in the Yard, particularly because I recalled how helpful some of my own proctors had been in my freshman year. I found that I greatly enjoyed counseling individual students who were making their way in a new environment. Occasionally, some who found their new total freedom at Harvard exhilarating, after the strict rules at most schools, also required other help, such as being carried upstairs to their rooms after late-night parties in town. Being a proctor had its advantages. I had my own spacious, ground-floor suite, and I even drew a salary of two hundred dollars a year.

My third and final year of law school proved to be the most difficult. Not only was it the busiest and most crucial period of my law school career, I was also hit with another serious ear infection. I had to spend three or four weeks in the infirmary and lost almost two months of class and study time. I was treated with one of the new antibiotic drugs, despite some misgivings by my fine conservative Boston physician, Dr. Gooddale. He said later that the new sulfanilamide had probably cured me.

During most of my stay in the infirmary, I was required to lie flat, which made it nearly impossible for me to write. So some of my friends, primarily Sinc Armstrong, helped by writing letters to my anxious parents from my dictation. Sinc was enormously helpful during this time, and his kindness and generosity continued after I was released: he and his new bride let me stay with them at their home while I made a full recovery, which took another three or four weeks. I managed to catch up with my coursework and graduate on time, but it was a struggle.

Although I started and ended my Harvard career with extended illnesses, I consider the seven years at Harvard some of the best of my life. In fact, I enjoyed Harvard so much that it took a world war to get me out of there.

CHAPTER 3

OVER HERE

*E*arly in my first year of law school at Harvard, it seemed evident to me that Europe and England were rapidly sinking into disaster. Winston Churchill seemed virtually alone in recognizing the folly of appeasement. In late 1938 a Gallup poll indicated that 65 percent of my fellow Americans approved of the Munich agreement. However, I firmly believed that America's interests required us to be active participants in what later came to be called the "Good War." It seemed to me clear then, as it does now, that we could not exist in a world in which our European friends were overrun by the Nazis (or later by the Communists). I agreed with Churchill that appeasement is the vain and foolish hope that if you keep on feeding the crocodile, he will eat you last. But my fervor was shared by few of my fellow students, and my parents were completely opposed to my desire to fight in Europe.

In the summer of 1940, when the Battle of Britain was at its height, the Royal Air Force (RAF), in affiliation with the Royal Canadian Air

Force, was doing some confidential—and, I suppose, illegal[*]—
recruiting at a San Francisco hotel. Filled with the crusading spirit, I
volunteered but was rejected because I had "no depth perception."
I asked if that really made a difference, and the examining doctor
said, "Not really—you'll simply try to land the plane fifty feet above
the ground and walk away from it!" For the rest of the summer, I did
eye exercises, but it was to no avail; the RAF would not take me. It
was only later that I realized what a major investment it was to train
a pilot.

My parents were relieved, to say the least; my father had tried to
dissuade me from leaving law school early, and I reluctantly promised
that as long as the United States was not directly involved, I would
not try to enlist.

As additional incentive to keep me out of the war, my father
arranged a postgraduation position for me on the legal staff of the
Securities and Exchange Commission, a new regulatory agency created under FDR. I, however, was determined to join the military after
law school, at the latest, and rejected the position.

My father, hoping to keep my participation stateside, then
arranged for me to talk with an army intelligence unit at the Presidio
in San Francisco. I did meet with recruiters for the unit but concluded that the work there would be extremely limited. I was also put
off by the Shell Oil Company maps on the walls; this did not seem
like the highly classified information I thought we should be working with.

As it turned out, the United States was not brought into the war
before I finished my three years of law school. I graduated with an
LL.B. degree in June 1941, and after passing the New York bar exam,
I came home and enlisted in the army in September 1941, asking for
assignment to the infantry.

---

[*] Because of our officially neutral stance.

The infantry was, in my mind, the most honorable way to serve, a sentiment which I suppose came partially from my mother's New England heritage and the ethic that only the most difficult, disagreeable path was morally right and that anything enjoyable must be wrong. But my fascination with the infantry was also strongly influenced by the novels of Siegfried Sassoon, particularly *Memoirs of an Infantry Officer*, which I had read in high school or early in college. The book by no means glamorized the infantryman's existence—quite the opposite—but Sassoon's eloquent account stirred my patriotic passions and brought out the idea of noble service and total dedication to a cause; even though Sherston, Sassoon's protagonist, was against World War I, he fought in it bravely. Martyrdom is perhaps too strong a term, but I seemed always to have this compelling inclination to do what I thought was the right thing, even if it was difficult, unpopular, or actually disagreeable. I thought it essential that this war be fought, and I could not imagine not being involved myself.

I was sworn into the army at the San Francisco Armory. Most of the other men had been drafted and had little interest in saving the world. I should mention here that my brother, Peter, was married and had one child at this time, so he was not eligible for military war service, though he did have a civilian job with the navy, first in Hawaii (before Pearl Harbor) and then in Fresno. He served in the army later, in Korea. In any case, he did not particularly share my crusading fervor. While he was supportive and understanding of my desire to fight, he was also very concerned when I eventually went overseas; I believe he could think of no one less able to take care of himself abroad than I.

But I was more than eager to jump into the fight. My first army assignment was to the Presidio of Monterey, which was basically just a holding site for new recruits while it was determined where we would go next. No real military training was conducted there except for some routine close-order drills; to keep us occupied, we were sent to a huge warehouse to receive canned goods for distribution to other military units in California. We would stack tons and tons of Del Monte canned tomatoes and apricots on one side one day and then move them all to the other side of the warehouse the next. For me, this was varied with latrine duty.

After three weeks in Monterey, when I was starting to believe my father may have been right, I was sent to Camp Roberts in central California. This was the Infantry Replacement Training Center.

When I arrived in October 1941, much of Camp Roberts was still under construction, so a good deal of our time was spent building its infrastructure. The first major task was digging sewers under the main parade ground. All men with college and graduate degrees had been assigned to one company—and this was our assignment.

Aside from digging the sewer, most of our time was devoted to marching and more warehouse stocking. What little training there was was far from realistic. We had no real weapons to practice with: we carried wooden "rifles" and used blocks of wood labeled "hand grenade." We had to pass a couple of World War I–era rifles around among us during instruction in what our regular army instructor called "the normanclature of the rifle." "Normanclature," we were told, "is a Latin word meaning 'parts.'" The complete lack of equipment and preparedness was a lesson that I carried with me to the Pentagon many years later.

It was also as an enlisted man at Camp Roberts that I got a good idea of what is important to enlisted men and their morale, which proved invaluable when I served as secretary of defense.

At Roberts, training meant long marches with heavy packs, slithering under old rusted barbed-wire fences, and on a few rare occasions "dry firing"—that is, *not* firing—at the rifle range. There was training in how to use the rifle sling and in the proper prone, kneeling, and standing positions from which to shoot. In later weeks, we had a strong incentive to keep down, as live firing exercises were conducted over the fences under which we were crawling.

Toward the end of my three-month stint at Camp Roberts, I was moved to a clerkship under a tough first sergeant. He was aptly named Tartar, and his favorite expression was "Soldier boy, you've been in the army long enough to know…" followed by a long and detailed list of various infractions and errors. One recruit asked our drill sergeant why we wore *two* dog tags. The answer, delivered in the army's best singsong monotone: "One is cut off and sent to the next of kin; the other stays on the body."

On the weekend of December 6, 1941, I happened to be home on one of my few leaves. Saturday evening, December 6, was innocuous enough; my father and I went to see *The Little Foxes*, starring my one-time interview subject, Tallulah Bankhead.

The following morning, we heard on the radio that the Japanese had attacked Pearl Harbor. At first I thought it was just another Japanese threat. But the reality was soon confirmed. Fear rippled through San Francisco as people realized that if Hawaii could be surprised by an attack, we might be next.

The army immediately canceled all leaves—all military personnel were to return to their bases. So my father took me to the train station late that afternoon. I'll never forget that ride through the city: the Japanese areas, and even Chinatown, were in a complete state of siege. The National Guard and police were out in force—partly to protect Japanese-Americans who lived there, but also to guard against sabotage from possible Japanese collaborators.

I took a troop train to Camp Roberts, arriving around 2 A.M. on December 8. Now there were armed sentries at each barracks. I was stopped by a guard of apparent Japanese descent, and my first thought was, "My God—they've already taken over!" But, of course, he was Japanese-American, and as loyal to the United States and the army as the rest of us. In fact, he hesitated to let me in because I could not come up with the correct password, which had been issued after the bombing.

On December 8, after the United States declared war on Japan, our training took on a new relevance—now no one was merely going through the motions; we were preparing to fight a specific enemy.

President Roosevelt's address to Congress and the nation that day, which I and my fellow soldiers gathered around the radio to hear, made it all too real, especially for those of us on the West Coast: "The attack yesterday on the Hawaiian Islands has caused severe damage to American naval and military forces. I regret to tell you that very many American lives have been lost. In addition, American ships have been reported torpedoed on the high seas between San Francisco and Honolulu. . . . I ask that the Congress declare that since the unprovoked and dastardly attack by Japan on Sunday, December 7, 1941, a state of war has existed between the United States and the Japanese Empire."

Soon thereafter, I heard about Officers' Training School and immediately applied. A lot of the men I was training with did not *want* to be officers, which I could not understand. I thought if anyone was in an organization, he would, of course, seek to rise to the top.

I nearly missed my chance, however, because the first order that came in was for me to be assigned, as part of a big bloc of infantry trainees, to a battalion in Alaska. But within a week, my application for officer training was approved and I was ordered to Fort Benning, Georgia, to attend the Infantry Officer Candidate School.

I joined Officer Candidate Class 14, along with about one hundred other soldiers, for thirteen weeks of far more rigorous training than at Camp Roberts. In addition to the standard requirements of physical exercises, negotiating obstacle courses, marching, and map reading, there was target practice with live ammunition and real guns. We learned how to conduct night maneuvers through swamps, how to dismantle and reassemble weapons under difficult circumstances, and what to do in various other demanding situations. Physical skill had never been my strong suit, and that deficiency was exacerbated by the fact that I had not had much real basic training at Camp Roberts.

There was one nerve-wracking exercise that made quite an impression on me—almost literally. Our whole officer candidate class gathered around a young lieutenant who was to give us our instructions. Before he began, he came over to me and asked if I remembered him.

"Actually, no sir, I really don't," I replied. This was before I ran for office and learned to be much more reluctant to admit I could not remember someone.

"Well, you should," he said, "because I met you when I was in competition for the *Harvard Crimson*."

"Ah, yes," I said, smiling cheerfully. "Did you enjoy the *Crimson*?"

He responded in an even tone of voice, "Not after you cut me from the competition."

This took me rather aback, and I was trying to think how best to respond to it, when he turned back to the group and began explaining the day's exercise.

This exercise was a result of French troops' not knowing how to deal with mass tank attacks. The tanks engendered a great deal of fear and panic, and the troops frequently surrendered or ran away. There was to be none of that in the American army, the lieutenant said, and we were going to practice some tactics that our strategic planners had come up with. This seemed reasonable enough.

Basically, what the exercise entailed was digging a small foxhole (easier said than done in the hard, red clay of Georgia), which had to be narrow enough that it would support the heavy weight of the tank without caving in, but also deep enough that you could get your entire body into it, crouching so that the top of your helmet was below ground level. This still seemed reasonable enough.

In addition, a new, small, plastic grenade had been developed, and we were to push one into the tread of the tank as it passed over the foxhole. Anticipating some of our worries, he explained that the timing of the fuse had been worked out so that it would not go off until about fifteen or twenty seconds after the tank had rolled on past. It was beginning to sound a little less reasonable, but still rather a neat idea—for someone else.

However, the lieutenant then announced that we did not have time for the whole class to practice this, and so only a handful of us would do it. I suppose I shouldn't have been surprised that he pointed a stubby finger at me first and yelled, "You!" Four other names were rattled off quickly, and we were given entrenching tools (the formal army name for the shovels we carried under our packs) and mock grenades made out of something like Play-Doh because we did not have any of the real plastic grenades.

A bugle sounded, meaning we had sixteen minutes before the tanks arrived. We started scrabbling away frantically at the Georgia clay, probably the most impermeable substance that had yet been discovered by man. Soon there was, in the distance, a rumbling sound, which we assumed were the tanks, although none of us had ever actually heard or seen a tank in action before. The rumble increased, as did our efforts, and finally I got to the point where it was possible, by assuming practically a fetal position, to wedge myself into the foxhole.

Shortly, the sunlight was blotted out, and I saw, too close for comfort, the tank tread above me. Somehow I was able to get one arm up and push the Play-Doh as hard as I could into the tread. I was never so glad to see the blistering Georgia sun as when the tank finally rumbled off. I counted fifteen seconds, but my Play-Doh did not explode, so the realism was over.

I extricated myself from the hole to see that my four colleagues had apparently long since emerged from theirs. Relieved laughter swept the group, and we stood around sort of anticipating the congratulations of our leader. But he had moved on to the next exercise—with what I thought was a fairly disappointed look.

In other training, I was surprised that I excelled at rifle practice, perhaps because I'd had no previous experience (except a BB gun at home and the dry runs at Camp Roberts). I simply did exactly what the instructors told me to do. Many of my fellow candidates had trouble, I suspect, because they had hunted extensively and had already learned other methods of shooting.

For the relatively short amount of time we spent in the barracks, a couple of vivid memories stick in my mind. Both involved the radio. A large, burly fellow infantry officer candidate named "Tex" Charlton had somehow hooked up his radio and phonograph so that when the lights came on every morning at 5 A.M. and the bugles blew reveille, his phonograph would blare out "Deep in the Heart of Texas." This was not then one of my favorite songs, nor did the passing mornings endear it to me.

The other thing I most remember was Prime Minister Churchill's radio addresses. The first of these talks that I heard was a rebroadcast of his address to the Joint Session of Congress not long after Pearl Harbor. I had been in the mud all that winter day, and all the equipment needed thorough cleaning before another execrable dinner. But Mr. Churchill's great prose delivered in those matchless tones (even on the small, tinny barracks radio) revived any flagging spirits, just as he inspired the people of England and of occupied Europe.

In May 1942 I was commissioned as a second lieutenant. My new officer's cap and gold bars made me feel important and proud of myself. I was sent home for a five- to seven-day leave before being deployed overseas. The week turned into two weeks, and ultimately into about five weeks, because there was no transport available.

Almost the last day I was at Fort Benning, we had been asked to fill out a questionnaire stating where we wished to be assigned. I put down England as my first choice and Northern Ireland as my second, since the United States was starting to build air bases there. But I doubt if anyone even read those questionnaires (a point I mentioned to the army many years later). Within six weeks I was on a ship to Australia.

CHAPTER 4

OVER THERE

Shortly before I shipped out, I had an inkling that I probably was not going to England. My orders said I was to go to "SUMAC." I assumed this was some obscure secret location, but I soon learned that SUMAC stood for "summer arctic," which meant that I would be in a climate that required both summer and arctic uniforms. Actually, on further reflection, I realized that could have meant England, but I guessed that it would most likely be the South Pacific.

My journey got off to a rather inauspicious start in July of 1942 when my mother and father were seeing me off at the dock in San Francisco. My mother had packed a box of her cookies and brownies for my trip. I set it down momentarily with my luggage while I went to the entrance of the pier to say good-bye to my parents, as they were not allowed beyond that point. When I returned, the cookies and brownies were gone. A rather traumatic departure, I thought.

The ship, the USS *Mt. Vernon*, was actually a converted ocean cruise liner, but needless to say, it was no longer a luxury ship.

Sandwiched into the five-high, sea-tossed canvas bunks were hundreds of other naive young men like me—in the same boat, literally and figuratively. Some were—or at least acted—swaggeringly confident and almost fanatical in their zeal to convince "the Japs" that *nobody* pushes the United States around. But in the creaking and pitching dark of the vast ocean, I am sure that most soldiers aboard felt at least some slight panic and nauseating aloneness. Those were the times, I suspect, when many of us clung to the images of such simple things as the curtains on our bedroom windows at home, our aproned mothers making our favorite meal, summer football games with our brothers and childhood friends. Those days seemed so innocent and so young and so far from where we were now, and as we sailed off to an uncertain future, it began to occur to us, perhaps for the first time, that maybe we were not all that invincible.

The cabin to which I was assigned was unbelievably hot because it was right over the laundry. Occasionally I slept out on deck, which was fine until the nightly General Quarters alert was called and everyone scrambled to their posts, usually trampling me in the process.

The eighteen-day journey to the Pacific theater did have its good points. Soon after we were under way, I noticed a young, red-haired nurse playing checkers with an "elderly" ship's officer. He must have been all of fifty years old. Later, I learned that this was the father of one of her friends. She was an army nurse, one of only four on board, being sent as a replacement to a station hospital in Brisbane.

I had found a sheltered spot on deck and taken refuge there with my books. After a while, I was interrupted by one of the nurses bent on rescuing a lonely soldier. She kept up a lively though one-sided conversation, asking if I played various games, to all of which I had to answer no. Finally she inquired what, if not cards, dice, or shuffleboard, did I play. In the hope of being left in peace, I admitted to chess—whereupon she insisted that I come down to their cabin to meet the nurse who played chess. I did, and to my surprise—or maybe to my hope—it was the one I had noticed earlier—Lieutenant Rebecca Jane Dalton from the state of Maine, as she informed me. She, too, was a second lieutenant, but outranked me, as she had been commissioned a few months earlier than I. She also outplayed me at chess, and having won that first match, she never played again, saying she had sense enough to quit when ahead. Luckily, I now have a delightful red-headed grandson who plays a great game.

Anyway, on that long-ago transport, chess no longer mattered, for as I started to leave that evening, thinking I had taken too much of her time, I said I thought I would take a walk around the deck. "Not without me, you won't," she replied, and that was the first of many star-filled evening walks. From then on, we spent every free moment together talking, walking, reading, sometimes just watching the sea, and mostly ignoring the rest of the world.

We could not share meals together since all the women—four nurses and eighteen Red Cross ladies—were required to eat with the higher-ranking army officers in the navy officers' dining room. But she took pleasure in smuggling me cakes and cookies, even a sandwich now and then, which were a great improvement over the meals served on the lower decks.

To our dismay when we disembarked in Sydney, we were separated: I went to a makeshift barracks at Randwick Racetrack outside the city, and Jane, to a hotel called 52 Maclay Street.

With a bit of rearranging, however, we were soon together again, and against all regulations, we were quietly married in Sydney. We had two days there before she left by train for Stuartholm, a convent that had been converted to an army hospital in Brisbane. I had been at the racetrack barracks when I returned to find that all the nurses were leaving with a train full of soldiers. Told that it would take a day or two for them to get to Brisbane and that there would be no food available except what you could purchase at stops, I quickly got a box lunch of sandwiches and cheese and a bottle of sherry. The train was about to pull out when I got there, but I was able to deliver the lunch to Jane and say a quick good-bye.

I informed my mother and father of our marriage by letter after the wedding. They were, of course, surprised because I was so shy, and my mother had all the normal reservations that all mothers have about any daughter-in-law.

Several days after Jane left, I took off by the same train for Rockhampton. Having been told how long each stop lasted, I was able to get off the front of the train in Brisbane, spend an hour with Jane at the hospital, and get back on board at the rear before it cleared the station. While she was in Brisbane, I was also able to visit now and then on supply trucks going back and forth between there and Rockhampton.

Then she was sent to Southport, a delightful little seaside town, to join a hospital group being made ready to relieve a unit at a camp in the Beanley Mountains. It was on the first of several visits to Southport that I had my first airplane ride. It was in a Royal Australian Air Force DC-3, whose pilot was quite willing to add me to his cargo of spare aircraft engines.

I was not there when the nurses left Southport by truck, sitting sideways on planks, for the long ride up the mountains. How they survived the trip is hard to imagine.

Jane and I did not meet again until she came back to Brisbane as a patient with dengue fever. Routine exams indicated that she was pregnant, and our marriage became public. Spouses were not allowed to stay in a war zone together. As a result, with other evacuees, she was ticketed for the next available transport home. I wrote my parents to expect her. When news of our marriage reached Jane's family, her somewhat catty sister-in-law said that "she always knew Jane would go and marry some soldier." One of Jane's favorite stories is to quote that and add, "Well, she was right. I did, and after fifty years, he is still *some* soldier."

Jane and I knew that we would miss each other dreadfully, but she would be safer at home and I would soon be moving up to New Guinea.

After a seemingly endless trip back to the States on a Danish freighter that kept breaking down, she arrived in San Francisco. She visited with my parents briefly before returning to Maine.

On the 27th of April, 1943, our child was born, weighing barely five pounds, but vigorous and healthy. A few days later I received a telegram: "Daughter born—all is well." Through some error, I received the same message three times in the next few days, so I wondered if we had had triplets. It turned out to be just one—Arlin Cerise Weinberger, named for Jane's adoptive mother, Stella Arlin Newcomb, and my mother, Cerise Hampson Weinberger—and my wife and daughter moved to San Francisco, waiting for the end of the war and my return. They stayed with my mother and father, an arrangement that underwent the normal strains of wartime living in close quarters. Jane and my father had an immediate fondness for each other, and my father was fascinated with Arlin. My mother, on the other hand, had some reservations about my new bride, as I suspect she would have had no matter whom I had married. Later, Mother came to like and depend on Jane.

I never met Jane's family. Her mother died before I made it to Maine, and Jane's father, a retired banker, had died earlier.

My mother and father and I continued to correspond frequently; my father wrote once a week, my mother more often, and Jane nearly every day. The mail arrived in batches, so I'd get four or five letters at once, sometimes two to three weeks apart. Finally, they started numbering their letters, so I would read them in the correct order. As every soldier knows, mail call is the highlight of the week (or whenever it arrived), and I was fortunate to have such a close-knit family and a devoted wife. Years later, remembering the trauma of waiting for the mail, I was determined as secretary of defense to improve the speed of mail delivery to the troops.

My own letters were written as frequently as possible. When we were in a rear area with some spare time I would write rather illegible scrawls. Occasionally I used "V-Mail," a form of photostatted mail that was designed to save space and weight but was very public. Years later someone saw a V-Mail letter from me to my family in a Seattle bookstore and bought it for me.

When I went overseas for duty, I was classified as a "Casual Unassigned." It was not until after I arrived in Australia that I was assigned to the Forty-first Infantry Division. The core of the Forty-first, a National Guard division mostly from Oregon and Washington, was already there but was understrength. We, the newly arrived crop of soldiers, were to "bring them up to strength," which seemed to me a gross misuse of the language, because we knew less than they did. Besides being very green we were also, I sensed, seen as interlopers. Indeed, as a National Guard outfit, most of the soldiers in my unit were from the same small town, Baker, Oregon, and had trained together for years. War does not allow much freedom of choice, so we inevitably grew to depend on each other, to have confidence in and trust each other, which is essential for a military unit.

After a few days in Sydney, I was sent north to Rockhampton for some field training. Shortly after we arrived, one of the men in my platoon was killed in an awful accident. We were practicing advances through jungle territory, putting out flank guards on each side of the line of advance and a point man in front. If the point man encounters opposition, you cover him, and he motions the rest where to go to avoid fire. We were using live ammunition, and when the maneuver called for shooting, someone behind me fired excitedly and hit the point man from behind. I actually heard the bullet on its way past my ear. That was my first experience with a casualty by so-called friendly fire. We had had a few live-fire exercises at Fort Benning, but no accidents. When I saw him go down, it seemed to me to be far too realistic a fall. I halted the exercise, ran forward, and tried to do what little I could for my fellow infantryman, a Hispanic corporal. I called for a stretcher and tried to comfort him and stop the flow of blood oozing from his back. We finally got him to a hospital in Rockhampton. He lived for two or three days, and I visited him in the hospital; when he died, I attended the funeral Mass in a small Rockhampton church. I wrote to his mother and father, telling about his burial after a high Catholic Mass. Ever since, the term "killed by friendly fire" has had a special and terrible meaning for me.

After more training, including night maneuvers, our regiment in early 1943 was sent up to New Guinea, landing at Port Moresby. Then we were flown to the Buna/Dobodura area on the north side of the island, over the Owen Stanley Mountains, one of the most rugged areas in the world. It probably would have taken two to three weeks to march over, and we all would have been in terrible shape by the time we got there. So the army pulled together air transport—a whole group of disparate planes—and that took quite a while. We had to wait twenty-four to thirty-six hours at the Port Moresby airstrip, during which time we had no food. (We were supposed to be fed when we reached Dobodura on the other side of the mountains.) Finally, they did issue us United States Army Field Ration D, which was a chocolate bar. Being a confirmed "chocoholic" and very hungry, I immediately devoured the whole thing. What I did not understand was that this was not an ordinary chocolate bar. It had, packed into it, a large number of highly concentrated and enhanced vitamins and, in fact, was the equivalent of a one-day, three-meal pack; you certainly weren't supposed to eat it all at once. Needless to say, I was terribly, terribly ill during the very turbulent flight over the Owen Stanleys. Once we landed, I, being the platoon leader, was supposed to organize the platoon and begin the march from the rudimentary airstrip to the sea, which I managed to do. I was almost hoping that the Japanese would attack immediately so that at least I could lie down. They did not, however, so we marched over a very rough log and mud road for

God knows how many hours and eventually got to our bivouac area in a coconut grove just inland from the beach.

While on the northern coast of New Guinea, we sustained a few Japanese air raids, generally just three or four planes at a time—nothing remotely resembling what Europe was enduring. When they came, you were supposed to get into a foxhole; the first time I did, I found a coiled snake as my companion. I decided that I would rather get hit by a bomb. From then on, I stayed around the tents (and later, shacks) during air raids, which was more stupidity than bravery.

Once in the Buna area, we mostly conducted patrols through the thick jungle. The Japanese were defending the Buna airstrip, and they had a nasty habit of tying snipers into trees. Once they even hauled a naval gun up a tree, and it and its crew stayed there for two or three days until we were able to locate and dispose of it. None of the infantry manuals prepared us for dealing with that. But we rarely encountered the enemy; eventually the Japanese abandoned the airfield, and we occupied it.

After several months in the Dobodura area, we were sent to Milne Bay on the eastern tip of New Guinea for more patrolling. We also patrolled further west for some months, and that was interspersed with building perimeter defenses and slightly more sophisticated living quarters. Every day we patrolled the jungle, manned the perimeters of our camp at night (the Japanese were always expected to attack at dawn), and cleaned and recleaned rifles and artillery pieces.

When our situation permitted it, I used to talk to the men in my platoon in an informal way, usually gathered in a rough circle, sitting on logs. They had all kinds of questions, ranging from trying to understand why particular orders had been given to asking why the mail took so long and who would get to go home. The most frequently asked question was, Why are we in New Guinea?

I tried to point out that we could not have stayed out of the war, that, that even the United States could be attacked, and in any event, we could not live in the world were both Europe and Asia overrun by the enemy. I told them I would much rather defend California or Oregon from New Guinea than from California itself.

Many seemed to enjoy these sessions. I found it a good way to try to keep up morale, for with periods of inaction and uncertainty about what we were to do, questions and doubts and the desire to go home multiplied.

There was a rough outdoor area used to show the very occasional film sent over by the USO to entertain the troops. There was also an area for religious services on Sunday mornings when the situation permitted. A rough entrance portal had been constructed and a handmade sign erected on which was a quotation from Emerson's *Sacrifice*—" 'Tis man's perdition to be safe, when for the truth he ought to die."

My law school education was put to use in a couple of court-martial cases that underlined why a new Code of Military Justice was enacted after the war. One was a desertion case, and when the jury showed signs of not believing the evidence, the regimental commander ordered the trial adjourned and summoned all to his tent. He said he did not want to hear any nonsense about an acquittal: "When I charge a man, he is guilty." He also mentioned that he made out the efficiency reports for all the officers. The implication was clear.

I was also assigned as a regimental gas officer and sent back to Australia for two weeks' training in dealing with poisonous gases. The school was just outside of Brisbane. There are two things I particularly remember about it. One was that the food was infinitely better than anything we'd had in months and months in the field; the second was that we lived in a big old house that was not by present standards luxurious but that at the time seemed like a four-star hotel.

Here we had very realistic training that included putting a drop of mustard gas on your arm so that you could see its actual effects. I still have the scar.

Shortly after I returned to my regiment, I became very ill with malaria and spent two or three weeks in the hospital. In New Guinea, 70 percent of my regiment had become ineffective because of malaria. Had we been subjected to a major attack at that time, we would probably not have been able to hold any of our positions.

In the field, we had introduced preventative water sanitation measures in an effort to destroy the mosquitoes that transmitted the disease. This consisted largely of turning over anything in the bivouac area that could gather water (usually old coconut shells) and spreading oil over any puddles to eliminate standing water where mosquitoes could breed. We created a fifty-yard perimeter with no standing water around our positions because fifty yards was supposed to be the flight range of the average mosquito. Our methods worked and the percentage of men well enough to fight increased.

For those not familiar with malaria, there are two kinds. There is vivax, or benign tertian, malaria, which is relatively mild, though it recurs for many years. When it does, it lasts for three days. Plasmodium falciparum, on the other hand, is a malignant, virulent, lethal strain. It has one advantage: if you get over it, it does not recur.

I had a fever of about 105, but the doctors could not identify which kind of malaria I had. They got me up one day and made me run up and down a hill behind the hospital tent. Then they were able to get a positive smear and found it was indeed falciparum. Since the treatment for both types (quinine, Atabrine, and bed rest) seemed to be the same, I did not understand why it was so important to determine which type I had. I was not in the best condition after my high-fever run, but at least it was an effective rapid-weight-loss treatment—had I needed to lose any weight then. I did eventually make a full recovery.

One other memory I have of that station hospital was a visit by Eleanor Roosevelt. We were supposed to have everything spruced up for her and then stand by our beds when she came in. After I used up some remaining energy cleaning the place, I took refuge in the gentlemen's lounge so that I would not have to see her. I took my politics rather too seriously then.

The only other health problem I encountered during the war was a slight hearing loss, due mostly to too much exposure to the 37mm antitank gun, which sounded like a loud, angry Pekingese. Ear protection during test firing was not introduced until much later.

Later in 1943, I was promoted to the rank of captain and transferred to General Douglas MacArthur's headquarters to serve in the Combined Operational Intelligence Center, a move to which I objected seriously. Being young and foolish and still filled with the crusading spirit, I wanted to stay in the field with my platoon and company and do some good, or so I thought. But the army wanted someone with legal and/or newspaper experience to join General MacArthur's staff in Brisbane, Australia.

When I arrived at my new post, I sought an interview with General Chamberlin, of General MacArthur's staff, to request reassignment to the division. It was a short interview. He looked me up and down and said, "Young man, in the army you go where you are sent. The army knows what is best for you."

I actually found my new duties interesting. I was on duty two days and two nights, then off a day, and back on for two days. My task was primarily to analyze intelligence reports coming in and then write situation briefs for the general. I would also draft communiqués that he would send to other theater commanders. In the jungle, platoon officers were lucky if they knew what was happening fifty yards on either side of them; from my new vantage point, I could see the whole Pacific campaign as it developed day by day.

General MacArthur was a tremendously imposing man. I worked on the same floor where he had his office—in the Australian Mutual Provident Society, or AMP Building. I could always tell when the general was on duty because he kept his hat on top of a file cabinet that I could see from across the courtyard.

One evening, after he had left—or at least his hat was gone—I walked out into the corridor, toward the elevator, and suddenly I saw him and his whole entourage heading for the same elevator. He saw me pull back and said, in those deliberate, sonorous, organ-like tones, "Come, ride along with me, Captain." I felt it was a royal command. We got in the elevator, and I stood at rigid attention—which was hard to do for eight or ten floors—the general in full uniform, with more rows of ribbons than I could imagine and a presence that inspired awe.

There was one other occasion on which we met at close range. The United States had a small amphibious invasion force at sea, preparing to land at dawn on a small Pacific island (I've forgotten which one). An intelligence signal came across my desk around midnight. Japanese naval units were sighted in the vicinity. I decided the situation was important enough to inform General MacArthur—and I was the only person on duty, so I had to be the messenger. I ran the four blocks from headquarters to Lennon's Hotel, where he lived, and eventually got through all the security to find the general in his bathrobe, but looking as if he were in full uniform, with impeccable posture and dignified formality. He read the intelligence report carefully. "Well, what do *you* think, Captain? What would you do?"

"Well, sir," I said nervously, "I think the Japanese are there by chance. I don't think they've discovered our plan. I don't think they'll interfere with the invasion."

"That's what I think, too. Good night." I raced back to my desk and spent the rest of the night fearing that I had been wrong. Much to my relief, our assessments turned out to be correct. Our landing succeeded unopposed.

My position gave me a minor part in discussing a possible landing on Japan, dubbed Operation Olympic. If we had not dropped the atomic bomb on Japan, we almost certainly would have lost more than two divisions in any ground assault on the home islands of

Honshu and Kyushu. Indeed, the first two divisions, one of them the Forty-first, were written off as assumed total losses. There would have been many more deaths in lost ships; a massive and prolonged engagement would have meant even more casualties on both sides; and there was no certainty that even a successful invasion would lead to a Japanese surrender. That is why I have always felt the decision to drop the bomb was correct.

After having been with MacArthur as his Intelligence Headquarters moved from Australia to New Guinea and then to the Philippines as the war progressed, I was offered the chance to go with him to Japan as part of the occupation force. But I was also offered, at about the same time—late summer of 1945—the chance to go home for good, because I had a very high number of points. (One received points for the number of months served overseas, the total length of time in the service, number of dependents, and so forth, so I was one of the first people selected to go home.)

I quickly decided to do that. My father had died the previous September when I was home on a brief leave, and I had had to go back to the war almost immediately, leaving the rest of my family to deal with the grief and not really dealing with it myself. I had carried a vague, dolorous feeling in the pit of my stomach since that time, but only now were the details starting to come back to me.

After returning from a business trip to Los Angeles, on the Southern Pacific train called the "Lark," and after a normal day at the office, my father had gone to bed. But my mother woke me close to midnight, concerned that he was feeling ill and short of breath. I ran up the street to get Dr. Shwartz, a friend of the family. When he arrived at our house, he immediately diagnosed heart trouble and called for an ambulance. The doctor at the hospital would not let my mother and me in to see my father for a couple of hours, and when we did go in, we were taken aback to see him in an oxygen tent; neither of us had seen such a thing before.

My father died about a week after the original attack, which doctors diagnosed as a massive coronary occlusion. I think he probably would have survived with current treatment and medications, but at that time, they could not do anything to unblock the clogged arteries. I'm afraid that his death was hastened by his constant worrying about my military service; he was only fifty-seven years old.

In any event, with the war essentially over, I wanted to return home to stay and get started on my law practice. By the end of September 1945, three years after I had gone to war, I was home.

My service in World War II was invaluable training for when I became secretary of defense in 1981. In particular, I was struck by the terrible lack of foresight that had left America so unprepared—materially, psychologically, and in trained manpower—for war.

In 1941 very, very few people were ready to teach new recruits. There was a total lack of preparation for many of the things we ultimately had to do and the conditions in which we had to fight. Those of us who were assigned to units in the Pacific had read about the jungles but had no training in jungle fighting or living in a jungle environment. In fact, we had no specialized training at all. For the most part, our knowledge of the South Pacific was limited to films that starred Dorothy Lamour.

The United States was totally unready for a war then. If anybody had been willing to look and listen, we could have seen it coming—at least a few months before it was upon us. Few did and most would not have believed any warnings. In fact, we made a large sale of scrap metal to Japan on December 3, 1941. Right up to that point there seemed to be no belief that we could ever be at war. We were not psychologically prepared as a nation. I learned many lessons from that and felt keenly the necessity of adequate training of men and procurement of materiel.

In 1981 I saw that, again, we had basically the same shortages of equipment and qualified personnel that we had had before World

War II and were facing—at the height of the Cold War—an aggressive global threat. I intended to rebuild our military strength very quickly, greatly improve our transport capability, and pre-position weapons in Europe so that we could mobilize rapidly. In World War II, we had had the blessing of time. But we could no longer take shelter behind our two great oceans when ballistic missiles could cross those oceans in eighteen minutes.

In 1981 General Jack Vessey and I were among only a handful of people left in the Pentagon who had seen active duty—as both enlisted men and officers—in World War II. Of the secretaries who immediately preceded me—Brown, Laird, Schlesinger—none had had any wartime military experience. I felt I was very lucky and was proud to have served in the infantry, and even given the vastly different situation of the 1980s, I knew the infantry was and is still the infantry. Without it and its ability to take and hold enemy ground, we would never be able to win wars.

CHAPTER 5

SETTLING DOWN

By late summer of 1945 I was quite ready to come home. The war had been won and I had been in the army for a little over four years. I was glad I had served, and still think that everyone should serve his country in some way.

But I never considered a career in the military. I was anxious to begin my law practice. I arrived at Fort Mason in San Francisco after a long, slow trip on a very crowded troop ship, the ship still zigzagging because the Japanese surrender had not yet been signed. From there I was sent to Camp Beale at Marysville, near Sacramento, to be officially discharged. It was there that I was reunited with Jane. She had taken a bus from San Francisco after receiving my one permitted call to say that we had actually docked. I suddenly realized I had never seen her in civilian clothes—but that made little difference.

The town was packed far beyond its capacity with returning soldiers and their families. We finally secured a room with a beautiful view of the freight yards—which also brought an all-night cacophony

of clanging trains. Still, Marysville was a neat, clean little town—
quite a pleasant contrast from the gritty army life. As Jane and I
strolled through its manicured park the next morning, we decided to
stop in a nearby church, which we later learned was Baptist. We
could not help noticing that the church reverberated with jubilant
singing, clapping, and shouts of "Hallelujah!" I had never before seen
people so thoroughly enjoying themselves at church; I had known
only Episcopal and Anglican church services—solemn, quiet events.
At first, I felt almost like a child reluctantly taking part in a prank at
which I was certain we would get caught. But the enthusiasm was
contagious, and I soon found myself enjoying the atmosphere.

After that, Jane and I continued our walk and pondered our future.
Jane wondered what we would do next. Quite spontaneously, I burst
out that I wanted to be famous. A Harvard classmate and fellow
Crimson editor, Hans Zinsser Jr., had hoped, before the war, that I
wouldn't be "just a lawyer." He had it exactly right—I wanted to
practice law, but not be "just a lawyer."

I think that, somewhere in my mind, I aspired—if only in general
terms—to the example of one of my great heroes, Theodore Roosevelt.
Ill and weak for much of his childhood, as I was in mine, he com-
pensated later by engaging in a mentally and physically vigorous life.
I had no desire to hunt buffalo in the Badlands or scale Europe's
peaks, but I felt I had to prove that I had overcome earlier weaknesses
and make something of myself. But at the same time, I felt the same
uncertainty that Roosevelt once expressed: "I wonder if I won't find
everything in life too big for my abilities." To overcome this, I sub-
consciously made extra efforts. Jane has often reminded me of our
talk that day.

After my separation from the army, we took a bus back to San
Francisco to the house where I had grown up and where Jane, Arlin,
and my mother were living. To my daughter I was a stranger, but she
seemed to me a beautiful child with a strong will and decided opin-

ions of her own. My mother looked much the same as when I had last seen her in 1944 and kept herself busy by doing radio surveys—something like the Nielsen ratings for television—by phone from home. A few months later she took a position at a children's clothing and toy store near our house. It bothered my brother terribly; he thought it was awful that she was working, particularly because she did not need to, but she seemed to enjoy it.

As for myself, I had an offer with a small New York firm and had passed the New York bar examination in 1941, but I wanted to stay in San Francisco and looked for leads at the San Francisco Harvard Club. The club directed me to a local attorney, Roger Kimball, who was interested in helping anyone who had been to Harvard and served in the war. He arranged a number of interviews for me, including a law clerkship with a judge newly appointed to the U.S. Court of Appeals for the Ninth Circuit. This was William Orr, former chief justice of Nevada. I met him in his chambers in the Post Office Building at Seventh and Mission. I had occasionally gone to that court with my father when he argued cases there, but I had never seen the judges' chambers. They were very grand—large, airy rooms with beautiful redwood paneling. The law clerk's office also seemed palatial as far as I was concerned, but then, I was coming practically straight out of a tent.

The entire building was a lavish federal building by any standard. It had been rebuilt after the devastating San Francisco earthquake of 1906. Something like $7 million had been appropriated for the reconstruction, but surprisingly, the final cost was way under that—somewhere around $5½ million. There was, at that time, a peculiar federal budgetary provision: by law, the surplus could not be returned to the Treasury. So they went back through the building and added embellishments. They paneled the offices with redwood and added a great deal of marble, among other things, so it turned out to be an extremely opulent building in an old-fashioned sense.

Judge Orr was cordial, pleasant, dignified, respectful, and a man of obvious talent. And he was a very western judge. From time to time, he wore a white cattleman's hat. He also had a dry, laconic, western sense of humor and knew numerous frontier jokes. He was a patriot as well, and admired anyone who had served in the war. The only clothing I had at the time that came remotely close to fitting (I had lost about fifty pounds) was my uniform. I wore it at our interview, and I think that was 95 percent of his reason for hiring me.

I was totally unprepared and ill-equipped to help a judge, or really to do anything except be an infantryman, and we had a great surplus of those then. I had been away for four years and had not even passed the California bar examination. Luckily, the judge had one other employee—an experienced, gray-haired lady named Grace Arnold, who had served with other judges and knew everything there was to know about federal courts. Shortly after she told me she had been a Red Cross nurse in World War I, she rather abruptly asked, "How old do you think I am?" Being stupidly more interested in accuracy than feelings, I did a rapid calculation and came up with precisely the right answer mathematically. "However did you know that?" she replied testily. It took several days to restore a cordial relationship, but she became a close friend of both my wife and me.

As soon as I was ensconced in my beautiful office and had begun my new job with the judge (less than a month after I had returned from overseas), I enrolled in a bar examination preparation course. It was an evening course given by Bernard Witkin, who had written a few textbooks and was famous in California law circles, both for his legal treatises and for his preparation course. The course accomplished its purpose, but it was the antithesis of Harvard Law School. There, they generally used the Socratic method in which professors would bring out the law by questioning you and having you give the answers. In the bar preparation course, in effect, Mr. Witkin bored a hole in your head and simply poured in, night after night, the things he knew you would need to pass the bar.

Meanwhile, my wife was busy house-hunting. Ultimately, she found a house in Sausalito for around $5,000. It was financed not by a bank but by the very effective California State Veterans' Program. If the state was satisfied with the price, the state would buy the house outright, and you would then pay the state back in very small monthly payments. As I recall, our monthly payment was about $40, which fit nicely with my court salary of $200 a month.

We moved in shortly after Christmas 1945. It was a very good first home. Perched on the side of a hill and nestled in a virtual tent of trees, the tiny house had three floors, but with basically one room on each floor. It was cozy, with a porch and a fireplace, and the living room had a cathedral ceiling. The trees framed a huge picture window that afforded an absolutely glorious, 180-degree view of the bay and of San Francisco. Leaf-blanketed log steps crawled from our street clear down to the center of Sausalito, at least one hundred steps that I counted every time I climbed them with groceries. I was in pretty good shape then, as walking was, and had been during the war, my primary mode of transportation.

Our lot was not only steep but narrow, so we were quite close to the neighbors' homes. We could hear their dog barking, and they could, on occasion, hear Arlin crying. A nice older couple who lived on one side of us often spoke of how terrible the war must have been, and whenever they heard Arlin crying, they sympathized with Jane. They were quite sure that I was suffering from war trauma and probably beating the child. Actually, the only "war trauma" I experienced, which no doubt was the same for many soldiers, was a recurring nightmare: for years I dreamed I was holding a hand grenade about to go off, and I would wake up perspiring profusely and grinding my teeth.

In January 1946 I took the California bar examination, and around May I was informed that I had passed and now had a chance to practice what I had been trained for. I enjoyed my work with Judge Orr, but there was no ladder to move up. Still, I knew it would be a wrench to leave Judge Orr, with whom I had formed a lasting friendship. He was not only a great judge but a first-class teacher and role model as well. He was the first to teach me, not by purposeful intention, but by example and by his kindness and great help, that not all Democratic appointees were necessarily bad! I fear the degree of my partisanship then was virtually limitless.

Judge Orr was a man of simple tastes who abhorred all pretense or affectation. He was completely a man of the people but not a populist, and he never forgot the dignity, without pomposity, he felt was required of a judge. He would frequently take me to a simple lunch at a cafeteria (I believe it was called, ironically, the Clinton Cafeteria) on Market Street, a few blocks from the courthouse.

In any event, I resisted the temptation to stay on, and I started looking for another job. Within a couple of months, I took a position as a very junior associate in the old San Francisco law firm of Heller, Ehrman, White & McAuliffe. At first, my new position seemed almost like a step down. My initial salary was barely more than before, and instead of having my own spacious, paneled office I now shared a tiny office with another associate, Robert Harris, and all of the firm's many years of files. I was the newest, youngest, and lowest in the firm, and the legal profession now seemed to me not quite the noble vision of it that I had carried in my mind since the day I graduated from law school. On that day, along with our diplomas, we were given Harvard's traditional dictum: "You are awarded the degree of Bachelor of Law, and admitted to the study and practice of those wise restraints that make men free."

The firm, located in the old Wells Fargo Bank Building (the bank was our principal client), had about eighteen people at that time:

twelve partners and six associates, an unusual ratio. Today, Heller, Ehrman has well over four hundred attorneys and offices in several cities. I have frequently pointed out to my former colleagues that the firm achieved its huge growth and prosperity shortly after I left them.

The job consisted almost completely of legal research in the firm's law library. Occasionally, abstruse points required a trip to the city law library, but generally you were "confined to quarters," to use the old army term. Very rarely did you get to court. When you did, it was to carry books and serve as a lowly assistant to the real counsel. But it was the best way to learn how to be a lawyer—something that neither law school nor the bar examination really taught.

One example of the large degree of naiveté I possessed at that time came in connection with our client Hiram Walker, the big Canadian distiller. The problem involved various state regulations concerning alcoholic beverages, and I was asked to get the regulations dealing with fermented wines. I promptly produced the regulations that governed the sale of distilled spirits. Not knowing there was a difference, I was quite surprised when this was pointed out to me rather forcefully. My "research" was immediately rejected.

Later, I also wrote briefs for cases on appeal and occasionally argued preliminary motions before trial courts, usually in probate matters involving wills and trusts. While these were minor problems, I prepared as carefully as if it were a law school mock trial. But some briefs were handed to me as I started on the streetcar trip to City Hall, and my preparation had to be limited to the ten minutes or so that those trips required.

One of my more interesting assignments was a criminal antitrust case brought against several California rice milling companies. This trial showed me how powerful, and absurd, the government can be.

The rice companies had been asked by the U.S. Department of Agriculture to get together as rapidly as possible and send a huge shipment of rice to war-devastated Japan.

They did so, and the U.S. Department of Justice then charged them
with criminal violations of the antitrust law for working together to
fill the order.

We worked on the case for nearly a year; it took about a month to
try, and the jury took only about thirty minutes to acquit all the companies. But there was no reimbursement to the companies for their
heavy legal expenses.

For me, the case offered a great opportunity to work with a number of San Francisco's best trial lawyers, representing the several
defendant companies, and to observe a not-always-courteous judge
in action. The principal lesson I learned from my colleagues was that
there was no substitute for the most thorough and detailed preparation of every phase of a trial combined with enormous patience for
snappish, irritable federal judges who had lifetime tenure.

Because the law firm was my principal source of income, I felt I
had to like it, but I felt then, and know now, that spending my whole
career as an attorney would have been stultifying for me.

A couple of years after I started at Heller, Ehrman, I began doing
some extracurricular work, which my wife came to call my "nonprofit
activities." Some of them did bring in a little extra money, but I was
motivated more by the need to do something other than practice law.

At that time, my brother was teaching a business course at Golden
Gate College, a downtown night school affiliated with the YMCA, and
he knew that the dean of its law school was looking for additional faculty to teach the big influx of law students coming in on the G.I. Bill.
The school was kind enough to take me on at my brother's suggestion
and let me teach a class one night a week. At about the same time, I
was also offered and accepted a teaching position at Hastings College
of Law, which was part of the University of California.

Hastings was noted for its "65 Club." This was an interesting plan
under which Hastings employed professors from other law schools
all over the country who had been compulsorily retired at age sixty-

five. This compulsory rule was nearly universal, but a great mistake because many of these professors were the most famous in the country. They clearly had seven, eight, nine years or more of good teaching left in them. So Hastings had an amazingly distinguished faculty in these professors, including many former law school deans. But even with the "65 Club," Hastings was still short of teaching staff, so it recruited some young practicing attorneys.

At Golden Gate I taught "Practice and Procedure," which was a good course for me because I needed to learn a lot about it. It covered the mechanical fundamentals of how to practice law—things that were not taught at Harvard Law School. I had to work hard to keep ahead of the class.

At Hastings, I was assigned to teach "Bills and Notes" and "Negotiable Instruments"—essentially the same thing—which was not my first choice, as it was a rather narrow area of law. Later, I was asked to teach the law of corporations, a somewhat more interesting topic. This teaching experience was very valuable for me. It helped me get over some of my natural shyness, and I learned how to answer unexpected questions. This stood me in good stead for later political and legislative debates. The second year of teaching was much easier because by then about 90 percent of the questions the students would ask were not unexpected. Aside from some brief experience training enlisted soldiers when I was an officer in the army, this was really the first public speaking I had done. I found that, both in the army and in the law schools, I greatly enjoyed teaching and taking questions, and I gradually became more comfortable speaking informally and without notes, appearing before groups, and answering questions. I have always tried to avoid reading speeches.

As if my schedule were not already full enough, I took up book reviewing. It was something I had always wanted to do, and my friend Bill Coblentz, another San Francisco attorney, had done a couple of reviews for the *San Francisco Chronicle*. The *Chronicle* was one of the few papers then that had not only a Sunday book review section but also a daily book review, and as a result, they received a great many more books than the permanent staff could handle. So, with Bill's encouragement, I called the paper and they agreed to let me try a couple. They seemed to like them, so I wrote reviews for them regularly for many years. Reviewers were not paid; the reward was the book. In addition, I could keep other new books I liked that the regular critic had decided not to review. So I would go up, usually on Fridays, and take at least five or six books (as many as I could conveniently carry) and review one or two of them. Occasionally books would be assigned, but generally I was able to choose which ones I wanted to review, which is why my library is so heavily overloaded with English history and biography. Art and music books and travel studies also caught my eye.

By the summer of 1948, we had saved enough money—roughly $2,000—to get a car, but money was not all you needed to buy an automobile then. There was almost as great a demand for automobiles as there was for housing in those postwar years. Factories were still making the transition from production of war materiel back to domestic production. Each auto company had huge backlogs of orders for new cars.

Again my brother helped. He knew a local dealer, and he somehow arranged that I could buy a car if I could pick it up in Detroit. By that time, I had two weeks of vacation due from Heller, Ehrman, so I took the train to Harvard for my tenth college class reunion.

Then, once I found the factory in Detroit on my way back, I had the great thrill of getting into the first car I ever owned. The gleaming, "Horizon Blue," two-door DeSoto sedan had literally just come off the assembly line, so when the odometer said zero, it *meant* zero.

As I slid in behind the huge steering wheel and first pressed the accelerator, I almost felt I was driving into a new phase of life, much as the country was at that time. After the clouds of war had finally drifted away, everyone breathed a collective sigh of relief, as when relatives who have overstayed their welcome finally leave. We were weary, but eager not to waste a minute of our new freedom.

Later that year, we began looking for a house in San Francisco proper. For one thing, in January 1947, we had welcomed a splendid new addition to the family, Caspar Jr., and we were rapidly outgrowing our little hillside home in Sausalito.

Cap Jr. had a big, welcoming smile almost from the first day. He was a healthy, happy baby, and as I recall, from the perspective of some fifty years, he slept all night—a very big plus.

We found a roomy, three-story, wood-shingled house on the narrow end of Pacific Avenue, overlooking the Presidio Wall* and the Julius Kahn playground, a key feature for a growing, young family. Even more important, the neighborhood boasted some excellent schools.

Pacific Heights was home to the old-money mansions of many of the city's leaders and business names, such as Spreckels, Sutro, Huntington, and Flood.

Fortunately for us, the house we liked was unusually low-priced, especially for that area. The owners had divorced, and part of the divorce settlement was that the wife would sell the house and the husband would get half the proceeds. She apparently disliked him intensely, so she deliberately sold it for a very small sum, about $27,000—unthinkable for a big house in that prize location. Our Sausalito house sold quickly, and we moved into our new home about the end of 1948.

I was always very fond of that house, with its fine view of the bay and the Golden Gate Bridge. A view has always been important to

---

* The southern boundary of the Presidio military base, headquarters of the Sixth Army.

me. Having a home in the city was also important because I was becoming more involved in local Republican politics.

The event that propelled me into an active role in politics was Governor Thomas Dewey's stunning loss to President Harry Truman in 1948. California did miserably for Dewey and Republicans, particularly in San Francisco. I decided I could no longer just sit on the sidelines and assume the right people would win.

Earlier that year I had campaigned a bit, working with a fellow attorney I had met in the bar examination course, Joe Martin Jr., a warm and witty man who had been taken prisoner by the Japanese early in the war and confined for the duration. He and I worked for William Farnham White, the Republican candidate for Congress from San Francisco. White lost ingloriously, as he deserved to, and joined the ranks of so many other fallen Republicans in that election.[*] It was during the course of this campaign that we discovered that there was no effective Republican organization in San Francisco.

The members of the County Central Committee, led by longtime chairman Herbert Hanley, had been entrenched in their positions throughout the 1940s and were mired in lethargy and incompetence. Their goal seemed to be to attend Republican events. They made no apparent effort to recruit more members into the party or to give more than token support to Republican candidates; they did not even recognize the Young Republican organization or work with other party groups.

We, on the other hand, wanted to win elections, and we knew that required aggressive leadership, active scouting for quality candidates, and expanding the base of the party, numerically and ideologically.

---

[*] Our support for him, based almost entirely on the fact that he was the Republican candidate, melted swiftly after he told a home meeting we had arranged that he preferred women who stayed home instead of "being political."

So Joe Martin and I, along with Robert Harris (the same with whom I shared an office at Heller, Ehrman), determined to oust the Hanley regime. In the 1950 primary we and a small group of like-minded Republicans—"Grand New Party" Republicans, as we called ourselves—put forward a reform slate of candidates to run for seats on the County Central Committee. With the help of newspaper publicity and an active and vigorous campaign—highly unusual for a county committee election, where incumbents almost automatically win—our slate took twenty-one of the forty seats, while the incumbents held on to eighteen. (An independent won the remaining seat.) Hanley's group contested the results immediately and went to court to try to prevent our nominees from being certified. I was one of the attorneys representing the new group, and ultimately we won. So, after a long and major effort, we became the majority party on the county committee and were able to throw out all of the previous officers who had done such a poor job.

In 1952 I myself ran for an open state assembly seat. Arthur Connally, a popular Republican attorney who had been one of San Francisco's assemblymen for several years, decided to retire and move down the peninsula. After encouraging calls and talks with several of our new Republican group (I must confess I did not require much encouragement), I decided to run for Connally's seat. Other potential and actual GOP candidates appeared, and for a time I thought I would not continue because I did not want to split the party. But finally I decided to stay in the race. My wife was very instrumental in this decision and, indeed, throughout my campaign. She knew that I was not deriving much satisfaction from the law practice, and she was well aware of my great interest in politics and saw this as a logical step. In fact, I think it is fair to say that if Jane had not vigorously encouraged me to run for office and stay in the race, I probably would not have felt I could do it after it turned into a contested primary.

When I first mentioned the idea of running for the assembly to the partners at Heller, Ehrman, they objected. Their immediate reaction was, "We employed you to be a lawyer, not a candidate." But when I kept raising the question, Lloyd Dinkelspiel, who was then the head of the firm, finally relented, saying, "You know, we spend a lot of time urging people to participate in government, and here we have the chance and we have turned you down. Well, we're changing our mind. The partners have agreed. You should run." Florenz McAuliffe, another senior partner and a major behind-the-scenes power in San Francisco politics, became interested in my race. He was the epitome of the old-style city politician—and an excellent lawyer. Many years of smoking long, strong cigars (probably Cuban since no one had heard of Castro then) gave him a throaty growl when he spoke, which could be intimidating. He was short with a bull neck and penetrating eyes, hidden behind thick glasses. He tolerated no shoddy work, and he was not troubled by self-doubts.

As I later learned, no one in the office felt I had a chance to win the race. Mr. McAuliffe decided he would try to make me a winner. His support and that of several of my fellow young Republicans— particularly Bob Harris, Joe Martin Jr., and Roger Lapham Jr., whose father had been mayor—were a huge boost.

My wife was an extremely active campaigner. She set up and manned the headquarters office (which was in our home) and put together a number of supporting women's church and neighborhood groups. They came to be known collectively as "Your Neighbors for Good Government," an organization that loyally resurrected itself for my subsequent campaigns. My children, aged ten and five at the time, also were recruited to help out at headquarters and to pass out campaign literature. They seemed very willing foot soldiers and particularly enjoyed putting up small signs called "quarter cards," which extolled my virtues and carried a retouched earlier picture.

For me, the campaign was another exercise in confidence building. I was constantly struggling to overcome my shyness at pushing my own candidacy. When I went door-to-door, I rather hoped no one would be home. But my confidence gradually grew as I found that the vast majority of people were nice and seemed both surprised and pleased that I was calling on them personally; it was unusual at that time for candidates for state office to do that. When I handed out my election card, many asked, "Are you him?" or they would call out to other family members, "It is Weinberger."

The Twenty-first District encompassed a large and reasonably upscale area of the city, including the Marina, Chinatown, the Presidio, part of the Richmond area, and part of Pacific Heights.

My principal opponent in the Republican primary, Milton Marks, was a young lawyer whose father had been active in San Francisco politics—so much so that when I tried to get supporters, many people said that they had to back Marks because they had roomed with his father in college. I began to think his father must have lived in the biggest dormitory in the University of California.

Marks ran a fairly traditional campaign, concentrating on getting endorsements from various organizations. I, on the other hand, tried to emphasize issues, particularly reducing the state budget and cutting state taxes. In addition, there was one local issue in which I was personally quite interested and which I brought up in the campaign: the restoration of the Palace of Fine Arts. This was a much-loved but crumbling relic of the 1915 Panama-Pacific International Exposition. The exposition site was located in the Marina, a major part of the Twenty-first District. It was highly unusual to have a local issue in the state legislative races, and the people seemed to like my pledge to try to restore the palace.

I did something else that was rather unconventional at the time. In San Francisco, it was considered bad form and bad politics to emphasize your party affiliation, especially as a Republican in a heavily Democratic city, but I did not hesitate to do just that. In fact, my campaign slogan (coined by my wife) was, "In a Republican year, elect a real Republican." This was in 1952, which indeed turned out to be a Republican year, with war hero General Dwight Eisenhower winning the presidency and the GOP gaining a majority in both houses of Congress. A lot of this was due to dissatisfaction with Truman.

Something I did must have been effective, because I won the Republican nomination in the primary by about eight hundred votes, and with cross-filing, then allowed in California, I even came in fourth (out of eight candidates) on the Democratic ballot. Marks actually had more total votes than any of us, but he finished second on both tickets. Under the law then, a candidate had to win the nomination of his own party to get on the ballot for the general election. So my emphasis on my Republican roots seemed to have helped.

For the November finals, I continued on in much the same way, but this time with substantially more support from many sources. The Democratic nominee I was running against in the general election was a large and deceptively old-looking San Franciscan named William Blake. He was a cheerful, friendly opponent who ran a ship-repair business on the San Francisco waterfront and had many friends among old-line San Francisco politicians. My friends turned it largely into a campaign for a new, young face in the legislature, and we managed to win by a substantial margin this time—about sixteen thousand votes. Blake remained friendly and supportive throughout the campaign. I think he was the nicest man I ever ran against. At one of our joint appearances, he even said to my wife after my speech, "You know, if I weren't running against him, *I'd* vote for him!"

CHAPTER 6

LEGISLATIVE LIQUIDITY

Dwight Eisenhower helped sweep many Republicans into office in 1952. Not only was he elected president, but the party also won control of both houses of Congress and increased its ranks in many state legislatures. Voters believed that Eisenhower and his fellow Republicans would clean up what was generally regarded as corruption and cronyism in the Truman administration and would reduce government intrusion into people's private lives. They also hoped that the military deadlock in Korea could be broken. General Eisenhower's pledge to go to Korea appealed to many voters who thought that his very presence there could accomplish wonders. I was, of course, but a tiny cog in the Republican wheel, but I could not help feeling a real exhilaration at being a part of this great new crusade under Eisenhower.

After two days of discouraging house-hunting, we found the perfect new, affordable apartment near the beautiful Capitol grounds. Our new landlord agreed that we could bring a "small dog." I felt our collie qualified, so we moved to Sacramento at the beginning of 1953. The regular legislative session ran from January through June in odd-numbered years, which corresponded nicely with spring semester in the schools.* The children were at an age where they were more excited about moving than unhappy about leaving their friends (they knew we would be back home on many weekends), and once in Sacramento, they seemed to enjoy it thoroughly. Arlin learned to ride her bike on the grounds of the Capitol, and both Arlin and Cap Jr. enthusiastically worked as pages on the floor of the assembly during the Easter school recess. I was much amused by the fact that as "employees of the state" for five days, both children had to take the then-required loyalty oath,† swearing that they were not then, nor had they been, members of a Communist organization at any time in the past five years. Caspar Jr. was about five at the time, so he was not forbidden by his conscience from signing.

My mother remained in San Francisco, which was only about an hour away from Sacramento, but I called her nearly every day and wrote her occasional letters.

I drove home whenever I could. I had the bad habit of driving much too fast as I was thinking about other things. And once I start toward a target, I like to get there as soon as possible. On one such occasion, I was stopped by a highway patrolman. When he came

---

* In the even-numbered years, the legislature usually met for only one month, and for those years my family remained in San Francisco.

† As relations chilled after World War II between the United States and our wartime ally the Soviet Union, a "Red Scare" swept across the country, permeating every level of government. This was similar to the atmosphere immediately after World War I. The House Un-American Activities Committee led the way in 1947, with hearings of a sensational and highly charged nature. The California legislature followed, requiring a loyalty oath for all state employees. It was not until 1967 that the state supreme court ruled that the oath, as formulated by the legislature, was unconstitutional.

up to my car, he said, "I'm very sorry, sir—you were going so fast, I didn't see your legislative license plate."* He had clocked me doing eighty-five miles an hour, and I acknowledge that that *was* entirely too fast regardless of my plates, but I must confess a bit of pleasure at discovering what kind of perks my new position afforded. I was not used to being the object of such deference.

When the legislature was not in session and there was no committee work, I spent substantial stretches of time in San Francisco. During these "off" times, I continued to work at the law firm, though it was understood that I could not be made a partner until after I left the legislature. An assemblyman's salary then was only three hundred dollars a month, plus a small per diem living allowance which generally was exhausted shortly after breakfast. But money, or the lack of it, was never much of a factor for me. State government held my interest because I could debate and work on issues of major importance, whereas my law practice often seemed to deal at endless length with rather petty matters. A friend of mine put it another way: "The trouble with Weinberger is, he can't stand making money."

I won reelection to the assembly in 1954 and again in 1956, running unopposed each time. I was glad because I preferred legislating to campaigning. When I learned that I was unopposed, I returned all individual contributions to the donors—which was unheard of. I was fortunate to have achieved some early accomplishments as a legislator and gotten quite favorable press coverage. The press corps even voted me "Most Able Member of the Legislature" in 1955.

---

* Legislators were issued special license plates: a green "A" designated an assemblyman, followed by the number of the district one represented, "21" in my case. A red "S" was for senators. I was quite proud of these, but after this encounter with a particularly kind patrolman, I realized that while rank had its privileges, rank was also supposed to behave well.

In the California legislature in those days, there was a friendly, collegial atmosphere that cut across party lines.* Most of us seemed to be there for something bigger than ourselves. Added to this was the fact that many of us were in our thirties or early forties, with young families, and we generally became good friends as well as colleagues.

Most of us shared offices (in the new Capitol Annex) with other assemblymen—in my case, a fellow Republican from San Jose, Bruce Allen. Bruce Allen was a taciturn, laconic, and skilled lawyer and legislator who was loyal, friendly, and much admired for his rugged, almost frontier-like honesty. He left the legislature when he was appointed a judge of the Superior Court and served in that post until his very untimely death. Our office arrangement felt almost like a college dormitory: we each had our own room, but we shared a common reception area where both of our secretaries worked.

If the Capitol offices were the dormitories, then the old Senator Hotel, just across Twelfth Street from the Capitol, was the student union. Most of the lobbyists lived there and lavishly (for the time) entertained legislators in their suites. Some lively cocktail party or meal or informal gathering was always under way.

Don Cleary was an amusing and popular old-style lobbyist for the city of San Francisco who often served grand gourmet meals at the Senator. Since they were for the cause of discussing legislation affecting San Francisco, I felt little compunction about going to those functions. Cleary always said, "With some of the legislators, you can get 'em with money; with some, you can get 'em with women. But with Weinberger, you need lamb chops." He was nearly right.

Fellow legislators also gave parties to showcase products from their districts, one of the best-known being Eureka assemblyman Frank Belotti's famous annual crab feed.

---

* The only major partisan issue seemed to be the reapportionment of legislative districts that took place after each census.

Legislators' wives added to the atmosphere of camaraderie as well, hosting luncheons and other activities. Jane was a popular hostess, entertaining with great style and graciousness. Her cooking and buffets became quite famous in legislative circles, primarily because she did it all herself.

Of course, none of these events was purely social; there was always a political undercurrent. Even so, I had little time for them. I was working far harder and far longer than I had at the law firm. I often began the day with a breakfast meeting around seven, followed by committee meetings around nine or ten. Then the assembly itself usually went into session at ten or eleven, and I tried to attend all of the actual sessions on the floor.* More committee meetings generally filled up the remainder of the afternoon and evening, and I often took reams of paper home to prepare for the next day's activities. That was a good eighteen-hour day—and I relished it.

Republicans had control of both houses of the legislature, but given the spirit of bipartisanship, divisions were more apparent *within* the party.

I was considered a somewhat liberal Republican, in part because I was one of the few who supported the Fair Employment Practice Act, which was basically a forerunner of later state and federal civil rights acts. Sponsored by Byron Rumford, a black Democrat assemblyman and a close personal friend from Berkeley, the act essentially tried to eliminate hiring discrimination against minorities. I had thought in the

---

* The assembly chamber was a large, well-proportioned room. Green was the predominant color—a throwback to the House of Commons in England. Red was the predominant senate color (as it was in the House of Lords). The members' desks—two abreast—were arranged to form a broad semicircle. The voting banks were at the front of the chamber, facing the desks, and to either side of the Speaker's rostrum. The votes were frequent and electronically recorded, and as each member turned the key on his desk, a green (yea) or red (no) light was illuminated after his name. Vote changes were permitted until the vote was closed. Frequently, on major issues, some would hold back until it was clear which side would win.

past that there had not really been any discrimination. But when I had tried to help some black and Hispanic friends get jobs in San Francisco, I found that there really were elements of discrimination. Many employers, particularly larger businesses like department stores, were reluctant to hire blacks because they were afraid it would hurt their stores' sales. So we did a survey of people coming out of a San Francisco department store, asking them if they had been waited on by a black clerk or a white clerk. Most of them had no idea, which confirmed my belief that the color of employees had no effect on business.

In general, I opposed government interference in the private sector, but in this case, it became increasingly clear to me that blacks would not be given a fair chance for employment (in many cases because of ignorance or unjustified fears) unless state law prohibited discrimination. The Fair Employment Practice Act did not become law until 1959, after I had left the legislature, but I had been an early and vocal proponent of the measure. This convinced some old-time legislators and lobbyists that I was not "fundamentally sound."

I think it is fair to add that another reason for my stand was my strong admiration for Byron Rumford. He was a large, capable, and friendly pharmacist who had been in the legislature for many years. Everyone who knew him liked him, particularly children—he always had a bit of candy or other gift for them handy. Our children were very fond of him and our families became great friends.

Byron was also particularly helpful on alcoholic beverage reform. He served on my committee loyally and skillfully, even though there were many pressures on him from old-time lobbyists to oppose everything we were trying to do. Much later, when I was chairman of the Federal Trade Commission, I had the great pleasure of appointing Byron to a key regional post in California where he again served with distinction.

Another action that placed me in the more "liberal" wing of the Republican Party was that I voted for the more moderate Republican candidate, James Silliman, for Speaker in the 1953 session. He was from the Fresno area and represented what he called the "Clean Government," antilobbyist approach, as opposed to the more traditional "old boy network" way of operating. A number of young Republicans—including Laughlin Waters, a Republican leader who later became a federal judge; Charles Conrad, an actor-legislator from North Hollywood; Luther "Abe" Lincoln from Oakland; and I—were part of the reform group that elected Silliman by a narrow margin.

It was fortunate that I, as a new assemblyman, had decided to support Silliman, because at that time the committee assignments were all made by the Speaker. As a freshman, I was assigned to my first-choice committees: Ways and Means, which heard the budget; Government Organization; Elections and Reapportionment; and Judiciary.

As it turned out, I spent most of my time and energy on issues before the Committee on Government Organization. My first major challenge came when I was made chairman of that committee's Joint Subcommittee on Alcoholic Beverage Control. It was considered sort of an in-house joke that this new, young, eager assemblyman was put in charge of this subcommittee. The truth was that nobody else would take it; everyone else was smart enough not to get anywhere near it. I don't think anyone really expected that anything significant would be done. The liquor industry lobbyists were considered the strongest in Sacramento. The Board of Equalization's administration of liquor licensing and other parts of the liquor law was scandal-ridden, but previous attempts at reform had gone nowhere because the Senate Governmental Efficiency Committee always killed everything that would have changed the status quo. That committee was considered the graveyard for liquor legislation.

I knew absolutely nothing about alcoholic beverage control when I was elected, but I worked hard to learn. The seeds of the problem seemed to lie in the Board of Equalization, a curious anachronism originally designed to equalize the distribution of tax revenues to

schools. There were many counties, particularly in the northern part
of the state, that had vast areas owned by the federal government—
national parks or national forests—which were exempt from local
taxation. Consequently, these counties had a very low tax base. The
Board of Equalization was created in 1879 to provide these areas with
the same kinds of educational opportunities as the more populated,
tax-rich areas of the state. Oddly enough, it was an elective board,
with one member from each of four districts whose boundaries—
despite massive population shifts—had been left virtually unchanged
since 1879. The board was completely independent of the governor.
(California was the only state where this was the case.) It was also
independent of the legislature, could not be impeached, and in practice usually left each member to make his own decision in his own
district. Few voters cared about it, generally automatically reelecting
incumbents, which left the board virtually autonomous.

These problems were compounded when the board fell under the
sway of the strong liquor lobbies. After Prohibition was repealed,
these lobbies succeeded in transferring to this strange board the
responsibility for collecting liquor taxes and the liquor licensing
function. The lobbyists were able to control the board because they
were the only major contributors to board members' elections. By the
time my subcommittee was assigned to study the board's operations
in 1953, corruption was pervasive. Liquor licenses were limited and
could be sold, and were sold, for ever increasing prices. Issued to
special friends of the board for $525, they were frequently resold for
$10,000 to $20,000. The new purchasers frequently did not meet
even the very lax standards set by the board for licensees.

Also, the basis on which licenses were granted by the board in the
first place was not apparent. Some district administrators who testified were evasive about how they decided who were to be the favored
few. But we soon learned that liquor licenses were being issued without anything resembling an adequate investigation of either the

premises or the individual applicants. Licenses for the sale of liquor were issued to vacant lots; to applicants who submitted blueprints of premises they promised to construct, but the dimensions of which could not possibly fit the premises; and even to cemetery lots and, occasionally, to people who were deceased. The decision of whether to approve or disapprove an application apparently depended solely upon the applicant's relationship with the district liquor administrator or the board member for that area.

I scheduled five hearings around the state for late 1953 and early 1954. It seemed to be general practice, at that time, for committee *staff* to determine the agenda and direction of hearings and then actually to run them, with the legislators asking only occasional questions. But I felt this was an important enough issue that legislators, and particularly I, should be more involved since this was more along the lines of a criminal investigation. The other members of the bipartisan subcommittee—Assemblymen Byron Rumford and Glenn Coolidge (a Republican) and Senators Hugh Donnelly (a Democrat) and Ed Johnson (a Republican)—were also quite interested and active and extremely helpful in the proceedings. The legislative auditor's office—primarily Arthur Buck, the staff member assigned to our subcommittee—was a major research asset. I did much of the preparatory work and questioning myself, including lining up many of the witnesses. The subcommittee heard testimony from everyone from Board of Equalization members to licensees to law enforcement officers to concerned citizens.

Our investigation uncovered numerous improprieties, weak or no law enforcement, outright fraud, and, indeed, a complete abandonment of the rule of law in favor of the rule of a few men—exactly the kind of concentration of power our government was supposed to forbid.

Many of these abuses were perpetrated and perpetuated by close cooperation between Artie Samish, the self-proclaimed "Secret Boss of California," who headed one of the big liquor lobbies, and William

Bonelli, the Board of Equalization member from the southern California district—the largest district, by far, in terms of population.

Bonelli felt he was absolutely invulnerable at the polls and simply denied any responsibility for the abuses we found.* Samish, on the other hand, flaunted his power and was almost clownish about it. He was quoted as saying, "I'm the governor of the legislature," and he claimed that he had "the damnedest Gestapo you ever saw." In his autobiography, he bragged about how he selected, elected, and kept in power those he believed would best serve the liquor industry's interests. He also was not shy about removing people from office if they did not play his game. As one example, he wrote, "I considered Senator Ralph Swing the best mind in the legislature. . . . But one year when he was chairman of the Government Efficiency Committee, he got in my way. All of a sudden he wasn't chairman of the Government Efficiency Committee any more." He made many of these boasts to writers in the old *Collier's* magazine, which then had a wide circulation in California.

After months of testimony at public hearings and long meetings to go over the evidence, we put our findings in our Subcommittee Report to the Legislature, and at our urging, Governor Goodwin Knight called a special session in early 1954, primarily to address the alcoholic beverage control issue and the recommendations we had made. Our efforts at reform were distinguished from previous attempts by the evidence we had gathered; by a dozen specific remedial bills and a recommended constitutional amendment attached to our report; and by the fact that our report was submitted to the legislature with the

---

* He publicly denied any responsibility for administering or enforcing liquor laws, saying that all he did was "rubber stamp" the recommendations of the district liquor administrator. (The liquor administrator disagreed.) I asked Bonelli in one of our hearings, "You really pay very little attention to the actual liquor control function?" To which he responded, "I don't have the time nor the inclination nor the responsibility."

unanimous support of the bipartisan subcommittee. I must take credit for the idea of making specific recommendations in the form of already drafted bills. I wanted action on these bills and the constitutional amendment, not just another report that would gather dust, so I worked continuously from the beginning of the hearings to try to get unanimous support. We also gained support from Paul Leake, the member from the Third District (encompassing much of northern California). Leake was an honest, straightforward Democrat and publisher of a Woodland newspaper. He had been appointed to the Board of Equalization to fill a vacancy in late 1952, and when he saw the tremendous corruption, he attacked it publicly and fearlessly, before the legislature did and before most people even knew of it. When my subcommittee began its investigation, Leake started out (as did many people) feeling that this was going to be just another whitewash. But when we named him as our first witness and set our first hearing in Woodland, he realized it was going to be a real investigation. We worked closely together and became good friends for the rest of his life. He was also particularly effective in persuading many of his press corps colleagues that we were determined to clean up this mess. In particular, Art White of the *Los Angeles Mirror* and Carl Greenberg of the *Los Angeles Times*, both of whom had covered San Diego and Los Angeles, where the worst of the liquor licensing scandals had taken place, were extremely helpful in working closely with the committee, as was another state senator, Arthur Breed of Oakland.

And as we began uncovering more and more evidence of corruption, the attorney general's office also became interested and started its own investigation, though I think that was essentially because Pat Brown, the attorney general, was planning to run for governor and did not want to be left behind.

Eventually, most everyone got on the bandwagon, for our evidence could not be refuted. A consensus agreed that something had to be done. And something was done.

The main recommendation we put forth was to create a Department of Alcoholic Beverage Control with a director appointed by, and serving at the pleasure of, the governor. The department would administer liquor licensing and would be assigned all liquor law enforcement responsibilities. The Board of Equalization would be stripped of all its power over alcoholic beverages. We considered it crucial that the director of the new department be appointed by the governor, be subject to confirmation by the senate, and be removable by either the governor or the legislature. As an extra safeguard against an all-powerful director of the new department, a provision was added later by the conference committee to create an Alcoholic Beverage Control Appeals Board to hear appeals from some of the director's decisions.

The constitutional amendment containing all of this was the centerpiece of our reform plan, and it was introduced by our committee as Senate Constitutional Amendment #4 (of which I wrote quite a lot of the final wording). It was adopted by a combined vote of both houses of the legislature, by a vote of 105 to 3. As with all proposed constitutional amendments, it was then placed on the ballot, where it appeared as Proposition 3 on the November 1954 ballot. It became law when voters supported it two to one.

The legislature also adopted several additional recommendations of the joint subcommittee. These laws were meant to crack down on the many illegal activities that seemed to be connected to liquor licenses—from narcotics dealings to prostitution. We also created a new Alcoholic Beverage Rehabilitation Commission, a particular interest of Assemblyman Glenn Coolidge, to study problems of alcoholism and its treatment. The commission would be financed by a license-fee increase we enacted. We felt there was a particular need for research into the causes and possible cures of alcoholism, because we had seen various figures on the amount of crime that was traced to alcoholism, much like drugs and crime today. Unfortunately, other committee recommendations, such as prohibiting the sale of licenses, were rejected by the senate after having been passed by the assembly.

As for the former liquor czars, many were indicted and convicted and served jail time. A 1955 indictment against Bill Bonelli accused him of conspiring to violate the election code and to obstruct justice. He fled to Mexico, where he apparently stayed for the rest of his life. Later there was a big question as to whether he could get his pension as a state officer. As I recall, the ultimate court decision was, incredibly, that he could. I have always wondered where they sent the check—some post office box in Mexico, I assume. He later wrote a bitter book about me and the subcommittee. Samish was convicted of tax evasion.

But the main victory, in my mind, was cleaning up the way the state's liquor laws were administered and enforced. The whole endeavor had taken a tremendous amount of work and time, as my young daughter pointed out when a teacher asked if her father could come and speak to her class. Arlin replied by repeating the joking response she had heard me make to similar requests: "Oh, no. Daddy's so immersed in alcohol these days, he doesn't have time for anything else." The teacher was a bit nonplussed.

In the 1955 regular session, I had another big assignment. This one involved the single most important issue in the state: water. There was no *shortage* of water, but 70 percent of it originates north of Sacramento, while almost 80 percent of the people live south of the capital. Just before World War II, the state's population was about 6.9 million, and by 1955, it had nearly doubled—with that population explosion concentrated in the south. As demand went up, water resources became more scarce, somewhat like the 2001 power crisis in California and other western states. The Owens River Project had been built many years earlier to get water from north and east of Los Angeles to the city, but the river was drying up; water from other sources, such as the Colorado River and Hoover Dam, was already overallocated; and attempts to convert seawater to potable water were prohibitively expensive. The need to move more water from the north to the south was an inescapable fact.

But the north had its problems as well. Flooding was far too regular an occurrence, and it reached unprecedented levels of devastation in December 1955 and January 1956. This dramatically emphasized the desperate urgency of securing flood control and regulating the runoff of the great rivers of the north, from which billions of gallons of water washed out to sea every year.

The obvious solution to help control floods in the north and deliver some of its surplus to the south was recognized in the early 1950s and evolved into what came to be known as the California Water Plan. This essentially entailed constructing a whole new river over one thousand miles long (most of California's major rivers flowed east to west). While this would be a huge and complex undertaking, it was felt, like most problems in California, to be entirely solvable. (We were all optimists then.) The new river would require a huge dam at Oroville, a whole series of aqueducts, pumps, reservoirs, and power plants to divert the new river around the mid-California delta (which was subject to heavy salt-water intrusion), and huge generators to create the power to lift the water over the Tehachapi Mountains just north of Los Angeles—higher than water had ever been lifted—before it would tumble down into southern California.

To me, the water problem was a fascinating subject that involved engineering, law, economics, and politics, and I flung myself into every detail—how to trap and transport the water; how much power was required to lift it over the mountains; how it would be distributed once it reached the south—to say nothing of the violent north-south fights on the political side.* It really was a full education for me; I did

---

* As Mark Twain once observed, "Whiskey is for drinking, water is for fighting over."

not have a rural, agricultural background. In fact, I knew nothing about water except that when you turned on the tap, the water came out. So to understand and convey the urgency of southern California's water needs through my many speeches and presentations on the subject, I asked audiences to picture what it would be like if they turned on the tap and nothing came out. And, to emphasize the need for a quick solution, I hammered away on the point of how long it would take to build the California Water Project and how few years we had before we would actually face real shortages.

Naturally, the plan for diversion of water to the south encountered major political resistance, primarily from many of the northern senators, who were absolutely determined that none of their water was going to go south. Many felt that their sparsely populated counties would someday be as large as Los Angeles if they could keep all their water.

Some of their objections were reduced when it was suggested that they could conceivably get "replacement" water from the Columbia River in Oregon, or even ultimately from the huge runoff of the rivers in Washington. We also acknowledged the need to help northern California with flood-control measures.

Another problem was the haphazard way in which the state government was organized to handle water issues. This was the area where I, as chairman of the Assembly Government Organization Committee, became most involved. As we studied our assignment (to recommend the best organizational structure to develop, use, and regulate California's water), we found that there were well over fifty California agencies that dealt with water in one way or another, very little coordination among them, and no one overall agency. Nor was much direction or control provided by the state. Much like the Board of Equalization before we reformed it, these state water boards and agencies were virtually independent of the governor and the legislature and had little communication with local boards and local governments. At the same time, none of these many agencies had the authority—or the expertise or the funding, for that matter—to build or manage a big water project. Before, they had been concerned mainly with water quality, water rights, and piecemeal flood control, not transporting or distributing water on a large scale.

My remedy for all of this, and the recommendation of our committee, was to consolidate the myriad boards and agencies into one streamlined department (under a director appointed by the governor) that could build and then efficiently administer the water project and effectively deal with any future water issues.

Our proposal, which came to be called the Weinberger Bill, was based on certain principles I believe should underlie any governmental organization: it should be integrated, unified, and capable of effective action—in short, it must have the power to carry out policies—and it must be responsible to the people by having its director appointed by, and reporting to, the governor.

Not surprisingly, there was strong opposition to the idea from the many employees of the various ineffective regional boards. And throughout the process, there was still the basic north-south rift. The south, of course, had a majority in the assembly, apportioned on the basis of population. The senate was still apportioned by counties, but the population-heavy south was about to change that.

The governor, at my urgent request, called a special session to consider our committee's recommendations and to try to solve our water problems. On the very last day of that 1956 special session, after extensive debate, the final conference report incorporating the unanimous recommendations of our bipartisan committee was adopted. I was greatly aided in the effort by the fine support of Senator James Cobey, a Democrat of Merced County. He was a particularly effective supporter coming from a nonsouthern county.

The bill created the Department of Water Resources. Responsibility for water quality and water resource development was transferred to this new department, thus eliminating the need for most of the separate water boards and agencies. Heading the department would be a director appointed by and removable by the governor. The only water-related function that was kept separate from the Department of Water Resources was the determination of water rights, for which our legislation created a State Water Rights Board. Water rights were as important as land titles in California, and indeed, a whole history of the state could be written based on fights over water rights. Unfortunately, the senate could not be persuaded that a constitutional amendment recognizing the need to protect the interests of both north and south was the fairest solution. But we did have a new, properly organized state department to finally fulfill the water needs of the whole state.

With the new administrative organization in place, a $1.75 billion bond issue (the largest ever considered by any state up to that time) to finance the California statewide water project was passed in 1960 by popular vote. The project's main beneficiaries, the water users, repaid most of the huge bond issue and paid most of the annual operating costs. Some state tidelands oil and gas revenues were also used, but little federal money (only about 1 percent of total project costs) was required, and that was mainly for some of the flood-control aspects of the project.

Actual work on the water project began shortly after the bond issue was passed, with the construction of the Oroville Dam on the Feather River, the first phase of the plan. By 1973 the bulk of the facilities had been completed, with water reaching the Los Angeles metropolitan area. I took great pleasure and, I must admit, some pride in coming out from Washington to attend the dedication ceremonies.* But the final phases to reach regions even farther south have yet to be finished.

---

* Governor Reagan turned on the activators to start the power generators. In a rather comic development (although not seen as such at the time), the first time he turned the switches, nothing happened! It finally worked the second or third time around.

The Department of Water Resources is still in existence today, with essentially the same responsibilities it was given at its creation—administering the use of the state's water resources and ensuring that there is and will be enough water for all.

But, unfortunately, water administration in California has again become fragmented and confusing, with a new proliferation of water agencies, many of which have overlapping responsibilities. A cursory perusal of the *California Water Resources Directory* reveals the extraordinary number of federal, state, and local agencies and departments that currently have some interest in the state's water. The fight to keep government streamlined, and bureaucracies from multiplying, is never-ending. I hope some young California assemblyman will take up the cudgels again.

The California Water Project moved from the drawing board to reality in the 1960s because we established the management and administrative foundation and framework that such a huge project required. We will have to keep and strengthen that unified administrative structure if we hope to ever realize the benefits of a completed system.

Though these major, statewide issues of alcohol and water were extremely interesting to me, as indeed was virtually everything connected with state government, one local subject was especially close to my heart. Relatively speaking, it was fairly unimportant, but I was sentimental about San Francisco's beautiful Palace of Fine Arts.

The Palace of Fine Arts was one of the many temporary exhibition buildings built for the Panama-Pacific Exposition of 1915 in the Marina District of San Francisco. The rose and blond structure, with its eclectic details and neoclassical rotunda and columns, was said to have been the re-creation of a dream its architect, Bernard Maybeck, had once had. My father was fond of the palace and spent a lot of time at the exposition, taking many photographs of it. It had captured the imagination and affection of many San Franciscans, and it was the only structure of the exposition that was not razed when the fair was over. My family often visited it when I was a child. Over the years, it had been used for art displays, tennis courts, and even army storage during World War II, and it had always escaped occasional calls for its demolition.

By the early 1950s, the elegant, much-loved, temporary building had fallen into disrepair. The city of San Francisco had not done anything to preserve or even maintain it, even though the palace was part of the city park system.

So I made it a campaign issue when I first ran for the assembly; it was the one local issue I took to the state level. In fact, it was the only issue of local concern in the campaign. All the other candidates talked about their own virtues and, in general terms, about education, welfare, and so on. I was the only one who talked about a real local issue and a specific plan. I think the voters liked that. I felt I could do something about it in the legislature.

Even before I took office, I had drafted a bill to present to the 1953 session that would make the palace and its grounds a state park. As such, it would be maintained and restored by the state. (One friend in the legislature, Assemblyman Thomas Caldecott, who ultimately supported the bill, joked that I was proposing to build the largest all-marble birdbath in the world.) After my bill was introduced, the State Parks Department people strenuously objected. They did not want comparatively scarce state funds used for a park they had not chosen. They wanted all the money they could get for their standard mix of campgrounds and beaches.

I tried to make the proposal more palatable by offering an amendment allowing the state to lease the Palace of Fine Arts back to the city of San Francisco, with the city responsible for maintenance and operation and the state responsible for only the original repair cost. The bill passed in both houses, after some strenuous lobbying on my part, but Governor Earl Warren vetoed it following the advice of the

Parks Department. Governor Warren prided himself on the distance he kept from partisan matters and from legislators in general. It would have been virtually unthinkable for him to sign a bill opposed by one of his department heads.

By the 1955 session, Goodwin Knight was governor,* having taken over when Earl Warren was appointed to the Supreme Court. Along with Warren, many of the state officials who had opposed the Palace of Fine Arts restoration had also left state government, so when I reintroduced my bill I was quite hopeful. But sadly, Governor Knight proved just as amenable to the State Parks bureaucracy as had Governor Warren, even though the bill had once again passed both houses of the legislature.

Despite these discouraging setbacks, I was absolutely determined to save the palace. In fact, on one occasion, although I had contracted

---

* Governor Goodwin Knight was an interesting example of a successful California politician. He had been appointed a judge in Los Angeles, but unlike many judges, he had his eye on higher political office. He was once asked by one of his early supporters, "Judge, would you like a little publicity?" Knight replied instantly, "No—what do I do to get a lot?" He was a Republican and spent a large part of his time strengthening his party ties and building his own political organization. He and his friends frequently presented him as a conservative alternative to Governor Warren, who took increasingly liberal or nonpartisan positions.

Ultimately, Knight was elected lieutenant governor, a position with few duties but with increased opportunities to demonstrate his opposition to Governor Warren's above-it-all aloofness from the internal machinations of California politics.

It was widely expected that he would run for governor himself at the first opportunity. That came unexpectedly in 1954 when President Eisenhower appointed Governor Warren to be chief justice of the United States.

Goodwin Knight was then governor and could run in that year's election as an incumbent, a powerful advantage. Feeling that he had most of the conservative Republican sentiment strongly in his pocket, he quickly began to court leaders of organized labor and supported many prolabor programs that he had previously criticized. He also supported my alcoholic beverage bills and, later, the water bill. He and I got along well, and I always admired and was amused by his buoyancy, general good humor, and easy ability to gain support from widely differing areas of the political spectrum. In any event he was retained as governor in the 1954 election and then set his sights, as he always did, on the next election.

mumps from my children, I insisted on presenting the bill to the committee session. Committee chairman Caldecott entertained a motion to move the bill out of committee as quickly as possible—along with the author.

When the bill passed a third time, in the 1957 regular session, Governor Knight signed it over the continued objections of the State Parks Department. By that time I had succeeded in getting the liquor and water reforms through, and I guess I was listened to a little bit more. So the palace became a state park and would be run (after restoration) by the city of San Francisco.

A provision that I had added to the bill somewhere along the line was that the state's financial contribution to the restoration of the palace—then estimated to be about $2 million—would have to be matched by the city of San Francisco. The most feasible way to do this, I felt, was through a city bond issue, which was put on the city ballot as Proposition B in November of 1958. Sixty percent of voters supported it, but that fell short of the two-thirds majority vote required for passage of a bond issue. Many civic groups backed the bond issue, but I suppose our defeat can be attributed to the fact that, outside my legislative district, where it received a big majority, city voters did not turn out in sufficient numbers to give us the two-thirds majority.

It was shortly after this defeat, when it seemed that our years of effort had been in vain, that a financial angel, in the person of Walter S. Johnson, came forward. He had made his comfortable fortune heading an early adding machine company, the Marchant Company, and had been active in the campaign to pass the bond issue. He loved the palace and appreciated its beauty, artistic quality, uniqueness, and its sentimental importance to the city.

At a meeting to discuss resubmitting the bond issue, Mr. Johnson turned to me and asked, "Wouldn't it be simpler if I just gave the money?" Completely astounded, I said, "Yes, I guess it would." He did, and, finally, the palace was saved.

The next problem, though a relatively simple one, was *how* to restore the palace. Since it had been built as only a temporary building, it was made of lath and plaster, inferior materials that were not designed to last more than a few years. It had deteriorated significantly and was literally crumbling and falling apart. Much of it had to be taken down and completely rebuilt. Some structural steelwork was done and concrete was poured, and also a new, fairly malleable kind of fiberglass was used to cover the whole structure. That made it easier for the sculptors to work on.

Once begun, the whole process took only about three years, from 1964 to 1967. It had been fifteen years since I started my campaign to save the building, and the number of defeats we had suffered along the way far exceeded the victories.

But in the meantime, there was the question of what to do with the space—not in the rotunda itself, which needed to be kept open, but in the semicircular exhibit hall behind it. A group of benevolent San Franciscans had formed the Palace of Fine Arts League in December of 1957 in order to determine just that (as well as to promote the 1958 bond issue). Many proposals were offered, everything from a concert hall to a museum. There was even a very small but vocal group that wanted nothing but tennis courts in the whole huge building. Eventually a theater was put in one end, and then, in 1969, the rest of the building was occupied by a science museum called the Exploratorium, which is still in operation today. It was one of the first of the "hands-on" museums, in which visitors could operate many of the exhibits. I am proud to have been a part of saving the graceful Palace of Fine Arts that my father had so loved.

All of my six years in the California legislature were most rewarding. It was gratifying to see the results and feel that I was accomplishing something of some lasting benefit. I particularly felt that that was the case with liquor control reform and California's water plan.

I was sorry when I thought it was time to leave the legislature, just as sorry as I had been to leave the law clerkship under Judge Orr many years before. Probably it was the more or less subconscious fear of changing the known for the unknown. Of course, while I was in the legislature I had not actually left the law firm, so I knew what was awaiting me there. I also knew that I owed it to my family to earn a more substantial living in the law practice, uninteresting as that sounded in comparison to the previous few years. But before I returned to practice law, there would be one more political campaign. I could scarcely have chosen a worse year!

CHAPTER 7

THE BIG SWITCH

*B*y 1958, I had been in the legislature for five years, so I felt it was time to do something else. However, I had enjoyed state government work much more than I had earning a living at the law firm. Some people, on the basis of my legislative achievements in the liquor and water areas, talked of my running for governor of California, but I thought that would be premature.

After the Alcoholic Beverage Control investigation and passage of the constitutional amendments in 1954, many people had urged me to run for attorney general. I did not want to do that then, fearing that people would think I was trying to turn the liquor investigation into a personal political campaign. Now, almost four years later, the idea of the attorney-generalship—representing all the people in the state and working on all of the highly varied legal activities and other major responsibilities that went with that post—seemed very attractive. It would also mean continuing to work on state governmental issues. And so I decided to run for that office in the 1958 election, although after five years on a legislator's salary, I should have returned to more gainful employment.

After considerable encouragement from my family, I announced my candidacy in September 1957. Soon thereafter, Governor Knight made one of his jokes: "Why would anyone want a good, honest man for attorney general?"

My campaign apparatus was a little rusty, but my wife soon resurrected "Your Neighbors for Good Government." Several of my fellow attorneys joined our team, as did former law school students and many other well-wishers. Especially helpful, of course, were the enthusiastic efforts of my children, my brother, and my wife. Jane spent nearly every day at our headquarters, writing letters, making phone calls, organizing volunteers.*

It was largely an all-volunteer operation. We did not have professional campaign "managers" or big fund-raisers, and that, of course, was part of the problem in statewide races.

Most of all, statewide campaigns needed money, and we had little. So initially our campaign activities were minimal—mostly just billboards and basic headquarters expenses. Fortunately, I had no Republican opponent for the primary, and I was hoping for major GOP financial support in the general campaign. Rapidly shifting politics changed that. The problem was "the Big Switch." Senator William Knowland (who had presidential ambitions) decided early in 1958 that, instead of running for reelection to the U.S. Senate, he would run against incumbent Goodwin Knight for governor of California in order to support a proposed "right to work" law that union membership could not be made a requirement for getting a

---

* A letter she wrote to potential supporters exemplified her characteristic deft blending of purpose, charm, and humor: "In giving me his permission to write these letters Cap said I simply couldn't ask for campaign contributions. I won't but ... Robert Harris ... is the Treasurer and I understand is joyfully accepting all offerings, great and small."

job. This was a very divisive issue and guaranteed fierce labor union opposition to Senator Knowland in the fall. But Governor Knight was vulnerable to a Republican challenge because he had become increasingly close to the unions. He was eventually persuaded that he would lose in the gubernatorial primary. So he decided to run for Knowland's Senate seat, rather than seek reelection as governor.

Vice President, and Californian, Richard Nixon tried to orchestrate Knight's switch, in order to avert a Republican primary fight and to keep a united California Republican Party two years later when Nixon would run for president. I do not know whether or to what extent Nixon was involved, but Knight was not a willing pawn. Initially, he had felt his chances against Knowland in the primary were good, especially with labor support, but when told that major Republican contributors would back Knowland for governor, Knight realized, as he put it, that "Standing on the burning deck in mid-ocean, I had no choice."

"The Big Switch" divided the party anyway, and not until Ronald Reagan ran in 1966 were the various rifts healed so the GOP could triumph again.

As part of the fallout from "the Big Switch," a southern California congressman, Patrick Hillings, who had intended to run for the Senate seat, decided not to challenge Knight in the GOP Senate primary. Instead, he entered the attorney general race, having previously assured me that he would not.

I never liked contested primaries, because they usually meant a divided party and wasted resources—things that Republicans could not afford. The demographics of the state were changing, and Democrats now had a strong majority of registered voters. If I had known that the primary for attorney general was going to be contested and the party so disastrously split, I might not have entered.

I think everyone assumed I would drop out, but I had already made what I felt were irrevocable commitments to my supporters. So now we had a hotly contested primary race that turned pretty much into a north-against-south fight, with many independent voters disgusted by Republican infighting.

Filled with practiced and carefully cultivated bonhomie, the ruddy-faced former Democrat Patrick Hillings had succeeded Richard Nixon as congressman from the Twenty-fifth District in southern California when Nixon moved up to the Senate in 1950. In the attorney general race, Nixon did not *publicly* endorse either of us, but Hillings was widely known as Nixon's protégé (oddly enough, because Hillings had been an active FDR supporter in college), and he opened practically every speech by saying, "I've just come from a meeting with Dick Nixon." Hillings was close to then-chairman of the Los Angeles County Republican Committee Robert Finch, who supported him with a million-person mailing to L.A. Republicans urging his election in the primary. And Hillings, not surprisingly, won the endorsement of the *Los Angeles Times*, though the *Los Angeles Mirror-News*, a smaller paper which was owned by the *Times*, endorsed me. And, during the campaign, I believe Hillings encouraged the sudden entry of several other GOP candidates for attorney general—to divide the northern California vote.

Indeed, almost all the party support that could be had in southern California had been nailed down by Hillings in support of his Senate candidacy. When he switched to the attorney general race, much of that support stayed with him.

Thinking that I would have no challenger for the primary, I had not yet concentrated a very large effort in the south. After Hillings came onto the scene, Jane and I established a southern California headquarters at the old Alexandria Hotel in Los Angeles, but by then it was too late to be very effective.

There was also a smear campaign against me by Fulton Lewis, a right-wing extremist radio commentator. He seized on an old article in a California Communist newspaper, *People's World*, which warned its readership to watch me carefully because I had been effective in the California legislature. Lewis alleged on his radio program that the Communists were praising me and suggested I was actually a Communist. This was ludicrous—but damaging, nevertheless, and played into Pat Hillings's strategy of painting me as a dangerous liberal.

Some in my campaign wanted me to sue Lewis and the radio station for libel, and I rather liked that idea because I thought it was a way to set the record straight. But we soon realized that nothing could be decided by the courts until years after the election. We did, however, demand an apology, which Lewis gave half-heartedly. But a lot of damage was done, and it takes a long time to eradicate the negative effects of even absurd attacks.

My campaign emphasized that I was a practicing attorney—Hillings had never done any actual law practice—and was far better suited by experience to run the largest law office in the state. It was, in fact, the largest law office in the country outside the U.S. Department of Justice.

I spent the last month before the primary campaigning exclusively in southern California, before returning to San Francisco. The early returns—which were largely from the Bay Area—showed me running well ahead, but I knew that my lead would quickly be diminished when votes in Los Angeles were counted. When a reporter asked me early in the evening for a victory statement, I replied that if I weren't running so far ahead, I'd concede right then! It turned out that I did win in most counties, except for Los Angeles and Orange Counties, but that still was not enough to win the race.

My defeat, I am sure, was partially the result of some of the political factors I have already mentioned, but I think the main problem was simply that we did not raise enough money. We had many dedicated campaign supporters and volunteers, and I borrowed from the bank a substantial amount, for me, which took about five years to pay off. These sources combined gave us roughly $50,000, but in those days you needed at least a couple hundred thousand to mount an effective statewide campaign. The race taught me at least one lesson: that if I ran for elective office again, I would never put my own money into it.

The California GOP also learned the cost of division. We had forgotten the cardinal rule for California Republican victory: our candidates needed to be able to win about 80 percent of the GOP vote and attract about 20 percent of the registered Democrats. I am sure Senator Knowland and Governor Knight could have done this and easily won reelection if they had stayed in their respective posts. As it was, nearly all of our candidates lost. Stanley Mosk, a strong Democrat with a lot of labor union support, beat Pat Hillings for attorney general in the general election—a race I think I could have won. Stan Mosk served well as attorney general and later became a most able member of the California Supreme Court and a good friend.

After this disaster for California Republicans, many felt it would take years to restore the party. In 1958 California elected Democrat Edmund G. "Pat" Brown as governor and gave him Democratic legislative majorities in both houses. This was part of a national trend. The Democrats in 1958 made their biggest gains in Congress since the New Deal and won a net of five governorships, probably because we had had six years of Republican victories and many people wanted a change.

You never know, but I still think the California GOP could have survived this 1958 tide had we stayed united. After all, just two years later Richard Nixon carried the state against John F. Kennedy in the race for president.

CHAPTER 8

〜

GRAND OLD POLITICS

*B*y 1960, Richard Nixon had already led a distinguished life in government—four years as a congressman, two years in the Senate, and eight years as President Eisenhower's vice president.

I had known him—I suppose as well as anyone could really know Richard Nixon—since 1950, when, as a California congressman, he ran for and won a seat in the U.S. Senate. It was during that campaign that I first saw him at a small gathering of San Francisco GOP supporters in a mezzanine room at the St. Francis Hotel. His main theme was that he wanted to "help clean up the mess in Washington"— mostly some real transgressions by some dubious Truman appointees (although I have to add, quite minor transgressions compared to today's). Nixon had a garden shovel that he displayed rather sheepishly as an instrument he would use in this cleanup endeavor. I sympathized with him; I would not have wanted to wave a shovel around either.

He was a good candidate and a good political speaker, expressing solid conservative views, and he was popular within the Republican party. He was a favorite son of the California Republican Party, but there were always liberals who hated Richard Nixon from the moment he defeated the radical Democrat Helen Gahagan Douglas in the 1950 Senate campaign. Mrs. Douglas was a media favorite and professional Nixon-haters always spoke of his "dirty tactics" in that race. But it was really the same atmosphere that surrounded any other hotly contested California seat.

In his memoir, *RN*, Nixon wrote:

> Throughout the campaign I kept her pinned to her extremist record. I pointed out that she had voted against Truman on military aid to Greece and Turkey, the key plank of the Truman Doctrine, which I had supported. She had also voted against bills requiring loyalty checks for federal employees and was one of only fourteen members of Congress who had voted against the security bill that allowed the heads of key national defense agencies, such as the Atomic Energy Commission, to discharge government workers found to be security risks....
>
> Mrs. Douglas had often appeared at meetings and addressed organizations that had been cited by the Attorney General's office during Truman's administration as "Communist and subversive."

Some in the Nixon campaign, if not Nixon himself, took to calling her the "Pink Lady." In return, Douglas dubbed Nixon "Tricky Dick." I think one of Mr. Nixon's main campaign problems was that he allowed some less scrupulous or less careful campaign advisers to take over. In the early days of Nixon's political career, a Los Angeles attorney named Murray Chotiner was a good example. He was a likeable enough rogue whose enthusiasm for doing in his opponents sometimes exceeded his judgment. Of Mr. Chotiner it was frequently said that "Wherever you find Murray Chotiner, there is a trail of blood behind." One of his favorite ploys was to telephone someone from a booth in a corridor of the Senate Office Building and to open the conversation with, "I am calling you from the vice president's office."

In 1960 I felt that, as the Republican nominee for president, Nixon deserved the support of the party—all our party. I was adamant that my other political supporters not hold a grudge because of the Pat Hillings race against me for attorney general. It is a fundamental law of successful GOP campaigns that they are a process of *inclusion*, not of continuing old enmities.

So when Mr. Nixon asked me, I became a campaign cochairman in northern California. Basically that meant I was to arrange speaking engagements for him in the area, help coordinate his campaign appearances, plan rallies, and try in the usual ways to drum up party and independent support for him.

I also attended the national convention in Chicago that year, as an at-large delegate selected by Nixon. The three major party leaders in California—Nixon, Senator Knowland, and former governor Knight—each nominated one-third of the delegates for the 1960 convention, a sign of how the division in our party still hadn't healed. This selection process was a way of avoiding a major fight as to who was the "leader of the California party." But at least it ensured unity behind Nixon.

The convention itself was fairly uneventful, although all the paraphernalia, noise, and standard demonstrations (such as stunts with live elephants) were there in full measure. There was no organized opposition to Nixon—only a brief and minor challenge by supporters of Governor Nelson Rockefeller of New York, far too late because the delegates were already pledged to Nixon. This was considered by Nixon managers to be the "last gasp" of the "Eastern Establishment" that had run the party.

The basic theme of Nixon's 1960 campaign was "Peace, Prosperity, Progress," which was a continuation of the Eisenhower years that had delivered these three P's in the sure hands of the experienced Richard Nixon against the young Democratic nominee, John F. Kennedy.

There were no major ideological divisions in the country. The Cold War was at its coldest, and both men promoted their qualifications for dealing with that. Senator Kennedy frightened people with talk of a "missile gap" between the United States and the Soviet Union (a gap that he later admitted did not exist). Nixon, of course, was the quintessential anti-Communist, and much of his campaign literature emphasized this. As vice president, he had stood up to Soviet premier Nikita Khrushchev in the "kitchen debate," extolling the virtues of capitalism as they toured a Moscow exhibit of a model American home with all of the latest technology. Also, as a congressman in 1948, Nixon had successfully uncovered the spying activities of former State Department official Alger Hiss.

In the final analysis, however, the personalities and personal appeal of the two men were the deciding factors to many voters. That, unfortunately, did not work to Nixon's advantage. As many recall, the presidential debates (the first to be televised) were significant. Kennedy appeared young, vigorous, and handsome, as indeed he was. Nixon, on the other hand, came across poorly in the first of the four debates. He had the flu, he had recently hurt his knee, and a nonstop travel schedule had not allowed him any preparation time. Moreover, his "five o'clock shadow" made him look rather sinister and, compared to Kennedy, quite old. He came across better in the subsequent debates, but the first, being new, had the most impact.

It is interesting to note the influence television was already having in elevating style above substance. People who watched the debates on television felt that Kennedy was the winner, but those who listened on the radio decisively picked Nixon as the victor. Sadly, even this did not help Nixon, since the television audience was about five times larger than the radio audience.

Still, the election turned out to be a very narrow defeat for Nixon—with considerable evidence of vote fraud, particularly in a few precincts in Illinois and Texas, without which the election may have gone in his favor. Local bosses in both states had, through illegal counting and manipulation, provided ammunition for a major challenge. Nixon, to his credit, immediately decided to accept the election results. He admired Kennedy as a former Senate colleague and did not want to embarrass the country and the new, apparent president with a vigorously pursued recount.

As 1962 approached, a number of people encouraged Nixon to run for governor of California, as a natural platform for another presidential campaign. I was then the state party vice chairman and I was one of those urging him to run for governor, because I thought he could be elected. After all, he had barely lost the presidential election in 1960 and had carried California against the popular young Kennedy.

When Nixon decided to run for governor, he asked me to be the full-time manager of his campaign. This was tempting, but I declined. I did not feel safe in giving up my principal means of income, my law practice. There were also many nonprofit activities I was engaged in (of which more later), and I knew that running a gubernatorial campaign was more than a full-time job in itself. I did, however, serve as an informal adviser, occasionally meeting with Mr. Nixon on strategy or issues, and I made a few speeches, but I did not hold any formal or paid position.

Nixon was a reluctant candidate in this race, because his greatest interest was foreign policy and he did not know state issues well, which is one reason I think he wanted me to run his campaign. Someone had asked him about a local problem in Los Angeles, and he said, "See, Cap, I don't know how to answer things like this. I don't know anything about the sewage disposal problems in Los Angeles." (He did not call it "sewage.") When I told him that governors do not deal with such issues, he replied, "Well, you see, I don't even know that!"

Another factor that substantially weakened Nixon in this race was the party split caused by a far right-wing Republican challenger, Joe Shell. Shell had been a colleague of mine in the assembly and was quite popular in southern California. He was a former football player at USC, which in southern California was practically a passport to political advancement. An ultraconservative, Shell supported the dubious John Birch Society,* a small but very vocal extremist faction of the party that Nixon had condemned in an act of political courage for the time.

Nixon won the primary, but he did so without generating much GOP enthusiasm, which was deadly given that he was running against an incumbent Democratic governor, Edmund G. "Pat" Brown, who had not done anything particularly iniquitous. In California, incumbents of either party are hard to unseat. So Nixon lost the election, and the next morning, feeling understandably depressed and regarding himself as a political failure, unable ever to achieve the presidency—the only thing he really cared about—he held his disastrous "You won't have Nixon to kick around anymore" farewell press conference, lashing out, rather incoherently, at the press.

* The John Birch Society was a relatively new organization, established in 1958. Anti-Communism was its main thrust, a prevalent sentiment in the country at that time, but its members' rigid intolerance of anyone whose degree of fervor was less than theirs struck me as somewhat hypocritical.

I remember one particularly raucous meeting of the Republican State Central Committee in early 1963 that exemplified this. During a roll-call vote on a resolution to restore cross-filing (which had been eliminated in 1959), Birchers loudly disrupted the meeting in an effort to keep supporters of the resolution from hearing their names being called. For maximum effect, they even positioned themselves in a diamond formation around the room, just as vote-recorder Emily Pike pointed out, "like the Communist handbook recommends it." Their opposition to the measure, however, was based on their basic belief that any Republican who would run for office on both the Republican and Democratic ballots was obviously not sufficiently conservative.

Shortly after that defeat, Nixon gave up California as a residence and political base and moved to New York. He also did a great deal of traveling and speaking abroad, where he was still very popular; practiced law;* and kept in close touch with his most loyal party supporters. One loyalist and admirer, Bob Haldeman, believed that Nixon's 1962 gubernatorial race was crucial to his eventual election as president, because it kept him in the public's mind as an active politician rather than as merely a former vice president.

I never knew if Nixon himself actually felt that his political career was completely finished after his gubernatorial defeat. He certainly seemed to think so the morning after that election, but he proved to be a most remarkable political phoenix. I am sure this was because of both his meticulous planning and his dogged perseverance in the face of overwhelming odds.

I regretted having urged Nixon to run for governor, because it was bad for him to have entered a race in which he had comparatively little interest. Admittedly, I had been thinking almost entirely of the welfare and success of the state Republican Party rather than that of Richard Nixon personally.

In spite of my own loss in the 1958 GOP primary for attorney general, I kept a hand in politics as well. That year, I had been asked by Senator Knowland and agreed to become secretary of the Republican State Central Committee (RSCC)—the official GOP organization.† Its main purpose was to raise funds for state candidates, persuade good potential candidates to run, keep county party organizations

---

* Leonard Garment, one of his law partners in New York, has written in his autobiography, *Crazy Rhythm* (New York: Times Books, 1997), the best history of this part of Nixon's post-California career.

† The RSCC then consisted of all Republican members of the legislature and all other elected state GOP officials. Each of these had the right to appoint three other people to the organization.

going, and draft state party platforms in election years. The chairman was spokesman for the party.

But in the early 1960s the California Republican Party was factious. The party was used to winning, but when it split over degrees of conservatism it almost guaranteed defeat.

This was very much in evidence when I agreed to the urging of many friends that I run for the vice chairmanship of the RSCC in 1960. Some of the legislative leaders I had known when I was in the assembly came to me at the state convention and said they knew I did not have enough votes and I would be humiliated, and they urged me to drop out of the race. But my strong impression was that if they had the votes to defeat me, they would not bother to suggest I drop out. That conclusion turned out to be correct; I won on a roll-call vote. My opposition was largely based on the impression that I was relatively more "liberal" than my opponent, Vernon Cristina, and hence less "reliable" in the coming fight for the 1964 presidential nomination. Cristina, who ran a trucking company south of San Jose, was a pleasant man whom I liked, so there was little personal rancor between us.

The vice chairmanship was very important because the vice chairman almost always became the chairman two years later. So the more "conservative" faction, including Joe Shell, kept trying to oust me at each subsequent meeting.

I called several additional meetings in an effort to keep everybody active and interested in the party. Those meetings were usually contentious. Far too many Republicans would rather pass a resolution, even if ridiculous or unhelpful in persuading voters, than win an election. I soon learned that it was quite unsafe to call very many meetings because I spent half my time trying to survive the attempts to replace me with a "Goldwater man."

Still, in 1961, I developed for the RSCC a strategy that came to be called the Weinberger Victory Program. One element of this program was to register voters and bring more of them into the party. This was fairly successful.

Another part of the program was to make a concerted effort, particularly in marginal legislative districts, to win control of the legislature, which had already become considerably more partisan than when I had served in the assembly. The legislature was scheduled to reapportion the state after the next census, and we strongly preferred that the reapportionment be done by a Republican majority. We concentrated our resources on the most promising districts, developing precinct organizations, setting up phone banks, and sending out mass mailings.

Of even more importance was recruiting promising candidates, endorsing them strongly, and providing them with plenty of public opportunities to present their views.

The key to all of this, I felt, was to start two to four years before an election, because if you followed the standard practice of waiting until only a few weeks before, it was too late, and you would probably be stuck with a candidate who was not electable. Having *continuous* party activity, even many months or years away from an election, was a new idea. Of course, all of this planning was made more difficult by the efforts of the Goldwater people, who were uninterested in promoting candidates they felt were not conservative enough.

At the state convention in 1962, I faced a challenge from Gardiner Johnson for chairmanship of the party. He was a fellow San Francisco attorney and a friend. Senator Knowland nominated him in a speech that lost some of its intended dramatic effect because the senator forgot to mention Johnson's name. Johnson's nomination was part of an additional effort by the Goldwater people to gain control of every state party in preparation for the 1964 election, so I never felt it involved any opposition to me personally, although of course it might have. I did manage to win the chairmanship, again by a close roll-call vote.

The Goldwater faction was persuasive, had money, made a lot of noise, and worked hard throughout the year, but it also kept us riven with internecine squabbles and hurt our efforts to attract independents and wavering Democrats.

When Barry Goldwater became the Republican presidential nominee in 1964, his people expected all the rest of us in the California Republican Party to fold up and resign our positions. That did not happen—moderates retained leadership—but I supported Goldwater because he was the nominee of the convention, and I urged others to do the same, even though I would have preferred Nelson Rockefeller. I thought he had been an excellent governor of New York and was more electable, but I was careful not to make any public statements to that effect before or during the convention. One fellow state committeeman, however, was not so reluctant. Joe Martin, a "Grand New Party" colleague from 1950 and the California member of the national committee, resigned from the state committee to support Rockefeller.

The 1964 Republican National Convention, held at San Francisco's Cow Palace,* was raucous and divisive. When Rockefeller spoke, he was booed and hissed. The hatred toward this Republican governor was palpable, and it was shocking to many television viewers.

Even though I backed Goldwater after the convention, his people still did not regard me as "reliable." They did not, for a long time after the convention, accept my offer to help. Finally, Goldwater himself did, and at his request I made a couple of speeches on his behalf in October.

---

* San Francisco had hosted the Republican convention only eight years earlier but was chosen again because it had a good convention hall as well as good and plentiful hotel space—and, of course, it is a very attractive city that everyone likes to visit. I had made a couple of presentations in Washington, urging the selection of San Francisco to the national committee, which selects the convention site. The Cow Palace was so named because it was the home of county fairs with agricultural and cattle exhibits.

Goldwater won only six states (he lost California). He had been labeled as an extremist, and many worried that he would expand the Vietnam War and cut Social Security. President Johnson won reelection easily—and went on to expand the Vietnam War. One cartoonist summed it up rather neatly by showing a caricature of President Johnson telephoning Senator Goldwater after one disastrous Vietnam debacle and asking, "Barry, what was it you were going to do next in Vietnam?"

Though considered extreme, Goldwater was simply a conservative and proud of it. He had none of the bitterness that extremists feel toward the less ideologically pure. In fact, later, in the Senate, he sometimes voted for measures considered quite liberal.

It was Ronald Reagan who made the most notable speech on Goldwater's behalf in 1964, and it was Reagan who would soon express the kind of conservatism that could win elections.

CHAPTER 9

TELEVISION IN CALIFORNIA

*I*nvolvement in politics kept me busy enough in the late 1950s and early 1960s to satisfy my addiction, but with a recent defeat in elective politics and a large (for that time) campaign debt to pay, I reluctantly concluded that I should concentrate on more profitable pursuits, namely, my law practice. Some people talked of my running for city attorney or mayor of San Francisco, but I really had no interest in those positions. I wanted to be where I felt I could make a real contribution in public service, not just run for an office for the office's sake. Besides, I'm sorry to say, municipal politics has never really interested me, even though I know it is a vital part of citizen participation in government.

Actually, even if I had wanted to pursue a position in San Francisco city government, I could not have because by 1959 I was no longer a resident. The previous year, after our vigorous campaign for attorney general, our family's summer camping vacations were replaced with a much-needed rest for a month in the hot, dry climate of California's wine country. The summer home we rented had a swimming pool.

This, in turn, led to family queries as to why this sort of thing could not go on all the time. So we moved down the peninsula to Hillsborough, where swimming is possible, if not all year, at least for a large part of it.

My professional life remained in San Francisco, though, and I soon understood all the jokes about commuting. I returned to Heller, Ehrman, and I became a partner in 1959. While I worked hard at the law practice and liked some of it, I never enjoyed it as much as what my wife called my "nonprofit" activities. I do not think I made a conscious effort to find other, more interesting things to do than the law, but I certainly did not resist too strongly when various offers presented themselves.

The first of those came around January 1959, just as my final term in the legislature was coming to an end. Jon Rice, general manager and one of the founders of KQED, San Francisco's local, and fairly new, educational television station, called and asked if I would be interested in being the moderator for one of their public affairs programs. I had always been interested in educational stations, and as an assemblyman I had secured passage of a bill amending the Education Code to permit public schools to spend money for educational television programs. This had provided KQED and other early educational TV stations with urgently needed public funding that helped them to survive.

Profile: Bay Area, the program I was asked to host, was essentially a weekly public affairs discussion program covering all sides of a wide range of topics of local, state, and national interest. *Profile's* first moderator, Roger Boas, had served as host of the show for its first year or so but then wanted to move on to a career in local politics. KQED liked the program and knew that a lot of people watched it (half a million, by some estimates). I had been on a few similar programs involving state legislative matters and enjoyed them. So Jon's offer fell on surprised but willing ears, and I accepted.

Our crew on *Profile* consisted of myself, a permanent studio cameraman, and the producer/director—a bright, brilliant, energetic lady named Virginia Duncan. She was largely responsible for the considerable success the program enjoyed.

Virginia and I worked closely together on all aspects of the program: deciding the topics to be covered, lining up the guests and interviewing them ahead of time to ensure that all points of view were presented on controversial subjects, writing the scripts and preparing questions, and so forth. All of this was time-consuming but quite helpful—indeed essential if we wanted to present an intelligent, fair, and balanced program.

Still, things did not always go smoothly. Sometimes pressing work at the law practice, or the lack of firm commitments from guests until a day or so before the program, made it impossible for me to interview or meet with the guests ahead of time. I always regretted this because I felt the preprogram interviews with the guests were a vital part of the program, particularly because frequently my knowledge of some topics was extremely limited, such as with modern art. For that program, we interviewed Richard Diebenkorn, the famous modern artist from Berkeley about whom sadly I previously knew nothing at all.

We generally wrote out an introduction and background for me to read, but I did not stick rigidly to the various questions we drafted. This allowed for more spontaneity and give-and-take among the guests.

The only special visual effects or graphics were pictures I was allowed to pick up from the *San Francisco Chronicle*'s morgue to illustrate the show's opening. I usually walked there from the law office around 6 or 7 P.M., selected the pictures, and then took them to the small KQED studio on Fourth Street, which was "South of Market"— a rather seedy part of town at that time, and quite a long walk. The *Chronicle* was very cooperative about letting me wander through its files and picture collection, even when its rival, the *Examiner*, was sponsoring *Profile*.

We did the program live at 9 P.M. every Thursday, which I much preferred to taping. Originally, the show was only a half hour long, but viewer requests for more thorough discussions allowed us to extend to forty-five minutes and eventually to an hour.

We always tried to have at least four guests, two on each side of an issue. I would start talking with the guests in the studio several minutes before airtime so that when the camera actually started rolling, they would be warmed up and ready to continue, rather than start, the discussion. I acted as moderator and did not impose my own opinions. We had many highly vigorous debates. In one program, on public education, an actual fistfight developed afterward between two academics.

Occasionally we received letters from viewers who said the program was slanted because I was a fairly prominent Republican. We always wrote back and asked these people to point out one specific incident where my personal opinion had intruded, and they were invariably unable to do so.

We covered a wide variety of topics, including riots at City Hall, political campaigns, narcotics, loyalty oaths, state water problems, the San Francisco Symphony, professional boxing, rapid transit, disarmament, baseball, and Vietnam. As Jon Rice said, "There's no subject the program won't tackle. It was the first in the nation to deal with the relationship between cigarette smoking and cancer." I remember that program quite vividly because one of the guests, a doctor who opposed theories linking smoking to cancer, defiantly and ostentatiously smoked cigarettes, blowing smoke over the other guests throughout the program. A few years later he died—of cancer.

Profile occasionally even directly influenced policy. One example was when we discussed capital punishment the night before one of the many scheduled executions of rapist Caryl Chessman. Chessman's attorney, as part of his *Profile* presentation, made a dramatic—and successful, as it turned out—plea addressed to the governor, turning to talk to him as if he were actually in the studio. The governor was indeed watching, and later that night he granted another stay.

Once, following the death of a boxer who had absorbed a terrible beating in the ring, our subject was whether professional boxing should be allowed. We had a retired boxer who was contemptuous of efforts to ban professional boxing and a brain surgeon who had told me that this barbarous sport should be banned. My first question went to the surgeon: "Why do you think professional boxing should be abolished?" "Oh, I don't. I've changed my mind," he replied. That left me with about fifty-eight minutes to fill with two guests who agreed with each other.

Our guests were as disparate as the subjects we presented. Among them were state and local political candidates; farm labor spokesman Cesar Chavez; the inventor of the hydrogen bomb, Edward Teller; and an extremely eloquent and persuasive Malcolm X shortly before his assassination.

The program I remember most vividly was one in October of 1966 that illustrated, with considerable force, the problems underlying riots at Hunters Point, a low-income, predominantly black area of San Francisco. The root cause of the riots seemed to be primarily the difficulty for residents there to get satisfactory jobs, so Virginia and I decided to devote a special two-hour show to the issue, to try to find out what obstacles they were facing and to discuss some possible solutions. Our panel included city, state, and federal employment officials, labor leaders, an NAACP representative, and several representatives of youth groups and residents of Hunters Point.

I felt that we had assembled a pretty balanced group of participants, but about an hour into the show, a handful of disgruntled, agitated young men from Hunters Point cut into the discussion from one side of the stage. They said that since they were the ones who were closest to the situation, their position should be heard. I agreed and asked for their point of view, but they simply kept repeating who they were and that we should listen to them. I quickly realized that this exercise was not productive, so I returned my attention to the invited panel.

Soon, however, the interlopers surrounded the table, pressing themselves and their indignation further and further onto center stage. I would have been pleased to hear their opinions and some of their suggestions, but it was difficult to have any kind of calm discussion about it because they all spoke at once and seemed determined to disrupt the program.

I was becoming rather irritated as well because our invited guests, who were kind enough to take time to be a part of our panel, were hardly getting a chance to speak. When I tersely suggested to the intruders that part of the problem might be that they were not willing to listen to anyone else, their anger—and volume—only rose, with fists pounding the table and fingers pointing.

Partly because I was trying to maintain order and partly, I think, because I represented to them every white man who had discriminated against them, I became a convenient target for their ire. The exchange that perhaps revealed their complete frustration and disillusionment best was when I said it was difficult for anyone to be heard when they kept interrupting, and one man got right in my face and replied, "You've been interrupting me since the day I was born."

That program won a couple of prizes for best educational television program, and much was written about it in the newspapers. It was lauded mostly for the "realism" and spontaneity provided by our unexpected participants.

The invasion brought home to many of our viewers, in a way that little else could, the desperate frustration of a group of people to whom most of us could not relate. Program panelist and city supervisor Terry Francois described it well: Though he "could not excuse the intemperate, rude behavior" of the angry young men who had invaded the studio, "the intense hostility, the feeling of alienation, and the total rejection of middle-class standards which were exhibited came as no surprise. We have told them that they didn't belong for so long and treated them as though they had no stake in society, that it is not surprising that they have come to see themselves as a group apart and not bound by any of the rules of the group."

Much later, we learned that a week before that show, this same group had poured into the reception area of the station and demanded to be heard on another program. A rather frightened manager offered them each five dollars to go away. So I think most of them came back not so much to disrupt *Profile* as to get their five dollars.

The program, and indeed the station, was run on a shoestring budget, supported largely by individual contributions, occasional corporate sponsors, and some school funds. The *San Francisco Examiner* sponsored *Profile* for a time, and we tried to get foundation grants, but most of the time only our permanent cameraman was paid; the producer/director and I received nothing at all. Over the roughly nine years I moderated the program, I doubt if I received much more than five hundred dollars in all. But we enjoyed it thoroughly and were dedicated to producing a fair and accurate discussion program.*

Aside from my continued but rather minor involvement in the Republican Party during these years, two other opportunities turned up that allowed me to combine my passion for government and my interest in journalism.

Around 1959 I made a speech to the California Newspaper Publishers' Association, the gist of which was that while there was plenty of coverage of local matters and a lot of coverage of national

---

* I remember how astonished I was when I appeared on NBC's *Meet the Press* in Washington for the first time, in 1970, after I was appointed chairman of the Federal Trade Commission. There were about thirty people in the studio—everything from cameramen to scriptwriters to assistant producers and directors to make-up people to lighting experts and graphic artists—all working on a single discussion program.

and international events, the state government was rather badly neglected in most newspapers outside of Sacramento. With such minimal coverage, I argued, there was very little understanding of it, certainly not as much as I thought people ought to have in view of the numerous ways the state affected the lives of so many people. One or two of the publishers came up to me afterward and said, "You're complaining about this; what are you going to do about it? Why don't you write us some stories, or even a column?"

That idea greatly appealed to me, so I started writing a regular column (a couple of times a week) about state government issues. I tried to explain each issue as objectively as I could and then give readers an idea of the pros and cons as well as the interests behind each side. My own opinion usually came out toward the end of the column. Occasionally, however, I would unabashedly push my view from the start, as I did, for example, when I advocated allowing taxpayers to file as their state income tax return a simple carbon copy of their federal return. I also gave my opinion frequently when writing about measures that would affect the areas I had worked on as an assemblyman, particularly alcoholic beverage control and the state's water needs.

Ultimately the column ran in twenty to thirty papers around the state. Each one paid a small amount (ten to twenty-five dollars as I recall) for each column. I did this for about nine years. It certainly did not bring in a large income, but, like my other extracurricular activities, I enjoyed it much more than my work at the law firm. My personal secretary at the law firm, Marguerite Klapka, did too, in fact. She was always enthusiastic and helpful with this, as well as with all of my other outside activities. I have been so fortunate over the years, for the secretaries and executive assistants with whom I have worked have all been very helpful, enormously able, and loyal, and have usually become good friends.

I also did a daily radio commentary for the local NBC station. The program initially was sponsored by a group called the Republican Alliance, which wanted to get Republican views on the air, but before long the only ones paying for the airtime (we had no "production costs") were old friends and Hillsborough neighbors, John Renshaw and his wife, Hope. They were longtime, hardworking Republicans. The station was reluctant to sell the time at first because it was afraid it would lose its audience and would have to offer equal time to a Democratic spokesman. Neither scenario materialized.

It was only a fifteen-minute, live program (daily, and later, weekly), sandwiched between the evening news and prime time. I would walk up to the station around 5 P.M., reading over notes I had made about some events that had happened during the week and that seemed to me to demonstrate the need for Republicans to be elected. I did not like to use a prepared script, as the studio urged me to do. I would go on the air and talk informally about these six or eight topics. Unlike on *Profile*, here I did express my personal views. The station was quite pleased with the program because it got far more favorable than negative reactions. We did it for about two years, until our efforts turned more directly to the 1966 governor's race.

CHAPTER 10

~

THE GOVERNOR WHO TURNED
THE STATE AROUND

*T*he main Republican contenders for governor of California in 1966 were George Christopher, former mayor of San Francisco, and a personable, handsome actor named Ronald Reagan. It may surprise some that I supported Christopher in the primary, but I had pledged my support to him before Mr. Reagan decided to run. Christopher was a fellow San Franciscan, a political supporter in my own bids for office who had made the very first contribution to my 1952 campaign. I was very busy with my law practice, so my support was limited to a few speeches in which I was always careful to extol Christopher rather than attack Reagan. I had no problem after the primary in joining the Reagan gubernatorial campaign because I admired him and appreciated all he had done for our party.

Ronald Reagan had a star quality and a popular message of personal and economic freedom that helped him win that primary and, ultimately, every major race he entered. He eloquently presented a picture of reduced state government expenditures and reduced government involvement in people's daily affairs, both of which meant increased power and freedom for individuals. It was exactly the message and the picture most people wanted to hear and to achieve.

Moreover, he was fully committed to rebuilding the party *within* the state and was enormously effective in doing so. His celebrity status helped, but even beyond that, he had an electric quality about him and a way of making each person in the audience, no matter how large or small the gathering, feel as if he were speaking directly to him or her. He could articulate their hopes and ideals—or persuade them to share his.

Also, as I had seen when I was chairman of the State Central Committee, Reagan was willing to go anywhere, however small or remote, even though he did not like to fly, to preach the Republican message—a message that no one could express more personably or with more inspiring vision.

I went with him to some campaign rallies, did a few radio programs on his behalf, helped draft some speeches, and gave a few of my own. I also met occasionally with his personal campaign staff. But in the 1966 general election, it was his own tireless efforts and the appeal of his philosophy that translated into his overwhelming victory over incumbent Governor Pat Brown.*

Reagan immediately set about translating his beliefs into action. In fact, he was so anxious to get started that he even asked to be sworn in, in the rotunda of the State Capitol, immediately after midnight on Inauguration Day, January 3, 1967, instead of waiting until the more traditional noon ceremonies.

* Governor Brown did his part too, though. A master of malapropism, he often hurt himself more than anyone else could. A good example was when he flew over a flood-damaged area and proclaimed, "This is the worst disaster since I was elected governor."

His goals in office were essentially his core philosophy that he had talked about in the campaign—that is, smaller government and more individual freedom and responsibility. He wanted to reform welfare by removing some of the incentives to stay on the welfare rolls and by adding a work requirement. He wanted to improve schools by raising standards, not necessarily by raising budgets. And he wanted to reduce taxes. But first, he had to get rid of the budget deficit that Governor Brown had left. The state constitution required a balanced budget.

During the transition, Governor-elect Reagan asked me to head a small ad hoc task force to recommend ways to make the state's executive branch more efficient, less cumbersome, less expensive, and more responsive to the governor's direction.

It was through this endeavor that I first met Bill Clark, a rancher and attorney who was, at that time, one of Reagan's senior campaign advisers. For Bill, the son of California ranchers, his greatest love, after his lovely wife, is indeed his ranch and ranch life. I believe that one of the reasons he had been attracted to Reagan's candidacy was the fact that Reagan personified the best of the frontier virtues that Bill admired. We each subsequently served in Reagan's gubernatorial and presidential administrations, and it was evident to me from our first meeting that Bill Clark was a thoroughly decent, completely honest man, totally devoted and loyal to the cause of Mr. Reagan's success. Bill always served Mr. Reagan extraordinarily well, because he innately understood the way Reagan thought and operated. He also understood better than most that extremist versions of Reagan's beliefs, which some of the governor-elect's friends were recommending, would hurt him at the polls and beyond.

As cabinet secretary, and later, as the governor's executive secretary, Bill did an excellent job of organizing the governor's office and staff; he worked well with all of the various interests competing for the governor's time and was well liked by the press. Bill brought order to the generally chaotic early days of any new administration. I have always thought that Reagan's enormous success as governor, particularly in his first term—the term that propelled him onto the national stage—was in large part due to Bill Clark. Bill has always been completely selfless, and although he was rewarded by high judicial offices, those appointments were the governor's initiatives, not Bill's. Of course, I was prejudiced in his favor. Bill has been unfailingly thoughtful and generous to me; indeed, Jane and I consider him and his wife, Joan, our closest friends. All in all, he is one of the most able people with whom I have ever worked.

We worked closely on the governor's reorganization task force in late 1966. This group, which included management consultants and business executives I had appointed, held a series of meetings in my San Francisco law office (and a few in Los Angeles) and prepared a thorough reorganization plan. Essentially, this called for clustering groups of state agencies together according to the types of things they did—agriculture and services, business and transportation, human relations, and natural resources. Each of these four broad areas would be headed by executive vice presidents or secretaries, who would then report to the governor. As it was, there were well over one hundred agencies reporting directly and separately to the governor, so our plan significantly streamlined communications.

To get legislative approval for this plan would probably have been very difficult and taken many months because the legislature was heavily Democratic and suspicious of any reorganization plan. So, at Bill Clark's suggestion, we put the essence of the plan into effect immediately by executive order, on the theory that the governor would use this new plan simply as a means of communicating with his appointees. This did not require any statutory authority. Governor Reagan used this organization for most of his two terms, and I believe that his successors have used some versions of it as well. Some aspects were subsequently enacted formally through legislation.

Several years later, President Nixon implemented a similar plan, essentially consolidating federal departments and agencies performing generally similar activities under four or five "counselors to the president." Mr. Nixon appointed me counselor to the president for human resources. Not surprisingly, individual cabinet members, and some of the White House staff, did not like the arrangement because it subordinated their role to these counselors. And members of Congress, as was the case with the state legislature, were wary of the reorganization because they felt it changed their relationship with the executive departments and agencies. Taking a page from Governor Reagan's books, President Nixon put the plan into effect without formal congressional approval. Actually, it lasted only about six months, and then Watergate overtook everything and nothing more was done about it—or indeed much else until President Nixon's forced resignation.

We tried to put in the same kind of plan later, when Reagan was president, but there was too much opposition from some members of the White House staff, who were afraid it would reduce their influence with the president, and from potential cabinet appointees who wanted to report directly to the president.

As Governor-elect Reagan's administration was taking shape, Bill Clark urged Reagan to name me director of finance. Bill liked my work on the reorganization task force and knew of my earlier work in the legislature, and he apparently felt, correctly, that I would be completely loyal to the governor. There was, however, strong opposition from southern California ultra-conservatives who still considered me a liberal Republican. In any event, interested as I was in helping the governor, I was preparing for a major antitrust case, so a full-time state job was out of the question.

There was, however, another way both the governor and Bill felt I could help. They asked me if I would serve as Reagan's first appointee to, and chairman of, the Commission on California State Government

Organization and Economy. This "Little Hoover Commission," as it was also known, had been in existence since 1961, and it had investigated a variety of individual questions, largely based, it seemed to me, on the personal interests of its members, some of whom were appointed by the leaders of the assembly and state senate, and some by previous governors. The commission had never looked at overall reorganization of the executive branch; it was our task force that really did the work on that.

It was difficult to reach a consensus on anything because the governor's appointees and those within the Little Hoover Commission appointed by the legislative leaders, mostly Democrats, were usually at odds. The majority of the commission also insisted on keeping a singularly inept and partisan staff, added to which were a couple of particularly unpleasant holdovers from the Brown administration.

Nevertheless, I have always found it difficult to say no to governors and presidents, and since the commission met only once or twice a month, I accepted the position. We managed to complete some reasonably useful investigations and projects, but I cannot say I enjoyed the experience.

As 1967 went on, more and more people inside the administration recognized the ineffectiveness of Governor Reagan's first director of finance, Gordon Paul Smith. Smith had come from a management firm and was not experienced at dealing with the legislature. He was generally not very knowledgeable about state government, and little had been done to deal with the state's deficit. So, toward the end of that year, Bill Clark, who was by then the governor's executive secretary, renewed his efforts to have me appointed director of finance. When Governor Reagan called me about the job, I was waiting for the jury's decision after a ten-week trial in the antitrust case. The case involved predatory pricing in the dried sandblast sand industry, and I had learned far more about sandblast sand than I wanted to know. So when Mr. Reagan asked again, my reply was, "No—when do I start?"

I planned to serve as finance director for only a year, and the law firm reluctantly agreed to my taking a leave of absence. I think by then the firm realized that practicing law was not my top priority.

The salary of the director of finance was about $30,000, which was a significant cut in pay from the law firm, and there was no living expense allowance. My wife noted that I had cut my own income and doubled my expenses—which made me seem a very dubious budget director.

In any event, I accepted the position, and we rented another apartment in Sacramento across the park from the Senator Hotel and fairly close to the one we had rented when I was in the legislature. Our new apartment was later Governor Jerry Brown's "pad," as he called it (which he chose over living in the newly built governor's mansion). Apparently, he moved all the furniture out and slept on the floor in accordance with his widely publicized monastic views, and he was pleased to describe it as spartan. But we found it very comfortable with the furniture in, and it had a splendid view of the beautiful park and Capitol grounds.

It was only a short, pleasant walk from there to my office, which was on the ground floor of the Capitol and faced the same beautiful park. The governor had flowers from the gardens in the park grounds brought to his office daily, and I quickly got my office on the list too. The gardeners were delighted to have somebody else who liked flowers. However, I was not fond of potted palms, which were the standard decor—I did not want any reminder of the jungle—so I immediately had the regular-issue plants removed from my office in favor of fresh, multicolored flowers.

I was sworn in on March 1, 1968, in the governor's office, with Jane and my brother, Peter, and most of the other cabinet members in attendance. As I recall, there was a San Francisco newspaper strike on at that time, so my hometown saw very little coverage of the event. In fact, the news apparently barely made it around Sacramento, as I learned shortly after I took office. I was to attend a press conference by the governor, to which only the governor's staff and cabinet and properly credentialed members of the press were admitted. I was held back at the door by a policeman who did not know I was the new director of finance. One of the governor's secretaries ultimately got me in. I found the whole thing very funny. Incidentally, that incident *did* make the papers.

What was not so amusing, however, was the shape of the state's finances. In fact, in a postscript on his letter of appointment to me, Governor Reagan wrote, "By now, you must think you've been appointed receiver in a bankruptcy case." The state was still operating in fiscal year 1967–68, the budget for which had been prepared by the previous administration. Governor Brown had left a deficit of nearly $1 billion, but by using some dubious accounting methods, he had been able to show the budget closer to balance than it actually was and thus avoid raising taxes in an election year. This accrual method allowed him to reflect, on the books, revenue to be received as if it had already been received, making it appear that there was enough revenue to cover expenditures.

The California State Constitution required a balanced budget, and Governor Reagan most reluctantly concluded that he could close the huge deficit only by raising taxes even though that went against everything he stood for. He succeeded in pushing a large tax increase through during his first year in office, and it did not meet with *too* much public resistance, probably largely because the governor was able to explain effectively to the people the nature and scope of the financial mess in which the state found itself. And the Democrats really could not criticize the tax increase because they knew the dire fiscal situation was largely their doing.

The combination of the governor's first-year tax increase and some budget cuts resulted in a surplus of about $100 million. Reagan wanted to give the surplus revenue back to the people. I said that sounded great, but of course it had never been done before. To which he replied, "Well, we've never had an actor for governor before either." Governor Reagan went directly to the people, immediately appearing on television to announce the surplus and the intended refund—a tactic which thwarted potential opposition in the legislature. Most of the refund was in the form of a 10 percent rebate on 1970 income taxes, and it was enormously popular.

But the governor believed that, in addition, there needed to be fundamental reform of the tax system. Californians were paying too much,* and the state was spending too much. The best way to impose fiscal discipline, Governor Reagan felt, was to limit the amount of taxes that could be collected by fixing an objective standard, such as the previous year's expenditures plus inflation. This novel idea was bitterly opposed by the lobbyists, particularly the education lobby. We actually qualified a revenue-limitation measure for the state ballot (by obtaining the required number of signatures), but sadly, it was defeated, largely because of the argument that it would force local taxes higher. This would have been true only if local governments refused to cut their own expenditures, but the scare tactic used by the governor's opponents succeeded in inflicting a rare loss on him. Even so, the people recognized that he had been the one trying to hold their taxes down.

Another component of the governor's 1969 tax reform plan was to reduce the regressive residential real estate tax and to shift more than half of it to three other imposts that are directly related to ability to pay: sales tax, income tax, and nonresidential real estate taxes. That new state revenue would then be used to finance a large part of the

---

* In the second decade of the century, it took the average citizen only a couple of weeks to earn enough to pay his whole year's taxes. By 1970, it took over three months, with thirty-seven cents of every dollar going to the government. Of course, it's even worse today.

cost of public schools. Unfortunately, several senators in the Democrat-controlled legislature blocked the proposal. It was not until much later that California's real estate taxes were finally reduced by the famous Proposition 13 in 1978.

In addition to the governor's tax reduction efforts, I recommended ways to improve the administration of taxes as well. I thought it would be much better to put all of the responsibilities for administering and collecting taxes into a single new department headed by an official appointed by the governor. The existing laws split the tax responsibilities between the Franchise Tax Board (consisting of independently elected state officers, serving ex officio) and the independently elected Board of Equalization. A new Department of Revenue, I estimated, could save up to $7 million a year, which was a fair-sized saving then.

Another of my suggestions was that the state adopt a carbon copy of the federal tax return—that is, when you filed your federal return, you would simply make a carbon copy for the state and pay California at a rate designed to bring in the same revenue as the state's income tax. This caused a great outcry, primarily among the Franchise Tax Board employees, who correctly saw that they would be out of a job. They raised the specious argument that the carbon copy tax return would infringe on "California's sovereignty," but the voters, in 1966, had only narrowly rejected a constitutional amendment authorizing the change. I had advocated both of these ideas back when I was in the legislature, but there, too, without success.

I made one additional suggestion to Governor Reagan, based on my legislative proposals. This was to get rid of duplicate taxation and burdensome and redundant filing requirements. I urged that we eliminate California's gift and estate taxes, as these areas were already taxed heavily at the federal level. In return, the state would get something back on the federal collection of income taxes. Unfortunately, this proposal was never put into effect either.

Along with tax reform, Governor Reagan and I believed that it was imperative to reduce expenditures significantly as well. Indeed, one of the first things the governor had wanted to do as soon as he took office was to implement a 10 percent across-the-board spending cut. But he found that was not possible because close to two-thirds of the budget was made up of dedicated funds—special funds automatically allocated by law for specific purposes—which had to be paid on a regular basis regardless of revenue or other factors. To change any of these automatic allocations, the legislature would have to agree, a most unlikely event, particularly since Democrats controlled the legislature for six of Governor Reagan's eight years in office.

So there was very little room for discretionary cuts, and those could be made only from the remaining one-third of the budget. That one-third of the budget comprised the General Fund, which funded things like some education programs, welfare, health, construction, bond interest, and conservation programs. So if there were to be any real overall reductions, we had to hit some of these politically sensitive areas very hard. For example, in the 1969–70 budget, in order to achieve a tax reduction and a balanced budget, and also to fund sufficiently the governor's priorities, such as school aid and care for the mentally ill, we had to reduce other General Fund expenditures by more than $500 million. Still, each year's budget was higher than the previous one, due largely to the untouchable dedicated funds. Initially, we were able, at least, to hold down the *rate* of increase.

As I had in the legislature, I tried, again unsuccessfully, to get some of the dedicated funds released. For example, I wanted to make some of the highway gas tax monies available for rapid-transit construction. But, as with all of the dedicated funds, the gas tax highway fund was backed by strong, entrenched special-interest groups. My suggestion was opposed by the highway construction lobby, gas companies, automobile clubs, and a number of labor unions, none of whom wanted any of "their" gas tax money diverted for other uses. There always seemed to be a large number of opponents to everything I wanted to do!

One way I *was* able to address the governor's desire for budget cuts was to switch from the standard, long-used budget procedure to the so-called program budget. Under the existing method, each agency's budget was basically determined by taking the amount it had had the previous year and adding cost-of-living and salary increases—in other words, automatically funding the same things each year, only at a higher price.

What I did, in effect, was to go back and start from zero (so-called zero-basing) and then try to determine what each department really needed for the programs we wanted to continue. The program budget incorporating these concepts (which we fully adopted for the first time in the fiscal year 1969–70 budget) thus enabled us to see more than just how much it cost a particular department for all of its employees, typewriters, automobiles, and so on. The program budget allowed us to determine the cost of a particular program, such as firefighting, educating undergraduates, or improving safety on the highways. It also gave us the opportunity, by measuring the amount of effort and dollars that we put into a program and, even more important, by measuring the results we got from that program, to determine whether the results justified the cost.

Oddly enough, one of the greatest difficulties we encountered in switching from the traditional to the program budget was the reluctance—and, in some cases, the inability—of various departments to put into simple, understandable narratives precisely what it was their department was doing, why they were doing it, and what results they hoped to achieve.

Hand in hand with the new program budgeting, I also tried to get away from the general practice of having the departments independently determine their budgets and then submit their requests to the Department of Finance. Those requests, for the most part, had been included in the state budget, so each year's budget was bound to be larger than its predecessor. Instead, we began giving the departments and agencies guidelines so that their budgets would fit into our overall estimates of revenue. This was important because of the state constitutional requirement of a balanced budget. This is also what I did later in Washington at the Office of Management and Budget.

It was bound to be an inaccurate science, because all revenue estimates were based on guesses of future economic activity—inflation, employment, sales tax revenues, and so forth. And these estimates (which had to be done eighteen to twenty months ahead) had one distinguishing feature: they were always wrong. But we always tried to make them as accurate as possible because, as I frequently pointed out to the governor, the state was not a business—we were not aiming for a surplus; we needed to have only enough revenue to pay for necessary and effective programs. The governor agreed and frequently used the phrase "If a government has a surplus, it is because taxes are too high."

It was also while I was director of finance that we began the practice of trying to make five-year estimates. With those, I wanted to show the long-term implications of passing a new program. We might be able to fund a new program this year, but what is it going to cost in subsequent years? By doing that, the governor, and particularly the legislature, could see what effect adopting a new program (or expanding an old one) might have down the road.

As director of finance, I tried to be involved in all aspects of the budget process. I held hearings and personally met with the department and agency heads to go through their budgets and to instill in everybody the Reagan administration's policy to *reduce* spending overall and not just to finance all program desires, particularly when doing that would require a tax increase.

I also, of course, represented the administration on fiscal matters in the legislature, as our first objective was to secure passage of the governor's budget. The first year I was there, the budget negotiations went into the night of June 30, the last day of the fiscal year and the date when the existing appropriations ran out. Around 3 A.M., the lights all went out in the Capitol. I joked that the Sacramento Municipal Utilities District had assumed that they were obviously not going to be paid, so they shut the lights off. Actually, somebody had accidentally cut a cable, but the timing could not have been more appropriate.

The following year, the legislature was again a few days late in passing the budget act—which has happened many times since, but that was one of the first times. When the press asked me what was going to happen, I facetiously said that the first thing we'd have to do if the legislature failed to pass any budget was to dismiss the guards at all the jails and mental institutions. This was quoted in newspapers across the state and might have helped put additional pressure on the legislature to pass our budget.

All of our efforts to keep spending down and to keep taxes and government intrusion from becoming onerous and stifling were important factors in maintaining the state's strong economy and impressive prosperity. By 1970, if California had been a country, its gross national product would have been sixth in the world, and Governor Reagan was determined not to let anything interfere with that.

My duties as director of finance, happily for me, went far beyond budgetary matters. I was a member of the governor's small cabinet, which met at least once a week in the large conference room just off the governor's office. The room evoked the Old West, with a huge Mission-style table and heavy, high-backed Spanish chairs. In many ways, the atmosphere reflected qualities of the governor himself: solid, uncomplicated, and surefooted.

As a cabinet officer and fiscal adviser, I recommended to Governor Reagan whether to sign or veto any bill that had a fiscal impact (and that was most bills).

During cabinet meetings, Governor Reagan would ask a few questions, but mostly he just listened as we made presentations to him and discussed the issues at hand. He normally did not make a decision right then, particularly on more contentious questions; he would take in everything that was said, and after his questions had been answered, he would move on to the next agenda item. Typically there were many items. Bill Clark, as the executive secretary to the governor, was instrumental in formulating an inclusive agenda and keeping all of us on track. In many ways, our cabinet meetings were more substantive and helpful than many of the federal cabinet sessions in which I later participated.

Governor Reagan has sometimes been characterized as being absentminded or uninterested because he was not more active in the discussions. On the contrary, he clearly weighed each issue carefully and thoughtfully, and it was important to him to hear all sides. It was clear from his questions that he knew exactly what were the issues and the implications of his decisions. He did not want us to present a united front just for the sake of consensus; he preferred to hear the pros and cons discussed in front of him, so that he could make an informed decision himself. And he was anxious that our comments not be filtered. Further evidence of this was that he established a direct phone line to his desk for each cabinet member, always assuring full access. I could see him virtually at will. When you walked in, he always seemed delighted to see you.

Of course, I tried not to take advantage of this wide-open access very often, but it was particularly important to have during the all-consuming task of preparing the budget.

In addition to my duties as a member of the cabinet, along with three or four others, I informally assisted the governor in preparing for press conferences, which he held at least once a week. We would brief him on a variety of issues that were likely to come up. With his extraordinarily retentive memory, he did extremely well in press conferences. Questions out of the blue did not faze him, but if he felt that someone else could answer a particular question better than he could, he would ask one of us, who always stood in the back, to supply an answer. Though he rarely needed to call on us, it was rather like modern-day presidential press conferences—anxious staff members were always there standing along the wall.

At the start, the press was somewhat hostile toward Governor Reagan because they felt it was a serious aberration in the state's history that this untutored movie actor was governor. Moreover, so many of his views violated the conventional wisdom that many in the press automatically opposed him. But that feeling was soon erased; it was impossible to dislike Ronald Reagan or to doubt that he was serious about improving state government. The press in Sacramento were much more objective than the press in Washington. Reporters in Washington were essentially advocates of liberal causes and very adversarial.

Occasionally I would also help Governor Reagan prepare some of his speeches, though he wrote quite a few of his own. I always felt his own were the best. But often he did not need a written speech or even very much lead time before an event. The governor had the impressive ability to absorb a cursory briefing—about his audience and its main concerns—in the car on the way to the speaking engagement, and then he would deliver a most eloquent, thoughtful talk that delighted his audience.

Humor, in both content and delivery, was one of the governor's strongest points. He liked people to be happy, and to leave people laughing, and so he would always try to open and close a meeting or a speech with a joke of some kind, most of which were very funny and set the stage for a receptive audience, no matter their initial feelings toward him.

Even hostile reporters couldn't hide Reagan's easy, genuine, and natural wit. It helped establish warm, personal relationships between himself and other leaders. This, in turn, often surmounted policy differences they might have had. I remember one meeting, when he was president, with Canadian prime minister Brian Mulroney. They each had thick briefing books covering serious issues like acid rain and trade. Reagan began by telling an Irish joke. Mulroney responded in kind, and they traded jokes for almost half an hour before they even touched the briefing books. It was frequently said of Reagan that he could quickly make a warm admirer out of almost anyone, but for the people who really hated him and his views, it sometimes took as long as ten minutes.

This great friendliness did not translate into going soft on his principles and beliefs. When he was governor, I heard some political advisers warn him that his proposed budget cuts in education spending were seen by many as dooming his chances for reelection. He responded, characteristically, "But I didn't come up here to get reelected." He also asked how, if teachers were not doing a good job (as was frequently pointed out), paying them more was going to help. No one could answer that.

This is not to imply that Governor Reagan was antieducation; he simply felt that no one should be exempt from fiscal belt-tightening, which was not stringent in any event. He proposed, for example, not *cutting* the budgets of the University of California and the state colleges but simply holding down the rate of increase and securing some revenue by small tuition charges.* As veteran political reporter Lou Cannon put it, "The university, which for years had demanded and received the cream of the state budget, was now being served skim milk"†—but it *was* being served.

---

* Charging tuition was a revolutionary idea for California at that time—and one only reluctantly agreed to by the UC Board of Regents. Governor Reagan felt strongly about this issue, often saying that "higher education in our state colleges and universities is not a right, it is a privilege."

† Lou Cannon, *Ronnie and Jesse: A Political Odyssey* (New York: Doubleday, 1969), 231.

Governor Reagan was heatedly opposed by narrow special-interest groups, but he enjoyed wide popularity and support. He was saying and doing things many people believed in but that had not been said before by government officials. By 1968, a group of Reagan loyalists was pushing the governor hard to run for president. I was not in favor because I thought he should finish his gubernatorial term. I'm not sure that the governor himself ever really authorized a campaign. It was only at the Republican convention that year that he reluctantly allowed his name to be presented as a candidate. But he was a realist, and though he received quite a few votes, he quickly told backers to support Richard Nixon, which they did—though the Nixon people continued to harbor a distrust of the Reagan people.*

Still, I campaigned for Nixon and thought he was far superior to the Democratic candidate, Vice President Hubert Humphrey, on the big issues of the day. I was, of course, so busy as director of finance of California that my participation was limited just to making a few speeches.

In fact, I was so completely absorbed with California's fiscal affairs and state matters that I did not pay as much attention as I should have to national and international issues. And there was indeed a great deal going on in the country and the world during those years—1968 and 1969. Of course, the biggest of all issues was the Vietnam War.

I thought America's involvement in the conflict was fair enough, but I was disturbed that we were trying only to "contain" Commu-

---

* Although I was basically opposed to a Reagan candidacy for president at that particular time, I did, as a member of his cabinet, attend the convention, as did my son. Cap Jr. had studied film at Harvard and had become quite fascinated with it. So, for the convention, he created and produced a triple slide show on Governor Reagan's record in California called "The Governor Who Turned the State Around." This was one of the early uses of three screens to show a series of slides simultaneously, creating the effect almost of a moving picture.

nism rather than win the war. I thought it was very wrong to ask our soldiers to risk their lives for a war we did not consider important enough to win. I also thought it impossible, as time went on, to fight a war abroad at the same time we were fighting the American people's opposition to the war at home. These vivid impressions influenced me many years later, when I was secretary of defense.

The Vietnam War affected my own family only peripherally. My daughter, Arlin, was married in 1965, and shortly thereafter she and her husband moved to Canada because both opposed the war and he was anxious not to be drafted to serve in it. Of course this was very distressing for me and our family. My wife and I were particularly unhappy that Arlin was not able to come back into the United States freely as long as she was married to someone who was evading American law. After a few years, she apparently reached the same conclusion. She divorced and returned alone to live in San Francisco, and my wife and I were delighted to have her back.

Our son, Caspar Jr., was not eligible for the military because he has no hearing in one ear. He graduated from Harvard in 1968, which coordinated nicely with my own thirtieth class reunion. My mother, my wife, and I attended Cap Jr.'s commencement, as well as some of my reunion activities. The atmosphere in Cambridge still had a comforting familiarity to it. There were a few visible signs of the tumultuous unrest sweeping college campuses across the rest of the country. (Later, of course, and to my considerable surprise, this unrest engulfed Harvard too, with University Hall being occupied by rioters.) Even the graduation ceremony was much the same as in 1938. There were a few changes: Cap Jr. received his diploma at Dunster House rather than in the Yard. And this occasion was particularly special for my mother because she and my father had not been able to attend my commencement.

After Cap Jr.'s graduation, he became a producer for KRON, a San Francisco television station owned by the Chronicle Publishing

Company. He enjoyed it and even won a prize for a documentary he produced and directed about the strains and stresses of being an air traffic controller.

In September of 1969, my wife and I went to Europe—our first vacation in several years. But after only a few days there, my son called from San Francisco and said he had some bad news. I assumed that meant my mother had fallen ill or died; she was then eighty-three. I could not believe it when he said my brother, Peter, had died. He was fifty-five—only three years older than I. He had had a sudden heart attack while in San Francisco.

It was a great shock, and naturally I began revisiting in my mind all the good times we had had together and the support he had given me, particularly in my political endeavors. He had come to my swearing-in ceremony and was very proud when I became director of finance.

About a year before that, he himself had been appointed to Governor Reagan's administration as director of employment, and in early 1969 he became head of the Department of Industrial Relations. People may have assumed that since he was my brother I would give his department special treatment or exemption from budget cuts, but that was not the case. He came in and made his presentation, and I asked the usual questions (bound to be found unpleasant by department heads), and ultimately we did knock his budget back a bit. I had not seen him much lately, however, as we were both busy with our respective jobs. As a result, my grief was compounded by my anguished thoughts of what I should have done differently and by wishes that I had spent more time with him during his short life.

I returned to San Francisco for his services and to try to be of some help to my mother and Peter's widow and their four sons. I was particularly concerned about my mother and how she would handle Peter's death. She simply refused to accept or acknowledge it—a reaction her doctor called "automatic rejection," or denial. From that time on, she was confused about who various people were. Her altered state of mind was very difficult to witness, but I think it was really the only way she was able to go on.

It became clear that she should no longer live by herself, so it was decided that she would move into our home in Hillsborough.

Peter's death was a shock, but I think Peter had been afraid of a heart attack ever since our father had died so unexpectedly of a massive and sudden coronary occlusion. He was similar in build—thick and strong through the chest and arms—and, also like Dad, Peter had always enjoyed good health, even prided himself on it. Neither had ever had any previous signs of heart trouble.

I have never paid much attention to my own health, and, aside from my childhood mastoid problems, I have been free of most health problems until very recently.

Of course, there were the usual stresses and long hours that go along with such a demanding job as finance director, and I undoubtedly added a lot to that by insisting on actually reading the entire budget. I also wanted personally to see as much of the correspondence, both incoming and outgoing, as I could, so I usually spent at least twelve hours at the office each day, and then I would take two or three briefcases of work home in the evenings.

But I did not mind any of that because the post was a marvelous platform from which to see the whole government in action. My longtime interest in state government never flagged the whole time I served in it. I enjoyed it all thoroughly—participating in the cabinet and staff meetings, advising the governor on a wide range of issues, hearing the department heads present their budgets, and trying to make all the pieces fit into an overall budget plan. I learned and gained experience in a number of areas that helped me later in the federal government: I was running a large organization and working with a large variety of problems that had an important bearing on the way the government works. I was also dealing with both the legislative and executive branches, as well as the press. For someone as fascinated as I was in all things governmental, being director of finance was really an ideal position. I always said it was no way to earn a living, but it was a lot of fun.

My wife, however, was not nearly as enthusiastic about it. She did not like the demands of the job, the long hours, the being "onstage" constantly, and she was anxious to get back to a quieter, more private way of life. She had always urged people to contribute something to their community, and she believed, as I did, that you cannot have a democracy unless everyone participates, but by this time, she had come to feel that I had overdone it. So she was not very pleased when, in the late summer of 1969, I got a call from Washington.

CHAPTER 11

JUMPING RIGHT OFF THE DOCK

*O*n August 5, 1969, White House aide Peter Flanigan called me in Sacramento and told me that President Nixon was interested in having me come to Washington to head either the Federal Trade Commission (FTC) or the Federal Communications Commission (FCC).

This took me completely by surprise. I was flattered and wanted to learn more about what they had in mind, but I did not feel that I could take the time out from my budget work just then to go to Washington. From midsummer to December was the heart of the budget timetable in California. Peter Flanigan then offered to have his deputy, Jon Rose, meet me halfway in Chicago so that I could return to Sacramento the same day. I agreed because I wanted to know far more about both the FTC and the FCC before I made a decision.

I flew to Chicago a few days later, but when I landed at O'Hare, there was no Jon Rose to be seen. Just as I was about to leave, a red-faced young man rushed up to me, out of breath and apologetic. He announced himself as Jon Rose, and he had apparently run the length of the concourse. Stout and short and a bit flustered, he quickly proved himself to be extraordinarily friendly and helpful—and clearly anxious to succeed in his mission, which apparently was to persuade me to take the post at the FTC.

We settled into a relatively quiet airport conference room, and he gave me a frank assessment of the sorry state of the FTC[*] and the heavy criticisms that had been levied at it from diverse sources. When I asked whether there would be any other Republican appointees named to the FTC, he said no, that I would fill the only GOP vacancy and that the president would name me as chairman. It could not be described as an especially appealing offer, but the challenge of trying to do something that obviously needed doing was a point in its favor as far as I was concerned.

In the following weeks, I met with Peter Flanigan and, later, with President Nixon himself at San Clemente to discuss it. This was the first time I had visited San Clemente, the president's home in California. The compound was on a bluff, with trails leading to the beach. The residence itself was in the Spanish Mission style and sat well in from the ocean. There were various other buildings, standard utilitarian temporary structures, where most meetings were held.

Physically, Nixon seemed much the same as he had been in the 1950s. But there was also an intangible aura about him, as well as numerous appurtenances that come with being president: Secret Service everywhere, numerous staffers hurrying about (staff people rarely moved slowly), and an occasional glimpse of a magisterial Henry Kissinger.

I told the president that I was actually more interested in the Federal Communications Commission because I was more familiar with, and had had some personal experience in, television and radio,

---

[*] I inquired about the FCC, which had sounded more interesting because of my interest in television, but Jon said he thought that was no longer on offer.

but the president felt that there was a greater need for management and guidance at the FTC. The Federal Trade Commission was, as Jon Rose had said, in terrible shape, and it had been the subject of several critical reports, including ones by the American Bar Association and Ralph Nader's group, all of which by that time I had read, along with reports of various congressional hearings. The president wanted me to come back and "clean it up." When I pointed out that I had no experience in consumer protection, an area that was rapidly becoming an important facet of the FTC's responsibility, he said he felt that my unfamiliarity was one of my strongest assets. We needed an "open mind," he said. I tried to tell him there was a difference between an open mind and an empty mind, but he was not interested in arguments. He was convinced that I was the man for the job.

While we were on the subject of the right man for the right job, I took the opportunity of this one-on-one meeting to tell Mr. Nixon that I was delighted to see him as president for several reasons, but particularly because I had always felt somewhat guilty about having urged him to run for governor of California in 1962. He said, "If I hadn't lost that one, I'd never have won this one."

Before we concluded our meeting, he said he wanted to assure me that I would have a full seven-year FTC term, which struck me not as an inducement but as a rather ghastly prospect. I certainly did not want to spend seven years cleaning up the FTC—in fact, I could not imagine doing *any* one thing for seven years. I said that if I came, I would come for only a year to implement the kinds of urgent reforms the commission obviously needed, but then I would return to California. The president smiled and said, "I doubt if you can do the job in just a year, and anyway, I doubt if you will need to go back after only one year."

I think the task appealed to me because it was a major challenge, especially in light of the heavy criticism the agency was receiving. And, too, the fact that this provided an interesting alternative to going back to the routines of law practice after two years as finance director was no small factor.

When I discussed the matter a bit later with Dick Guggenhime, the managing partner at the law firm, he very kindly said he would hold my position for me during my year at the FTC, but my feeling was that if I went to Washington, I might get into a possible conflict-of-interest position without even knowing about it. So I decided I would have to resign entirely from the firm and relinquish my relatively new partnership.

My primary concern, of course, was my responsibility as California's director of finance and my commitment to Governor Reagan. I told the governor and Mrs. Reagan of the FTC offer at their large, ranch-style home in the Los Angeles hills in mid-August. I assured the governor that if I took the Washington post, I would not leave Sacramento before the end of the year, so that I could get the 1970–71 state budget finished. He said he wanted me to stay on in Sacramento but would not object if I went to Washington. As usual, he was able to see the situation in a positive light. It would help the Nixon administration to have more Californians at a federal level, he said. And it might give me some national exposure, which could help if I ever decided to run for the Senate, a thought that he always seemed to have in the back of his mind. Nancy Reagan (who provided the governor with a healthy-looking salad lunch) was more firm in her opposition to my leaving the governor's administration.

I finally concluded that I had done as much as I could do as director of finance in the nearly two years I had been there, and I kept thinking that I should not turn down a request from a president. I suppose I accepted mostly out of a sense of duty and a desire to help the Nixon administration, which I had strongly supported.

On August 29, I called the White House and accepted the FTC chairmanship. Then I told the governor I had decided. He was very complimentary about my service as finance director, and he said he hoped I'd be a frequent visitor in Sacramento.

My wife was not enthusiastic about moving to Washington, or, perhaps more precisely, moving away from our home and family, and I admit I too was not all that eager to pull up my California roots and sell our lovely home in Hillsborough. On the other hand, we both knew that I would find little satisfaction if I returned to the law practice and that this new opportunity might be something I would really enjoy doing. As she has so gallantly and selflessly done so many times, before and since, Jane rallied to support the decision.

I was fortunate to have my own personal "advance man," so to speak: my good friend Bill Clark, who had left Governor Reagan's administration to become a California judge.* He knew that I was busy with the budget until the end of the year, so he took a leave of absence from the bench and, with his family, went back to Washington for a couple of months in late 1969 and, in effect, laid all the groundwork for me. He made it a smooth transition indeed. He set up my office; he met a lot of the permanent civil service staff and advised me as to which ones he thought were the most reliable; and he interviewed a number of people for appointive positions and recommended good candidates to me. He was extraordinarily helpful and truly a great friend to spend his time, including his Christmas, smoothing the way for me so that when I arrived in Washington, everything was ready. This enabled me to concentrate on finishing my work on the budget and to prepare for my confirmation hearings and our move.

* Bill later was appointed to be a justice on the California Supreme Court and, still later, came to Washington as President Reagan's deputy secretary of state, national security adviser, and secretary of the interior.

On October 1, I held a press conference (embargoed until the next day, at Washington's request) in Sacramento to announce my appointment. It was important to me to make clear that I was not leaving Governor Reagan's administration because of any dissatisfaction with him or with my job there, and I tried to convey that in my announcement. It was also at this press conference, I believe, that I was asked what was the prime requirement for a director of finance. I replied, "Survival," almost without pausing to think.

On October 2, I flew to Washington for the official announcement at the White House, followed by a press conference with the White House press corps. This was my first encounter with the Washington media, and they seemed notably different from their California counterparts. Reporters' questions in Sacramento showed genuine interest in government and in establishing facts about a policy. In Washington, however, the questions were designed to elicit controversy. They seemed particularly interested in my views on smoking and tobacco policy. Some appeared quite gleeful when I said I did not smoke.

I later learned that the Senate disapproved of press conferences held prior to confirmation, because senators wanted the first chance to question an appointee. I never held a preconfirmation press conference again.

My arrival in Washington also meant my first visit to the White House. The building inspired a feeling of awe and wonder—accompanied by some degree of astonishment at my being there at all. No matter how often I was there after that time, those feelings were just as strong, and the sense of history was palpable.

In mid-October, I made another quick trip to Washington, making the required courtesy calls on several senators and congressmen. I called not only on the senators on the Commerce Committee, the committee that would vote on my confirmation, but also on senators and congressmen with whose committees I would deal after taking office (assuming I was confirmed), such as the Appropriations and

Judiciary Committees. Generally, they were courteous and interested in my views and experience (which was virtually nil at the time), and some went out of their way to make me feel at home.

When I returned to Sacramento, I spent as much time as I could trying to prepare for my confirmation hearing, which was very much like an oral examination for a degree. I felt it especially important to try to be familiar with everything the commission might have done or might be doing in the future. I tried to anticipate the questions as much as I could; I succeeded to some extent, but I was pretty much on my own as far as learning about the FTC ahead of time.

I talked with members of the commission, most of whom were Democrats. One, however, was particularly helpful—retiring commission member James Nicholson.* Nicholson was a Democrat, but he was interested in reforming the FTC and thought I could bring positive change. He even came to Sacramento to help me in my preparation and provided me with valuable thumbnail sketches of my new colleagues-to-be. He was most helpful, and I immediately felt I could trust him completely.

My confirmation hearing took place in mid-November 1969 in a Senate committee room, the physical arrangement of which was most imposing. The committee members were seated a long way from the witnesses—and several steps above them and the audience. Authority was clearly delineated by the massive, curved wooden bench from behind which they peered down. The arrangement was similar to the grand dais with which I had become familiar in appellate courtrooms, but this was on an even more intimidating scale. I was surprised and impressed also with the large number of staff,

---

* It was his resignation that created the vacancy I filled. I replaced him as a commissioner, but he had not been chairman. Rand Dixon had been chairman for many years, and when President Nixon named me as chairman, he had to step down but remained on as a member of the commission.

press, and others who were present. I suppose this was probably in part because I was a new appointee and also because of the vast number of special-interest groups that were concerned with the FTC.

Some of the committee members' questions were designed to discern my attitude and the positions I would take on various matters, such as consumer affairs, warnings on tobacco products, and advertising. But the senators were mainly concerned with my thoughts on the FTC's relationship with Congress and with the president. I told them frankly that since I would be head of an independent regulatory agency, appointed by the president, the Congress would not be my primary allegiance. Many in Congress believed they owned these independent agencies. My incautious remarks angered several senators and congressmen, particularly Senator Warren Magnuson, chairman of the Commerce Committee, who rather pointedly asserted that the Federal Trade Commission was an arm of Congress and that the only connection the president had with the agency was the power to appoint commissioners. Chairman Magnuson then and later was generally pleasant to me personally but remained prickly on several issues.

On November 19, the day after my hearing, the full Senate confirmed my nomination.

On that same trip to Washington, Jane and I looked at homes in the Georgetown, Kalorama, and Capitol Hill areas. We finally settled on a narrow, yellow, three-story row house on Capitol Hill, mostly because it had a small pool, which Jane would enjoy. It was not all that far from the Federal Trade Commission building at Sixth and Pennsylvania Avenue, and local legend had it that Abraham Lincoln had lived nearby during his one term in Congress. On pleasant days, I walked down the hill to the FTC building, even though I had a driver assigned to me. Our real estate agent tried to talk us out of living in the Capitol Hill neighborhood because of its higher crime rate, but it seemed all right to me, and besides, I did not expect that we would be there more than a year. I often walked our beautiful collie, "Mr. Buffington," on the grounds of the Supreme Court and around the construction site for the new Library of Congress Madison Building, and never had any problem with crime, although the papers reported various holdups and shootings in the area.

There was one other interesting thing about the neighborhood, which I learned after we were actually living there: for a time, whole blocks were classified by the always strange District government as eligible for welfare benefits, so at one point we qualified simply by virtue of where we lived, and an "outreach office" suggested that we should apply.

After my confirmation I returned to California and the governor held a splendid farewell dinner for me at the executive residence.[*] Governor Reagan appointed the able and affable Verne Orr to succeed me as director of finance. Orr had been a deputy in the Finance Department and was later appointed, at my request, to be secretary of the air force when I was secretary of defense under President Reagan.

In late December 1969, with the California budget completed and ready for submission to the legislature, and after a final Christmas in our wonderful, large Hillsborough living room (which looked as if it had been designed for Christmas), my collie and I flew to Washington to start moving into our new home in Washington. Bill Clark assisted even with that, helping me and the movers carry pieces into the house. On December 31, Jane and my mother followed. Arlin came down from Toronto to help, too, and that is how I met the press.

* The partners and staff of my law firm also gave a fine farewell dinner for me at a private San Francisco luncheon club, the Villa Taverna. I have always been fond of the Villa Taverna, which was named after the U.S. ambassador's residence in Rome and offers a most pleasant atmosphere in a simple, Italian tavern–like setting.

Jane had arranged for someone to come help for a few days. So when the bell rang (our first visitor), Arlin went to the door to see a pleasant, brisk, tall young lady—obviously the new helper. Arlin was unpacking and making up beds and invited her to help. The lady said she would like to meet me and promptly began asking pertinent questions about the FTC. When I arrived and began to question her, she turned out to be Nina Totenberg, a TV and radio reporter at PBS, hot on the trail to get the first interview with the new chairman of the FTC.

In addition to the huge task of moving out of Hillsborough and getting the Washington house settled, Jane spent a great deal of time taking care of my mother—and did all this admirably and without complaint. On January 1, we had our first Washington dinner at a small nearby Italian restaurant which had the great advantage of being open New Year's night. We went out because none of our china or utensils had yet been unpacked, there was no food, and the refrigerator did not appear to be working.*

Almost as soon as we arrived, we experienced firsthand, and more glaringly than anywhere else, poor customer service, outright fraud, and other consumer frustrations—the very issues that would occupy much of my time as FTC chairman. Washington is an interesting and most beautiful city, but living there does take patience; I was certain that neither my wife nor I would suffer Potomac Fever.

In the first week we were there, our pipes froze. When the plumber finally came, he said he couldn't do anything about it and that he would be back "in the spring." We were, of course, billed for his "service." (Jane solved the problem by holding a lighted candle up to the pipes until they thawed—a risky procedure, but it worked.)

---

* My wife's description of our move is far better. See *As Ever* by Jane Weinberger (Mount Desert, ME: Windswept House Publishers, 1991).

Prices of furniture went up between the time we looked at it and the time we called to order it only a few hours later. It took weeks to get lamps delivered. I had assumed we could pick them up at the store that afternoon, but a horrified salesman told me they had to come from a warehouse that was at least nine miles away. After living a short while in Washington, I never doubted the need for stronger consumer protection.

There had been complaints that the FTC coddled big business and neglected consumer complaints. President Nixon clearly wanted to change that. When I was sworn in, the president said, "Business had better look out now! On the basis of what Cap Weinberger did in California, he'll make life difficult for them."

My swearing-in, on the afternoon of January 13, 1970, was held at the White House in the Roosevelt Room,* giving my appointment more ceremony than usual. Even President Nixon attended. So did my mother, and when the president came in, she loudly asked, "Why is *he* here?" I explained as quietly as possible that he was the president and he *lived* here. At which point she announced, "I've never liked Nixon." This was quite out of character for my normally quiet and reserved mother, but at least the press seemed not to have heard her.

When asked to raise my right hand to take the oath, photographers and several reporters noted, I for some unfathomable reason raised my left hand. Then, assuming the Bible was mine to keep as a memento, I took the Bible home. Within an hour, H. R. Haldeman's office was on the phone asking to have it returned, presumably so it could be used for the next event.

The chairman's office at the FTC was still occupied by the previous chairman, Rand Dixon, a hearty, southern, courthouse-type politician

* When a Republican is president, Theodore Roosevelt's portrait hangs above the mantel; FDR's portrait graces the spot in Democratic administrations.

and Democrat. He was even friendlier when I told him he could keep his big office and that I would take another. This was as practical as it was generous. I did not see any way he could possibly move out—it was the most cluttered place I had ever seen. It looked like about six antique shops merged into one big room.

The office I took was big enough for me, and comfortable. My secretary thought it needed a fireplace, but when she gave me the General Services estimate of the cost, I decided I'd much prefer not to read about the expense in the press.

Occasionally, the other commissioners and I held formal hearings up in the commission room, which looked much like an appellate courtroom. We had only three or four formal hearings during the time I was there. Most of the real work was done in closed, once- or twice-weekly informal meetings, which were held in the conference room adjacent to my office. These were more relaxed, and many staff would attend, in addition to the five commissioners.

The commissioners, most of whom had served for several years and had fairly firm agendas of their own, presented quite a set of contrasts. Everette MacIntyre, a Democrat from North Carolina and a longtime commissioner, had formal and courtly manners. I think he did not care for my informal meetings. I generally did not call on people to speak unless two or three were clamoring to do so all at once. If somebody wanted to say something, he or she would just say it, and this went against MacIntyre's style. He was rather like an old English solicitor, slow-spoken and precise, and he always called ahead if he wanted to come in to my office and talk (which was good, because if you were going to have a discussion with Everette MacIntyre, you had to set aside a couple of hours). But he was kindly, extremely polite, and plainly rather puzzled by this California attorney.

Phil Elman was another Democratic commissioner; indeed, he was an almost doctrinaire Democrat. Normally he and I would have been on opposite sides, but we were agreed that the FTC urgently needed reform. We worked well together on procedural matters and had a good personal relationship.

There was only one other Republican commissioner besides myself: Mary Gardiner Jones, an ambitious lawyer who was quite put out when I was appointed chairman. She was a tough lady, more aggressive than I had been used to dealing with. Once, she came into my office and startled me by snarling, "I want to get right down to the facts of this case," as she swung her feet onto my desk. She also smoked cigars.

It was not only among the commissioners that Republicans were in the minority. Almost all of the top staff were Democratic appointees. I felt rather like the British holding India with one battalion; of the roughly 1,200 people at the FTC, I found only one Republican. This was Basil Mezines, who had been a permanent staff member for years and who knew exactly why the commission needed dramatic reform. Bill Clark had told me Mezines could be trusted completely, and Basil soon became my closest adviser.

I brought in some new blood as well. I recruited San Francisco Republican Joe Martin to be general counsel; unfortunately, his arrival was delayed—almost to the time I left the FTC—because the White House staff discovered rumors that Joe's wife was a Communist, which was entirely mad. Joe eventually came on board and did a fine job of furthering my reforms. I also brought in Byron Rumford, my Democratic friend from the California legislature, who was a pharmacist and did a lot of work for us on fair drug pricing. The White House initially opposed his appointment as well, for partisan reasons.

In addition, I decided we should recruit the very best law students to strengthen our legal staff. All large law firms did this, and indeed I had done much of the interviewing at Heller, Ehrman. It seemed, however, an entirely new idea at the FTC—and one that was not looked upon kindly. Two or three of the permanent staff people told me, "This is exactly what we *don't* want. We don't want people who are that good because they're going to leave shortly. We want people who have tried and basically failed elsewhere, and will stay with us for the rest of their career." To me, that attitude explained a great deal about the FTC's problems.

In any event, we recruited several bright young attorneys, starting with the three law clerks authorized for the chairman. The first of these was Will Taft, who, as it turned out, stayed with me all the way to the Defense Department and did a superb job in every post.[*] In 1970 he was fresh out of Harvard Law School (I was willing to overlook the fact that he had gone to Yale for his undergraduate degree). He had been involved in Ralph Nader's group and its critical report on the FTC. Nader recommended him highly. I interviewed Taft myself and was impressed with how knowledgeable and pleasant he was. I instinctively liked him, and I brought him on board as my chief law clerk and legal adviser. He proved to be an extremely hard worker, and indeed indispensable, especially when it came to doing in-depth research, interpreting staff papers, and things of that kind. Besides his professional contributions, he was simply great fun to work with. He laughed at the same things I did, and he was familiar with the literary allusions I would make from time to time. It made for an easy camaraderie that I have enjoyed ever since.

My other two clerks were Robin Freer and another fine lawyer who was shy and reserved but knowledgeable about the commission. Freer was an ambitious and able young lawyer, eager to work, and energetic. Both were exceptionally good and helpful and had fine subsequent careers.

---

[*] After his great service at Defense, Will was appointed to be our ambassador to NATO.

Even before I learned firsthand about the FTC's problems, I did not have a very favorable impression of the commission. My only previous association with it had been when my wife and I took our children on a tour of Washington many years before. When we passed by those dreadful, early Soviet powerhouse-style statues of strange-looking men trying to control mighty horses, placed at the sides of the building, my son asked, "What are those?" The guide, an unwitting wit, said, "Oh, they represent the government restraining trade." I fear that was about what I thought, although I had had virtually no experience with the commission in my own practice.

But some had just the opposite opinion. As an *Advertising Age* article put it in 1970, the Federal Trade Commission had been called "the little old lady of Pennsylvania Avenue for half a century, because its timid performance never managed to make any significant impact on the marketing practices it was supposed to police."

In any event, as I started wading into the, for me, unknown depths of the FTC, I began to fear I may well have jumped right off the dock this time. The fact that the American Bar Association (in a study requested by President Nixon) and Ralph Nader's consumer group, which normally would have widely differing viewpoints, had reached similar conclusions after their separate studies should perhaps have given me a hint of what I was getting into.

Among the criticisms of the agency were that its activities were mired in a maze of antiquated procedures and incredibly slow execution. The entrenched, largely incompetent staff would spend two to three years and no one knows how much of the available resources on relatively small or unimportant cases. For example, an inordinate amount of time seemed to be devoted to whether the Robinson Patman Act was being sufficiently enforced. This aroused enormously strong emotions in grown men—including a couple of the commissioners. Rand Dixon had a fixation about upholding and strengthening the act, a measure designed to eliminate any purchasing advantages big business might have had over buyers of small to medium quantities. The problem with that was that it generally meant higher prices for consumers. So it was essentially an expensive subsidy for small business. I thought it was an important enough statute but not one that warranted the whole trade commission devoting so much attention to it.

I also found a curious situation in which the Federal Trade Commission and the Antitrust Division of the Department of Justice had overlapping responsibilities, with no clear line separating the authority between the two. On top of that, the liaison officers between Justice and the FTC were not speaking to each other. One of the original mandates of the FTC was to maintain fair competition in business, but by the beginning of the 1970s the consumer movement had become a groundswell, and I felt that taking on the responsibility for protecting consumers directly was more important than fighting with the Department of Justice over who was going to break up which monopoly. Of course, attacking monopolies was also a broad form of consumer protection, although regarded by consumer activists as too slow and cumbersome.

One of my top priorities at the FTC was to dismiss bureaucrats who did little but attend to the narrow special interests of certain congressmen. One congressman in particular—Joe Evins, a Democrat from Tennessee—was apparently under the misapprehension that he owned the FTC, and probably all of the other independent agencies, for that matter. He had, for a long time, been able to get the commission to do what he wanted because, as chairman of the House Appropriations Subcommittee for Independent Offices, he controlled their budgets. When I let some of his henchmen in the FTC go, Evins immediately retaliated by reducing our appropriations. But this did not have the usual desired effect—I fully agreed that our budget was much too big and should be cut. This confused him and caused quite a stir. Congress had never had anyone ask for a budget reduction.

We replaced marginal staff with bright and vigorous attorneys and professors who had no congressional ties and were eager to work. Then we cleared the dockets of old, relatively trivial cases. One of the more absurd examples that I recall was that the FTC had spent about seven years trying to determine whether Listerine really freshened your breath and whether its advertising was truthful. We also accelerated timetables to resolve cases and reduced the numerous cumbersome tests that were used to decide if a citizen's complaint warranted an investigation.

We reestablished communications with the Department of Justice and also divided our antitrust responsibilities with its Antitrust Division—actions that reduced wasteful bickering over turf. We encouraged businesses to set up policies themselves so that we didn't have to intervene.

Another priority of our reform program was decentralization. I personally visited some of the field offices, including those in Boston, New York, San Francisco, and Chicago, which, I discovered, were not allowed to do much on their own initiative. In late January 1970 I called the heads of each field office to Washington to get their ideas for improved performance. As a result of this and other meetings, we expanded the functions of the regional offices so that they could lead investigations, issue subpoenas, and take cases of deceptive trade practices and restraint-of-trade to trial. We also encouraged them to take an active part in protecting and educating consumers. To this end, I established consumer advisory boards, made up of businessmen and consumers as well as representatives from each level of government, for each of the eleven field offices. These boards basically determined if consumer complaints could be dealt with best at a local, state, or federal level, and by private or governmental organizations. Thus the attorneys-in-charge of the field offices were enthused and the officers reminded that their primary responsibility was to help consumers. This shift from essentially protecting small business—and bureaucratic institutions—to protecting consumers was literally an innovation, the first time the 1938 expansion of the FTC's responsibilities had actually been put into force.

A prevalent consumer complaint was mislabeling. Sometimes labels were just plain false, such as claiming an item was fireproof when actually it was only fire retardant, if that. Other labels were confusing. My favorite was a clothing label that said "Do Not Wash" on one side and "Do Not Dry Clean" on the reverse. In addition to dealing with these problems, I also thought that the public should be given much more product information on the labels so that they could make more informed decisions. We were able to make substantial strides in this area by vigorously enforcing the Truth in Labeling Act, which had been passed by Congress in 1966, and by working with various trade and professional organizations. Of course, advertising was another area where we cracked down on deceptive practices. I always preached that it was not only right but also very good business for all manufacturers and sellers to protect the public.

One company that I frequently cited as an example of how good business practices were indeed good for business was the Chrysler Corporation, which was giving its customers relatively lengthy and nearly unconditional warranties on its new cars—a program that boosted Chrysler sales. Warranties were not federally regulated until the Magnuson-Moss Act was passed in 1975, but many companies had proved the merits and profitability of offering customers such guarantees.

The cigarette industry was another big issue for us. When the surgeon general issued a report in 1964 confirming the link between cigarette smoking and various illnesses, including lung cancer, bronchitis, and even heart disease, FTC Chairman Rand Dixon announced that all cigarette packages and all tobacco advertisements would be required to print a health warning. Tobacco lobbyists argued, successfully, that the FTC's ruling was an usurpation of Congress's power.

The result was the Cigarette Labeling and Advertising Bill of 1965, which was essentially a victory for tobacco. The law made package warnings mandatory but prohibited the Federal Trade Commission, for four years, from requiring any warnings or statements in cigarette advertising.

In 1968 the FTC had strongly recommended banning radio and television cigarette advertisements. This cause was supported in Congress by Senator Warren Magnuson of Washington, chairman of the Senate Commerce Committee, and his Consumer Subcommittee chairman, Frank Moss, a Democrat from Utah. The two senators pushed the Public Health Cigarette Smoking Act through both houses of Congress in March 1970, and President Nixon signed it on April 1 of that year. This act accomplished three things. It prohibited cigarette commercials on television and radio, beginning January 1, 1971; it lifted the ban on FTC action regarding warning requirements for other forms of cigarette advertising; and it strengthened the health warnings already required on package labels. Instead of "Caution: Cigarette smoking may be hazardous to your health," the labels now had to read, "Warning: The Surgeon General has determined that cigarette smoking is dangerous to your health."

Now I notice this has been changed on some ads to the very innocuous "The Surgeon General has determined that smoking contains carbon monoxide."

Predictably, these measures prompted an outcry from the tobacco industry and the television and radio networks. But the cigarette companies, the advertising agencies, and the networks all survived. I hope many American people survived too, thanks to the dangers of smoking being made clear to them.

I personally was convinced of the need to protect the public from the perils of smoking, but my opinion had been formed long before and was based on much less erudite reasoning. When I was four years old, I had found a half-smoked, still-burning cigar on the street near our home in San Francisco, and naturally I tried to smoke it as I had seen others do. I still remember how ill it made me, and I never touched tobacco again. More important, I felt the dangers of smoking were an important consumer issue. Among my advisers on this and other consumer matters were Virginia Knauer, the president's special assistant for consumer affairs, and Elizabeth Hanford (better known now as Elizabeth Dole), who was then her deputy. We even, along with a number of others, held an unplanned "meeting" when we got stuck in an elevator after a White House Correspondents Dinner at the old Sheraton Park Hotel. After about an hour and a half, someone finally rescued us through the trap door in the ceiling of the elevator.

There were a great many dinners and events like that to attend in Washington, which was a comparatively new experience for me. Simply by virtue of being an officeholder, I was automatically invited to many of them—particularly the annual dinners of various trade associations—and I felt that I should appear at a fair number of them to show the government's interest in their activities. But adding this to what were very long days was a novelty that soon wore off and I grew weary of being "onstage" so much of the time.

Indeed there was a great deal to do during the days. As I had in my state government posts, I probably brought a lot of it on myself. The "in-basket" was overflowing at all times, and I tried to look at as much of it myself as I could. A large amount of it was simply informational—various studies, articles, and so forth—and there was a good deal of mail. As always, I particularly wanted to see the mail, congressional and other, and I personally dictated many of the responses. There were also numerous commission staff reports, recommendations for action, and meeting memoranda.

Aside from the paperwork there were regular meetings with the other commissioners, fairly frequent appearances before various congressional committees and subcommittees, phone calls to be made and returned, occasional travel, and many speeches to give. I wrote many of the speeches myself, often in consultation with Basil Mezines and Will Taft.

One of the first talks I gave in Washington was to the antitrust section of the American Bar Association (ABA), and I admit to feeling quite a bit of trepidation. There is always an element of considerable risk in talking to a group of experts about their own specialty. When I was in the California legislature, I found it far easier to talk to people who were not specialists in legislative affairs. My favorite group in that category was the Northern California African Violet Society, which asked me back several times.

Somehow I made it through my rather long-winded speech to the ABA, talking mostly about its report criticizing the FTC and the ways in which I had already addressed, and planned to continue tackling, the problems it raised. The whole evening was made more difficult because the dinner was long delayed but the cocktail hour was not. The lawyers were getting more raucous as time went on. I was pleasantly surprised when Supreme Court Justice William O. Douglas, whom I regarded as an irremediable liberal and who was at the head table, leaned over and said, "Very good, young man," after I finished. I think I liked the "young man" part of the compliment best.

Overall, I feel that we accomplished a great many things during the short time I was at the FTC. We also seemed generally to receive favorable press reports. The press seemed to think that what we were doing was right and necessary, and a number of positive editorials were written. Even Ralph Nader reluctantly gave us some credit.

I enjoyed working on these important issues at a national level, though it certainly was not easy. The biggest challenge was trying to persuade people of many different viewpoints—commissioners, permanent staff, business, consumers, and, of course, members of the

Senate and House—to get together and support the reforms that I felt were necessary. But it was gratifying when that did happen, and we were able to achieve, or at least set in motion, many of those reforms.

I was looking forward to continuing my work through the end of 1970, at which point I planned to return home to San Francisco and, presumably, to the law practice. But in May of that year, I learned that President Nixon had other plans in mind for me.

CHAPTER 12

DR. NO, ALIAS "CAP THE KNIFE"

*M*y wife and I returned from a meeting in Paris of the Organization for Economic Cooperation and Development (OECD) to a sultry June day in Washington. I had attended this OECD meeting as chairman of the Federal Trade Commission, and it was one of my first experiences at an international gathering representing the United States. When we landed at Dulles Airport, there was a message that the president wanted to see me, and I was to report to the White House immediately.

I was shown into the Oval Office, where President Nixon told me he intended to create a new Office of Management and Budget (OMB), as well as a Domestic Council—two things that had been recommended by the president's Advisory Council on Executive Organization. As the president explained it, "The Domestic Council will be primarily concerned with *what* we do; the Office of Management and Budget will be primarily concerned with *how* we do it, and *how well* we do it."

I was not sure exactly why he was telling me all of this, but I listened with interest. The Domestic Council was basically to parallel in domestic affairs what the National Security Council did with foreign affairs. The OMB was to replace the existing Bureau of the Budget and separate the management and budget-planning functions. To this end, there would be a deputy director for management and a deputy director for the budget. On the basis of my work in California as finance director, the president wanted me to be his first deputy director of OMB on the budget side.

"I want you to do for me what you did for Governor Reagan," he said.

George Shultz was to be shifted from secretary of labor to director of OMB, but the president assured me that I would have full authority and control over the budget; he wanted me to make the same deep budget cuts in the fat federal budget as I had in California's state budget.

The president quickly dismissed my concern that I had not finished my work at the FTC, where I had been less than six months, saying I had made a good start and somebody else could take it from there. Besides, he said, "That's not nearly as important as running the budget of the United States." I agreed to take the post—but one important matter needed to be settled first. Jane was not eager to stay in Washington and had grave reservations about Nixon and my working with him. But, as always, and to my gratitude, she supported my decision.*

On July 2, 1970, George Shultz; Arnold Weber, deputy director for management; James Hodgson, Shultz's replacement at Labor; and I

---

* I was concerned too about my FTC driver. I mentioned this to the White House chief of staff, Bob Haldeman, my friend from California days. I later learned from his book, *The Haldeman Diaries*, that he apparently felt that I wanted to keep my FTC driver simply as a "perk" that I expected in my position. The truth was that I wanted to be sure my driver's tenure would be protected if he came with me to OMB, as he wanted to do. And I was very fond of him. "Sarge" was quite a colorful character. As

were all sworn in at San Clemente, the "Western White House." Jane had come out with me from Washington, and our son and his wife came down from San Francisco. The OMB was now a reality.

Federal law says that a person "cannot hold two positions of honor and trust under the Federal government at the same time," so I drew only one salary, but for a couple of months I handled both my FTC and OMB jobs. I had recommended Bill Clark to succeed me at the FTC, but he declined to take it. He had returned to his judicial duties in California some months before and did not want to change again. Eventually, Miles Kirkpatrick, an excellent lawyer who had written the ABA report on the FTC, was chosen, and he did a fine job continuing the reforms I had begun.

Moving over to OMB meant moving into an office in the Old Executive Office Building. It has always been one of my favorite buildings, with its grand, sweeping staircases, mahogany railings, black and white tile floors, and high ornamental ceilings crowning great long corridors—a total waste of space that would never be permitted in government offices built these days.

My new office had previously been the secretary of war's office, a huge room with a balcony overlooking the Renwick Art Gallery across Pennsylvania Avenue. I have always been fond of light and open spaces, so I had one of the large windows made into a door so that I could go onto the large balcony. My friends joked that this would enable me to make speeches to the huge crowds gathered below. The massive, ornate desk had been Secretary Henry Stimson's

---

an enlisted man in our military, he had been in a Turkish prison for doing considerable damage to a non-U.S. soldier in a bar fight. I never did hear all the details, but it was enough to make it difficult for me to arrange the necessary security clearances for Sarge to follow me to a White House position. I always felt completely safe with him, and he was fiercely loyal to me. Happily, he was able to come to OMB as my driver and retain his same government benefits, so it worked out well for both of us.

and, earlier, General John Pershing's. The whole grand office, with its intricate moldings and a magnificent inlaid hardwood floor (which I discovered when I had an old and very ragged carpet removed), inspired awe and transported one to another era.

There were moments when I could hardly believe it was actually I in these rooms where so much history had happened. I had read volumes of history and had often believed the makers of that history to be larger than life. But now I, a schoolboy from California, was making decisions that might affect the course of history and, indeed, the course of many individual lives.

In the course of one's normal duties and the press of the nation's business, it was easy to forget to appreciate *where* one was. Sometimes, as I passed through the rooms of the West Wing, the White House itself, and the Old Executive Office Building, flashes of history came alive in my mind, from photographs I had seen or simply my own mental pictures that I had attached to the accounts I had read: Lincoln convincing at least some of his cabinet that the time had come to issue the Emancipation Proclamation; Franklin Roosevelt's somber moments in the Oval Office contemplating the speed of our regaining a war-fighting capability in World War II; even Teddy Roosevelt's brood frolicking through the state rooms.

I would generally have lunch in the White House mess, which was in the basement of the White House West Wing. The mess served excellent food, of which I particularly remember the splendid chocolate sundaes; indeed, they were the main reason I liked to go over there.

There were, in fact, *two* White House messes, this being a true Nixon operation. There was a "B" list and an "A" list. Nixon's people were always big on that sort of thing. This was simply due to overzealous, overprotective staff who wanted to insulate the president from any other influences, but it seemed to be a consistent characteristic of the people about him throughout his political career, or at least as long as I knew him.

There were, however, times when appointees were *expected* to be in touch with the president. He was always extremely interested in feedback (assuming it was favorable) on his public speeches, particularly his major Oval Office addresses. There was a standing request for us to listen to all of these speeches, no matter where we were, and to call in our opinions as soon as possible after he finished speaking.

It was from Don Rumsfeld, then head of the White House's "War on Poverty" office, that I learned a good bit of the art of supporting the president. Don and I and several other mid-level administration officials were taking a rare afternoon off in California to visit a new technology exhibit at Disneyland. On our way back to the hotel, we listened to the president on the car radio. No sooner had he finished than Don pulled into a service station, raced in to the telephone, and called in the required message of congratulations. I was impressed.*

I always felt somewhat of an outsider in the Nixon administration, and I doubt that I was the only one. Bob Haldeman and John Ehrlichman were the president's gatekeepers, and they granted minimal access to him.

I had known John Ehrlichman back in California, when he was one of Nixon's advance men and I was the state party chairman. At that

* I have been even more impressed with Don's later work, particularly the superb job he did in securing a unanimous report from a highly bipartisan commission of experts as to the nature and proximity of a nuclear threat to the United States. That report, completed in 1998, has done a great deal to convince many doubters that we should proceed with missile defense, and it was, I believe, one of the strong factors influencing President George W. Bush to name Don as defense secretary. This is the first time in our history that a person has been twice named to hold that position, and I know he will serve the president and the country with the same extraordinary skill and dedication as he always has.

time, he was open and friendly, but he had changed a good bit by the time he came to Washington. He rarely returned phone calls. When I walked over to his office to get answers I needed for my budget work, he was annoyed, distant, and buttoned up. George Shultz spoke highly of him, but I lamented the way Ehrlichman had changed.

Haldeman, on the other hand, had not changed at all. He had always been stern and brusque, but at least he would talk to you, and he was extremely efficient. I liked him, and we usually got along well. Haldeman was totally loyal to the president and venerated the office. A good part of his later trouble came from the fact that he seemed to believe that if the president wanted something done, not only did it have to be done but it also must be legal—just because the president wanted it.

The Nixon "inner circle" were difficult to work with, but I was later grateful that I was not close to them or privy to their activities.

I remember one morning when I came into my office and found white plaster powder on the floor near one of the telephone jacks. The White House "plumbers" had put a wiretap on my line (and, I assume, on others' as well) because Haldeman was trying to find out who was leaking to the press. I called him about it that day. He was furious that the workmen had been so careless—but that was all.

Most of the limited contact I had with Haldeman and Ehrlichman was at the daily White House staff meetings in the Roosevelt Room, attended by senior and deputy White House aides and various special advisers to the president. These were basically crisis avoidance meetings, at which participants would give progress reports on whatever issues they were handling and whether any problems were likely to arise. I would report on how the departments and agencies were meeting the budget goals set by the president. Generally, the OMB director presided at these sessions, but I also went because George Shultz did not go to many of our internal budget meetings and I had the most current budget information.

I gave Shultz progress reports almost every day, but he was hard to read and rarely expressed his own opinions until late in a conversation, if at all—all of which I found frustrating. He always seemed perfectly friendly, but I often felt I was representing OMB by myself because of all the meetings I attended. Even though I was only a deputy director, once I was told to be at a meeting of the Defense Policy Review Committee in the White House Situation Room—itself a rather intimidating setting. National Security Adviser Henry Kissinger rushed into the room late, announcing that he had just come from seeing the president. Then he looked around the room and, fixing his gaze on me, he growled, "I thought this meeting was for *senior* officials only." Feeling rather as if my credentials were being challenged, I could only smile and prepare to justify my presence. However, we quickly moved on to substantive matters. I greatly admired Henry then, and my admiration for him has only increased over the years.

After that rather humbling experience, I was surprised by the reaction some of my remarks generated soon after I came to OMB. In a television interview, I mentioned how vital I thought it was to balance the budget, and the next day the stock market plunged. Wall Street did not *want* the budget balanced because that would reduce government spending, and Wall Street *liked* government spending in those days.

I threw myself into this new job, working fourteen or fifteen hours a day. I did not begrudge the long hours for a moment; the OMB offered an unparalleled platform from which to see it all, and it was particularly good fun for someone as fascinated by government as I am.

I made it a point to be extremely well prepared for my congressional testimony on budget issues, especially when I was advocating unpopular budget cuts. I probably spent three times the length of each actual hearing in preparation for the hearing, including having staff people, playing hostile congressmen, bombard me with questions as difficult as they could devise. I was probably a bit too combative in some of my responses, using tactics from debates and cross-examinations in legal trials. I had seen many people testify who were obsequious and sub-servient, so I probably overdid it a bit in the other direction. I was also conscious of how the hearing would be reported in the press. I knew that if I made concessions for the sake of getting a favorable nod from a congressman, it would be reported that the administration was aban-doning its program or wasn't sure of its position.

Hearings were physically wearing, sometimes running up to six hours at a time, during which time congressmen could come and go, but the witness could not. All the while, you had to pay the closest attention to every detail of what was said. My wife often says that I "tune out" sometimes in conversations, but you cannot do that in a hearing. One silly or ill-informed response would be the press focus of a six- or seven-hour hearing.

Dealing with Congress made my position one with inherent diffi-culties, because with more than three hundred congressional com-mittees and subcommittees authorizing, as President Nixon put it, "spending for their favorite programs without direct regard for what the others are doing," fiscal irresponsibility was the norm, and con-vincing Congress of the need for fiscal discipline was not easy. There was also an increasing and unfortunate tendency to commit the fed-eral government, through legislation, to outlays many years in advance. I preferred the California style, where the budgets of all departments were included in one bill, which was then considered as a whole by the legislature. In many other respects, the work at OMB was not that different from what I had done in California; you just had to add about nine zeroes to everything.*

---

* It was rather overwhelming at first, dealing in such huge numbers—hundreds of bil-lions of dollars, as opposed to millions, which had been daunting enough. But I grew used to it and occasionally tried to lighten the weight a bit with humor. Shortly after I

The budget process within the OMB began nearly a year before the document was completed and submitted to Congress. In late spring each year, the OMB would hold its Spring Previews, which really entailed first a review of how, and how well, each department was using its previous year's funding. We looked not only at how much was needed in order to continue effective programs but also at what could be reduced or eliminated altogether. I felt that this could be most effectively accomplished by using zero-based budgeting, as I had in California—that is, starting from zero rather than the traditional method of simply increasing the previous year's amount enough to keep up with inflation. I believe I may have been the first to introduce zero-based budgeting on the federal level, and, needless to say, it was not accepted warmly by those who were used to receiving automatic increases without having to justify them.

By early summer, we would arrive at a tentative budget total and then adjust it as necessary according to estimates of revenue, the impact of inflation, any new high-priority programs of the president, new security problems, and so forth. Ultimately, of course, the total was set by the president, based on these factors as well as on OMB's recommendations.

Then we would give the departments the amounts each had to work with for the coming fiscal year and would ask how they would allocate it so that we could measure that against the performance data gathered during our Spring Previews. OMB did not just give a department a lump sum to do with as it pleased; we wanted to know specifically how it intended to use the money. Invariably, every department asked for more—requests I almost always turned down, although I admit I did have my own biases.

---

left OMB, I was asked at a dinner party how a certain agency could have an overrun of $127 million. I couldn't resist responding, "Don't nickel and dime me to death."

I was personally most interested in space exploration and cultural endeavors; many on our staff said I was "soft" on space and the arts. These areas were easy targets for budget cuts because neither had large constituencies. They needed advocacy, and I advocated for them. I was actually able to ensure useful and adequate budgets for them, despite regular calls by some members for reductions or eliminations.

I felt that the government spent a great deal on programs for the aged, the handicapped, and so forth, but very little on things other than redressing existing problems. Of course, funding was needed for many of these programs, but, in my opinion, not enough emphasis was placed on the future of the country—things like programs for gifted children, medical research and development (especially for *preventive* purposes), the arts and humanities, taming the space frontier, and, naturally, a strong defense.

Even then, more than a decade before I went to the Pentagon, I felt that a strong national defense was extremely important. I was and am convinced that if we do not have enough money allocated for defense, we will never know it until it is too late. Nothing can be accomplished if our borders are not safe—that is, unless we have both peace and freedom. So, to me, defense needs must always come first, and I was worried that the winding down of our involvement in Vietnam was leading to unjustifiable defense cuts. In fiscal year 1968, at the height of the Vietnam War, 45 percent of every dollar spent went to defense. The proportion going to human resources and similar programs was 32 percent. Those proportions were exactly reversed in 1973.

My responsibility as deputy director of OMB was to fit every department's budget into the overall budget total set by the president. This usually entailed denying many appeals for increases. My job, much like being director of finance in California, was clearly not conducive to popularity.

In the Fall Reviews, each department had the opportunity to present its problems and requests to the OMB. I met with the department secretaries and their representatives, usually in the same conference room where we held our daily OMB staff meetings, and we took up their requests one by one. They would all try to demonstrate what incredible damage we were doing to the Republic by imposing such a low spending ceiling.* These meetings would be followed by weeks of negotiating with the department heads, in person and by telephone, on the budget figures. They had their responsibilities and I had mine, but I always had in mind that increases in one year would inevitably mean even bigger increases in the following years. Occasionally, a cabinet officer would appeal directly to the president. Since I was in effect representing the president's overall desire for budget cuts, these appeals rarely met with success unless the White House saw some major political advantage in granting them.

Then would come the Director's Review, which took six or seven weeks, ordinarily in the late fall. Despite the name, I was often the one who ran this part of the process as well, even when I was deputy director. I determined all of the departments' final allocations, which were reached after considering and trying to reconcile myriad often-contradictory factors—the departments' own requests and appeals, the president's priorities and the initiatives he wanted to introduce (which would mean cutting back something else he wanted, in order to stay within the overall total), revenue estimates, economic conditions, and factors like that.

* No doubt, some of these ceilings may have seemed so low that department heads might have thought they were typographical errors. But in order to avoid raising taxes and fueling inflation, and to allow for administration initiatives, it was imperative that overall federal spending be reined in.

Finally, there was generally a list of ten to twenty decisions that the president would have to make. Getting a response from the president on these was easier said than done. For one thing, as I mentioned earlier, his aides rarely granted direct access. I probably met personally with President Nixon only half a dozen times during an entire budget season, which ran for nearly a year.

One of those times I particularly remember. The president was flying to Paris in November 1970 to attend French president Charles de Gaulle's funeral, and he wanted me to come along to discuss the budget on the flight, even though I was not originally scheduled to attend the funeral. This budget meeting was remarkable not just for the setting, on Air Force One, but also because President Nixon, on his own initiative, wanted to talk about the budget. He was much more interested in foreign affairs than domestic issues, and the budget was generally considered only a domestic matter, although the Defense and State and foreign aid budgets illustrated how thin the boundary between domestic and foreign policy had become. Many people said the president had MEGO—My Eyes Glaze Over— syndrome when they tried talking to him about domestic matters. But on this occasion, he did seem interested in the budget as a whole, and I was able to get some decisions from him.

I also particularly remember this meeting for another reason: Air Force One. It was, of course, very comfortable, as one would expect, but also grand in its simplicity. The most lavish thing about it was that meals (not your standard airline fare) were prepared by the White House chefs and served on White House china. There were several roomy cabins, a couple of conference rooms, and private quarters for the president and his family. A few senior staff and the press were always aboard, assigned to the back of the plane. At one point—I am not sure if it was on this trip—a blue jacket with the Air Force One logo on it was given to each passenger as a souvenir. Unfortunately, mine was later stolen.

Once the president signed off on the budget, it was then sent to be printed. Then the OMB staff and I, along with some White House aides, would spend many hours preparing the President's Budget Message, which accompanies the budget when it is sent to Congress. The budget has to be submitted on a fixed date when Congress reconvenes in January. This is roughly six months before that budget's appropriations are to take effect on July 1. In 1974 Congress moved the start date of the fiscal year to October 1 to give itself more time to consider the budget, but it still managed somehow to delay passage of several of the appropriations bills until after even that new deadline.

The OMB director would hold a major press briefing on the president's budget on the weekend before it went up to the Hill. This was to give the press time to write their stories, which were on an embargoed basis until the budget was released. I was always on hand for this briefing to follow George Shultz's overview with specifics and to answer most of the questions.

Once the administration's budget is in the hands of Congress, it wends its way through all of the various committees and subcommittees, where it is debated, challenged, and invariably criticized as containing not enough of this or too much of that. My primary role during this process was to represent the president and defend his authorization and appropriation budget before all of those committees and subcommittees.

Whether we were dealing with Congress or the executive departments, we in OMB were confronted with near-constant disagreement with the president's budget, so it was important to have a clear objective and remain firm. It was also vital to be ready to explain and defend an enormous amount of detail completely accurately. Even a few slight errors would be seized upon as an excuse for negative votes.

President Nixon's main budgetary concerns were to reduce both the high inflation and unemployment rates. Each was only around 5 percent in 1970, which seems moderate and acceptable now but was considered alarming at the time. I felt, and President Nixon agreed, that the spiraling inflation rate was due largely to the Johnson administration's government-spending policies. President Johnson had tried to conduct the Vietnam War without asking the American people to make any sacrifices at home. He was afraid that making cuts in domestic programs or raising taxes would weaken support for the war, so he charged ahead with full-tilt spending on both the war *and* domestic programs. The deficit as a percentage of gross domestic product soared above 10 percent in the early 1970s.

To combat inflation and bring down unemployment, President Nixon announced on television his New Economic Policy (NEP)* on August 15, 1971 (a Sunday evening, purposely chosen before the markets opened Monday morning). One component was a tax package that included personal income tax reductions and a job development tax credit. The NEP also suspended the convertibility of the dollar into gold, an action popularly known then as "closing the gold window," to stop the outward flow of our gold reserves.

But the cornerstone of the president's New Economic Policy was a ninety-day wage and price freeze, instituted by executive order. I personally opposed wage and price controls, because they simply do not work. They create a completely artificial factor in the economy and interfere with the operation of a free market. They really only postpone the real problem, because as soon as the controls end, everybody raises prices to make up for perceived "losses" during the period of the freeze. Thus, the overall inflationary effect is usually higher. As Herb Stein, a member of the Council of Economic Advisers, explained in a memo to the president, "Tightening the price-wage control system creates the danger of keeping the con-

---

* Only after it started using the term "NEP" did the administration learn that Lenin had used the same acronym for his own economic plan years before.

trolled rate of inflation too far below the free-market rate of inflation, so that the controls become impossible to terminate." George Shultz, whose concerns on this point also were ignored, compared it to Vietnam: "Once the troops are in, it's hard to get them out." The problem was also aptly described in one of the administration's own earlier issues papers: "Mandatory wage and price controls won't work. They deal with symptoms not causes. They are like clamping a lid on a boiling pot without turning down the heat—they can only produce a later explosion."

The thing that really brought home the absurdity of the whole idea, and that went against all of my core conservative beliefs, was an exercise conducted by the Cost of Living Council.* This was the group, mandated as part of the NEP, to oversee the new price controls. We met regularly and considered requests for exemptions from wage and price controls. One afternoon, council members spent about two hours trying to decide whether a shirtmaker could get a price increase if he put a pocket on *both* sides. The government has no business trying to restrain or control the free market, much less determining such things as how much a two-pocket shirt should cost.

Besides the economic effects of wage and price controls, as a practical matter, enforcement was a gigantic problem; with billions of transactions a year in our free market, it was nearly impossible to prosecute individual violations or even to know of them.

At first, President Nixon opposed wage and price controls, as did Director Shultz and I. Having expressed my opinion to Nixon and feeling confident in his concurrence, I had spoken to a Ditchley conference near Oxford and assured all in attendance that the president

---

* The Cost of Living Council was made up of five cabinet officers, representatives of the OMB and the Council of Economic Advisers, and several special assistants to the president.

would not institute wage and price controls. Within two months, he did just that. The planning for it had been done in great secrecy to avoid having businesses raise their prices before the controls took effect—such secrecy that I believe that John Connally, the newly arrived secretary of the treasury, was the only cabinet member who knew of the president's decision until very shortly before it was announced. President Nixon did tell a few of us on the night of August 14 at Camp David, but we were all sworn to secrecy until the full meeting the next day. As I recall, we were even told not to make telephone calls that night.

I think the president changed his mind on controls in large part because Secretary Connally, a lifelong Democrat, was a very persuasive advocate of wage and price controls. The president wanted to do something dramatic about inflation, and Secretary Connally convinced him that the shock effect of the controls would tame inflation. It did, but only for a short time;[*] soon after the controls were lifted, prices jumped even higher. Over the next three years, the president continued to use various forms of wage and price control, but none with lasting or good results.[†]

---

[*] The NEP, particularly the wage and price freeze, was initially very popular and temporarily calmed consumers' fears. Indeed, the day after it was announced, the stock market gained thirty two points—the largest one-day gain in history up to that point. The new confidence even carried the president to reelection victory, which was perhaps part of his intent. But the euphoria was short-lived, as the longer-term effects became more apparent. In fact, as late as the fall of 1973, 89 percent of Americans still considered "the high cost of living" the country's biggest problem, even though the Watergate scandal was taking over the headlines.

[†] Besides the fact that wage and price controls were counterproductive, some economists had said, before the controls were even implemented in mid-1971, that they were unnecessary because the economy was already showing small signs of improvement on its own. The main evidence they pointed to was that the inflation rate had stopped rising and, according to other economic indicators, seemed poised to begin subsiding.

Another means by which President Nixon addressed the problem of inflation was the use of the so-called Full Employment Budget. As the president's 1972 reelection campaign factbook explained, "By pursuing a policy of deficit spending at the level of full-employment revenues, sufficient expansion of the economy is assured to provide full employment, increased federal revenues, and thus automatically *remove the deficit* and excess economic stimulation before its effects lead to inflation [emphasis added]." In simpler terms, the Full Employment Budget was based on what the revenues and expenditures would be *if* the economy were at full employment. The theory was that if more people were working, they would pay more taxes, which would bring in more revenues, and at the same time government expenditures would be less because unemployment insurance and other federal relief payments would be low.

George Shultz was a big advocate of the Full Employment Budget. I most definitely was not. Operating *as if* the economy were at full employment was little more than a method of presenting things to look better than they really were, and a way of enabling political speakers to claim balance even though the actual budget was quite badly *out* of balance. It had no real effect on tax receipts or on the allocation of money to any departments or programs; Congress still looked at the *actual* numbers and I continued trying to balance the *actual* budget. I felt that anything we did to mask how large the deficit really was would weaken our attempt to cut spending.

As had been the case in California, only about 25 percent of the federal government's spending was discretionary—the rest was legally required, as written into the funding provisions of almost innumerable programs. These usually start as a pilot project, which turns into an essential program in about three years and becomes an urgent priority in three years more. The distance from an urgent priority to an untouchable sacred cow is usually no more than five fiscal years.

One of the first things I did when I became deputy director of
OMB was to ask for a study on real ways the budget could be cut, and
whether any so-called uncontrollables could in fact be changed. I
also went through the budget myself, line by line. Everyone was horrified at some of the things I suggested as possible cuts, including
such obvious impossibilities as postponing interest payments on the
national debt. I felt it was essential to get everyone to realize how
drastic was the need to cut and that we had to look at every possible
option. My budget-cutting zeal earned me the nickname "Cap the
Knife," coined by presidential speechwriter, and now distinguished
columnist, Bill Safire. The biggest item that was relatively "control-
lable" was national defense, but both President Nixon and I were
extremely reluctant to scale back the defense budget.

Contrary to his rhetoric,* the president was reluctant to make the
deep cuts in popular programs that I thought were necessary.
Spending reductions were especially unwelcome in a campaign year.
In 1972 I strongly advised him against signing a debt ceiling bill
because that bill also contained a 20 percent increase in Social
Security. It was a well-known tactic of congressmen to include their
favorite bills in the debt ceiling legislation because the latter eventually had to be signed. The president signed it, telling me bluntly he
could not veto a Social Security increase in an election year. When
Nixon asked why I was less successful cutting the federal budget
than I was in cutting California's state budget, I told him, probably
too bluntly, that it was because California had a chief executive who
gave budget cuts the highest priority.

---

* In his second inaugural address, President Nixon put a conservative spin on the
appeal President Kennedy had made to the American people exactly twelve years
earlier, saying, "Let each of us ask—not just what government will do for me, but
what can I do for myself?"

To his credit, President Nixon did, at least, slash the rate of increased government spending. His 1971 budget provided only a 1.5 percent increase over the previous year's spending, compared to an *annual* increase *averaging* 17 percent for fiscal years 1965–68.

The president also called for a $250 billion spending ceiling for fiscal year 1973, the budget I spent most of my time on during my tenure at OMB. I was able to keep the budget outlays under that— $246.3 billion—despite the protest of almost every executive department and agency. The bills incorporating the ceiling passed both houses of Congress, but in one of the Senate committees, various amendments were added that would have required the president to cut equally from all programs if he cut from any. This was administratively unworkable and required reductions in effective programs. So we opposed it.

Ultimately, Congress restored most of the funding we had cut from the $250 billion spending cap. Sadly, it is often the case that an administration's efforts at fiscal responsibility are thwarted by Congress's zeal to ensure that every pet project is fully funded. I frequently urged President Nixon to veto such inflated appropriation bills, but he rarely did.

One thing he did do, however, was to withhold some of the congressionally appropriated spending. This "impoundment," as it was called, dated back to 1803 when President Thomas Jefferson declined to use funds that Congress had appropriated for two gunboats, because the Indian wars for which the gunboats were appropriated had ended. Every president since had occasionally "impounded" funds, and it was a useful way to postpone a portion of spending until it was really required. The best way to visualize this is to think of all of the money that Congress appropriates at any one time as going into a large tank out of which several hundred little pipes lead. The valves on these pipes are opened and the money drops out into the proper slots and program allocations from time to time, as the given conditions are fulfilled—as contracts are prepared, designs are agreed upon, the site is selected for a building, and so on. I would think that every president would, at some time, use the impounding authority—because there's nobody to give the money to, or because it violates the debt ceiling, or because conditions have changed since the appropriation.

If President Nixon had had the line-item veto (a power that most state governors had), holding funds in reserve would not have been necessary. He did veto some appropriations bills in their entirety; on a few occasions, Congress then reduced the appropriations, but often the vetoes were simply overridden. When that occurred, the only option left to the president was to withhold funds.

Of course, this "impoundment" infuriated Congress. Congress held hearings on the subject and even considered impeachment of the president for executive intrusion on legislative authority. It was a fierce constitutional fight, and ultimately President Nixon was persuaded to sign away his authority (and that of all future presidents) to withhold funding, as part of the Budget and Impoundment Control Act of 1974—at a time when Nixon's political capital had been whittled away by the Watergate scandal.

A precursor to this act was a 1970 hospital construction authorization bill, in which Congress included language requiring that the entire annual appropriation be spent every year. President Nixon balked at this and vetoed the bill, but Congress overrode the veto and won another victory for mandatory spending.

President Nixon's policy of revenue sharing was more successful. I was and am a great advocate of revenue sharing because it makes for more efficient and effective spending. Essentially, it works like this: the federal government gives states a lump sum to pay for federally required programs, thus eliminating expensive federal bureaucracy and freeing the individual states and cities to determine their own funding priorities under broad federal guidelines. I have always felt

1920: Not even three years old, and already stubborn.

My mother, Cerise, was an accomplished violinist.

I'm on the left, with my father, Herman, and my brother, Peter.

At Polytechnic High School in San Francisco, 1933.

A newly commissioned infantry officer, 1942.

Personal collection/Office of the Secretary of Defense

The nurse who became my wife, Jane.

On duty in New Guinea, 1943.

On the campaign trail in 1952 for a seat in the
California State Assembly.

McCurry Photo Company Collection/Sacramento Archive and Museum Collection Center

In the California governor's office with Governor
Ronald Reagan. I served as his director of finance.

The White House/Oliver F. Atkins

Sworn in as President Nixon's secretary of health, education, and welfare at
his western White House in San Clemente. Left to right are Governor
Reagan; President Nixon; my wife, Jane; and Judge Thomas Caldecott.

Bettman/Corbis

At the White House with Nixon, discussing health care issues, 1974.

Showing my perfect shooting form, even in cufflinks, with a radar-tracking gun—one of the perquisites of being secretary of defense.

Personal collection/Department of Defense

Sworn in as President Reagan's secretary of defense, January 21, 1981.

Personal collection/Department of Defense

Showing Mrs. Lagorio of Italy and Mrs. Rinaldo Petrignari, wife of the Italian ambassador to the U.S., around the Air and Space Museum.

The White House, courtesy of Ronald Reagan Library

Discussing strategy with Secretary of State Al Haig and Deputy Secretary of State Bill Clark in the Roosevelt Room of the White House, 1981.

The White House, courtesy of Ronald Reagan Library

Meeting in the Cabinet Room with the Joint Chiefs of Staff and the National Security Council in 1982. Left to right are General Barrow (Commandant of the Marine Corps), Admiral Watkins (Chief of Naval Operations), General Vessey (Chairman of the Joint Chiefs of Staff), General Meyer (Chief of Staff of the Army), General Gabriel (Chief of Staff of the Air Force), Robert McFarlane, Bill Clark, Ed Meese, George Bush, Ronald Reagan, and James Baker. Missile defense was on the agenda.

With my stalwart friend Bill Clark in 1983.

Personal collection/Department of Defense

Greeting Vice
President Bush at
the Pentagon, 1984.

The White House, courtesy of Ronald Reagan Library

Meeting Mrs. Weinberger.
Left to right are General
Secretary Gorbachev,
President Reagan, and
Chief of Protocol Selwa
"Lucky" Roosevelt; my
wife, Jane, is seated.

The White House, courtesy of Ronald Reagan Library

Saying good-bye to the president in the Oval Office. Left to right are my
daughter, Arlin; my grandson, James; President Reagan; my wife, Jane; my
granddaughter, Becky; my son, Caspar Jr.; and my daughter-in-law, Mavis.

The White House, courtesy of Ronald Reagan Library

Announcing my resignation and the appointment of Frank
Carlucci as my successor to head the Defense Department.
Behind me are President Reagan, Frank Carlucci, and a
young Colin Powell, November 1987.

The White House, courtesy of Ronald Reagan Library

With President Reagan at my retirement ceremony.

The White House, courtesy of Ronald Reagan Library

My last cabinet meeting as secretary of defense, November 19, 1987.

Associated Press

Outside of Buckingham Palace, displaying (at the request of the British press) the Knight Grand Cross just awarded by Queen Elizabeth II. Jane is with me.

Personal collection of Colin Powell

With Colin Powell at my eightieth birthday party.

Courtesy of Christian Frost

What I do now, touring the world for *Forbes*. Here I am with Kip Forbes, Steve Forbes, and Christian Frost on Wake Island.

that those closest to a problem are the ones best able to find and administer an appropriate solution.

The president had proposed revenue sharing in 1969, before I joined the administration, but I hope that my strong and active support for the idea had something to do with his making it the centerpiece of his recommendations for 1972.

In October of that year, President Nixon signed a $30.2 billion revenue sharing bill. But this came only after another protracted battle with Congress. Unsurprisingly, Congress opposed revenue sharing on the grounds that states would not spend the money or administer the programs as wisely or as well as the federal government did; the *real* reason was that congressmen liked doling out money to favored constituents.

By this time, June 1972, I had become the director of OMB. When John Connally resigned, George Shultz became the new treasury secretary and President Nixon asked me to direct OMB. Aside from taking over the management side of OMB, my duties grew but didn't change that much, though now I operated from a second-floor office in the West Wing of the White House.

Arnold Weber, who had done an excellent job as the deputy director for management, had recently resigned to return to university teaching. He was replaced by Frank Carlucci, who had done an admirable job running the Office of Economic Opportunity and serving as an associate director at OMB. He did a fine job on our management team as well.[*]

When I asked for staff suggestions on how to improve OMB, the responses focused on the need for more guidance and involvement from the director. This I was happy to do, as I had been involved

---

[*] Frank was a former career Foreign Service officer, and later he served with me at the Department of Health, Education, and Welfare and the Defense Department.

much more in the day-to-day activities of the budget than George Shultz had been.

I was constantly motivated by the size and scope of the job and by the idea that maybe what I was doing could make a difference. It was a continually challenging enterprise—and a vast improvement, in my mind, over the law practice, where one usually dealt with tiny, narrow disputes.

In early 1971 a number of my California Republican friends urged me to run for mayor of San Francisco against the incumbent, Joe Alioto. Some also wanted me to run for Congress.* But I thrived on the long days, heavy workload, and detailed policy of the budget, and did not let my mind think about much else, which, I am sure, made me a very dull fellow.

Fortunately, my wife, Jane, had become involved in a number of her own activities. When we first moved to Washington in 1970, she had immediately become active in the Folger Shakespeare Library, which was just down the street from our little row house on Capitol Hill. This more than fulfilled her long interest in Shakespeare and was a very good thing for the Folger. Later, she became chairman of the board.

She also continued some of the hospital volunteering she had done at St. Luke's in San Francisco. Being a nurse, she was drawn to this kind of work, and she enjoyed visiting patients in the wards of several area hospitals every week, as well as serving on the hospital boards.

In addition, she campaigned with some of the other cabinet wives for President Nixon when he ran for reelection in 1972. She was basi-

---

* My name bounced around quite a lot in this period. I later learned—to my great surprise—that Len Garment, a major adviser and the counsel to the president, suggested to the president that I would be a good appointee to the Supreme Court.

cally a rather reserved New England lady, but she became very effective at public speaking, television appearances, and fund-raising.*
None of this came naturally to her; she had taught herself the necessary skills, starting way back when she ran my first campaign for the
California assembly in 1952.

Although I think she would have preferred to be home in California, I was pleased and proud of her successful activities and that she
adapted so extraordinarily well to her role as a "Washington wife."
Once again, she proved to be of tremendous support to me, and she
found the bright side of the situation for herself as well.

We were both comfortably ensconced in our respective routines in
1972, but President Nixon's reelection that year brought an unexpected change.

---

* Jane even wrote and published her own how-to book on fund-raising called *Please
Buy My Violets*, which was highly regarded and much in demand. It was one of the
great successes of her publishing business, Windswept House Publishers, which she
started in the early 1980s, operating out of the top floor of our home.

CHAPTER 13

A FIRST LESSON IN REALLY BIG GOVERNMENT

*O*n Wednesday morning, November 8, 1972, the day after President Nixon's landslide triumph at the polls, the cabinet and the president's staff assembled in the Cabinet Room for what we expected would be the president's warm congratulations and hearty thanks for the work done on his behalf, and perhaps some indication as to what his immediate goals were for his second term. When he finally came in, he looked particularly angry and glowering, and only nodded when one or two people ventured to offer some congratulations. The first thing he said, as he picked up a stack of papers, was, "Can you imagine a million people voting for a fellow like that Schmitz?!" John C. Schmitz was a far-right California congressman who ran on the American Independent Party ticket. I thought it a rather odd comment from someone who had won 47 million votes.

After grumbling about that for a few minutes, the president said he had noticed in his study of history that second terms of administrations tended to lose a lot of energy and just coast along without accomplishing much of anything, and, by God, that was not going to happen in *his* second term. He was going to do some major reshuffling; he wanted everybody's resignation on his desk that day. With that, he got up and walked out. We did not hear the slightest sign of pleasure at being reelected. As we all sat there in rather stunned silence, Bob Haldeman cut in with what I thought was the most unnecessary comment of the year: "In case any of you didn't understand, the president wants your resignations." For anyone who was really obtuse, he added, "I have them here. You can all sign them now." So everybody resigned from office just as if we had lost the election.

As we all dispersed into the hall, there were some puzzled comments—and nobody had any idea what was going to happen next[*] or who was going to be in what position. I thought that, having recently started as budget director, I would probably continue there, if anywhere. In any case, it was quite apparent that there were to be many changes and that "energy" was to be infused into the second term.

Over the next couple of weeks, the cabinet members and other presidential appointees were taken by helicopter, in turn, up to Camp David to be told their fate. I rode up with Pete Peterson, secretary of commerce, who suggested a way we could tell, even before we reached Camp David, what the verdict was: "If there is a trap door in the floor of the helicopter, they're going to let us go halfway there. Then we can be reasonably sure we're not going to be retained." We both examined the floor fairly carefully but made it through the trip.

The Camp David proceedings were conducted with enormous secrecy—a phenomenon typical of Nixon's second term. Several of us had the same experience: as soon as we entered a room where the president, Haldeman, and Ehrlichman were, all talking immediately

---

[*] I think most assumed that the president would simply not accept the resignations until he was actually ready to move someone to another position or out of office entirely. Of course, having a formal resignation was a totally unnecessary step because we all served at the pleasure of the president and could be removed at any time.

stopped and everybody looked self-conscious. Clearly, he and his staff had been discussing things much too important to be heard by anyone else.

I cannot say that I would have been terribly disappointed if I had been let go, but apparently that was the farthest thing from the president's mind. When we met in his quarters at Camp David, he was cordial and complimentary, and said he had decided he wanted me to run the Department of Health, Education, and Welfare (HEW). The current secretary, Elliot Richardson, was moving over to Defense, an option the president said he had considered for me as well. But he felt that HEW was more in need of fiscal and managerial discipline; it was, at that time, the highest-spending department. The president said he thought it would be an interesting twist to send a budget cutter to HEW and a big spender to the Pentagon. Indeed, he felt I was better suited to HEW and shared many of his general goals for the department, such as reining in a runaway budget and devolving a good deal of power back to the states and the private sector.

I accepted, because I thought heading up HEW would be a great challenge and interesting work. My wife would have preferred to go home to California, but as always, she was supportive. In fact, she became very involved and did extraordinarily valuable work with many of the constituencies that HEW served, particularly in the health field and with organizations that represented some of the most needy groups in Washington.

My wife was not the only one who was less than thrilled with my appointment to head HEW. Outgoing secretary Elliot Richardson and much of the department staff were alarmed that a budget cutter was taking over, as were many senators and congressmen. Democrats like Senators Edward Kennedy and Harold Hughes of Iowa were particularly vocal in their opposition at my confirmation hearings, and liberal Republicans like Senator Jacob Javits had serious reservations about me. Javits's main reservation about voting to confirm me, he said, was that he was afraid I was not 100 percent in favor of all of HEW's programs. I told him that was absolutely correct—I felt that we needed to look closely at each one and have the courage to stop doing things that were not working so we could free some resources to try something else. This was not a satisfactory answer to him because he wanted the secretary to be a complete advocate for everything the department was doing.

I suspect that some congressional resistance stemmed also from irritation at President Nixon's thus-far-successful practice of impounding funds that Congress had appropriated. The vote on my confirmation was delayed for over a month, I'm sure in part to pressure the administration to release those funds. But the president did not yield, and finally, on February 8, 1973—long after most of the other cabinet members had been sworn in, and even after the inauguration—I was confirmed by a vote of 61 to 10, with the dissenting votes all cast by Democrats.

Frank Carlucci, my deputy at OMB, came over to HEW with me, at my urgent request, and was confirmed as undersecretary at around the same time. I was also fortunate enough to be able to bring Will Taft, who later became the department's general counsel and who served with all his usual skill and effectiveness. Also following me to HEW was my faithful driver, Sarge. Having familiar, competent people at one's side makes tackling major new challenges seem easier.

The delay in my confirmation meant that, officially, I was only secretary-designate of HEW during the inaugural festivities in January. The sign on my car in the parade said as much, as if to announce that I was not quite official. But that did not dampen my enjoyment of the grand quadrennial inauguration festivities.

The inauguration wrapped Washington in a jovial, celebratory atmosphere. As society writer Betty Beale described it, "This city has been a cross between Mardi Gras in New Orleans, peak hour at LaGuardia Airport, and the investiture of a new pope."

The occasion also provided a welcome opportunity to see some of our faraway friends. Governor and Mrs. Reagan, Ed Meese, and Mike Deaver came to Washington for the celebration, and Jane cooked a marvelous dinner for them the night before. Later that evening, we all attended a concert by the Philadelphia Symphony at the brand-new Kennedy Center.

The next day we invited our California guests back for breakfast. Jane had set the table the night before, only to find, when she came downstairs, that the party rental company had retrieved its table sometime during the night. Completely unfazed, Jane simply served breakfast buffet-style. She carried the whole thing off with her usual flair and good humor.

Later that morning, Jane and I assembled with the other cabinet officers and their families inside the Capitol, and then we were seated outside on the presidential inaugural platform built out over the east steps facing the Supreme Court building. There were people as far as the eye could see, from the driveway at the bottom of the stairs, back to First Street and beyond.

The seamless transition of power in a democracy is an event that many of us take for granted, but to witness it up close is a moving experience, even though some of that impact is lost when the president is sworn in for a second term. The oath, administered precisely at noon, when the previous term expires, never varies; it is prescribed by the Constitution. Also unvarying is the ceremony of a berobed chief justice swearing in the president, followed by the inaugural speech, delivered from the place where so many previous presidents-elect have stood. I wondered how some of these men, in the days before public address systems, could have been heard by more than a few rows of spectators. Indeed, many people probably could not even see their new president.

Immediately following the ceremony, we joined President and Mrs. Nixon, congressional leaders, and other cabinet members for lunch in the Senate Dining Room in the Capitol—a pleasantly spacious but rather featureless room near the Senate chamber.

Then my wife and son and I rode up Pennsylvania Avenue in the inaugural parade, in a top-down convertible sporting a large sign indicating my "half status" as secretary-designate of HEW. The rear seat was designed for only two people, and my son is not small, but the three of us squeezed in, which made for a warmer ride to the White House. As is typical in January, it was very cold, and I greatly admired the stamina of the Secret Service agents who trotted along beside the car for the whole length of the drive. The large crowds lining both sides of the avenue were generally friendly.

Upon arriving at the presidential reviewing stand on the north side of the White House, we took our assigned seats to watch the rest of the parade go by—which it did for hours. Fortunately, the reviewing stand was partially heated (and the seats for the president and vice president were, of course, protected by bulletproof glass).

The evening's activities included a dinner honoring Congressional Medal of Honor winners. As always, being in the presence of the bravest of the brave was a most moving experience.

Then there were numerous inaugural balls around town; we went to the one at the Smithsonian's beautiful Museum of Natural History, where the immense elephant greets everyone from his platform at the head of the main stairway. Inaugural balls are primarily huge crowds of people milling about a too-small dance floor. It is impossible to dance, and the crowd keeps growing as all await the arrival of the new president. He goes to all the balls and makes a few remarks at each, and perhaps enjoys a few brief dance steps with the first lady. Then they depart hastily for the next one.

The inaugural events provided a brief respite from the daily rigors of trying to rein in the federal budget at OMB, a pause that helped gird me for the challenges that lay ahead.

I was sworn into office on February 12, 1973, again at the Western White House, where President Nixon seemed to be spending much of his time. I was permitted to use our family Bible this time and made a conscious effort to raise my right hand instead of my left.

Between 1969 and my confirmation as secretary in February 1973, HEW's health budget had grown more than 100 percent, its education budget by more than 30 percent, and its welfare budget by roughly 75 percent, making it the largest of the executive departments and very unwieldy. When HEW was created in 1953, its budget was $7.6 billion. In 1973, only twenty years later, it had an $89.2 billion budget. Worse, only 6 percent of its budget was discretionary, the rest being mandated by law. Changing these automatic increases required the approval of Congress, which was not forthcoming. Congress, lobbyists, and departmental bureaucracies—the "Iron Triangle," as Theodore White called them—put up formidable opposition to any attempt to change the status quo. The special-interest groups who benefited directly, the civil service groups who did not want to lose their jobs, and the staffs of the congressional committees who didn't want to lose their control opposed our proposals to cut spending or even just to hold down the rate of increase of various programs. Indeed, in most cases, congressional committees appropriated more funds than the administration requested.

The more I thought about the difficulties of trying to control federal spending, the more I became convinced that we could never solve the problem solely by making cuts in various programs. The only way to achieve real budget reform was to limit the revenue government received—subject, of course, to various escape clauses for national emergencies and wars. By late 1974, close to 40 percent of the gross national product (GNP) went to support government. Many, myself included, felt that if that figure got much higher, it would be increasingly difficult to maintain our free-enterprise capitalist system. We needed to limit tax revenues to a fixed—and much lower—percentage of GNP. I outlined this idea to President Ford in November 1974, but he refused drastic policy changes until he could be elected president in his own right—but he wasn't, and my proposal went down to defeat with him.

It was also my feeling that a great many things HEW was doing could be performed as well or better by the states or by the private sector. I did not think that the federal government should try to operate general schools or public hospitals, for example. We ought to give the state and local governments grants they could use as they saw best, for what they determined to be their highest priorities. This was achieved, to a small degree, through revenue sharing, passed by the Congress in 1972, but this was not nearly as ambitious a program as the administration had wanted.

With regard to higher education, the Nixon administration was committed to ensuring that *all* qualified young people, be they rich or poor, black or white, male or female, could attend college. A key administration program passed by Congress in 1972 was the Basic Opportunity Grant program, under which federal assistance went directly to the *student*, who made his or her own decision as to which college he or she wanted to attend. This reversed the previous system of giving colleges the federal funds to disperse. But funding of the Basic Opportunity Grants was limited because Congress continued to prefer the traditional method of aiding schools rather than students.

All higher education institutions receiving federal contracts were subject to affirmative action requirements, both in their hiring and in student admissions. The colleges weren't happy about this, and I wasn't either. If a fair and broad search for qualified candidates—the proper goal—degenerated into fear that a college's federal funds would be endangered if it did not fill a specific number of vacancies with black or Asian or women appointees (or some other specific group), then we would achieve only quotas and reverse discrimination. That was certainly *not* my goal. Discrimination cannot be cured by practicing it.

In a celebrated case in 1973 and 1974, Allan Bakke, a white male, was denied admission to the University of California Medical School at Davis, even though his grades and test scores were higher than those of several minority students who were accepted. Bakke decided to sue the school, and the case went all the way to the Supreme Court, which, in 1978, ruled that racial quotas were not permissible and that, while an applicant's race could be considered, other factors such as aptitude and ability must be considered as well. This decision was a step in the right direction, but it provided rather nebulous guidelines.

Another education issue was school vouchers that would allow all parents to send their children to the school they prefer. I had supported this idea from the time I had been in the California legislature because I felt that poor children should have the same educational opportunities as any other children, but I was never able to persuade the administration. Organized public education lobbies, the National Educational Association, and various teachers' unions always violently opposed anything that enabled parents to choose private schools—because they feared the competition.

The main education issue on the table during my tenure was Title IX. Congress had passed Title IX as part of the Education Amendments of 1972 (to the Higher Education Act of 1965). Title IX was intended to prohibit sexual discrimination in educational programs that received federal money. HEW was assigned the task of developing the regulations—to set out in detail how Title IX would be administered.

It took three years from the time Title IX was passed to the time the president signed the final regulations. Many in HEW were reluctant to prepare the regulations, probably because the educational and college lobbies opposed the new law. If I had not kept pushing for it, I'm not sure the department would ever have finished the regulations. I felt that equal educational opportunity was very important and *needed* to be pushed instead of defeated by inaction.

Nondiscrimination in hiring at and admissions to federally funded educational institutions was at the heart of Title IX and encompassed the areas of financial aid and scholarships, but the most talked-about and controversial issue was athletics. As I studied the matter, I became convinced that women did not have nearly enough opportunities to participate in college sports. I was struck by the argument that women's athletics were supported by bake sales, while men's athletics were supported by football game revenues.

But remedies had to be tempered with common sense; as the final regulations explicitly stated, equal opportunity did not necessarily mean equal spending for men's and women's teams. For example, not as many women as men may *want* to participate in a sport. The intent of the law was that anyone who *wants* to participate in college and school athletics must have the opportunity to do so and must be provided with the necessary equipment, travel allowances, and so forth.

In June 1974, HEW published the proposed Title IX regulations, and I allowed ninety days for public comment on them. I took it one step further and held hearings around the country, in much the same way I had done around California when I was investigating the liquor laws in the 1950s. In general, it seemed that the NCAA and representatives of established, successful men's athletic programs objected to the idea that the revenue their sport produced would have to be shared to help support what they considered less important programs—women's sports. On the other side, the Association for Intercollegiate Athletics for Women felt that the regulations did not go far enough. As the Cedar Rapids *Gazette* put it at the time, "You know you have been fair if both sides are displeased."

Finally, in 1975, President Ford signed into law regulations designed to make access to all educational opportunities—academic as well as athletic—equally available to everyone.

Personally, I was especially interested in educational programs for gifted children. These children, in the same classes as everybody else, would finish their work sooner and quickly get bored—and bored children often get into trouble.

I believed we should cultivate gifted children—our future leadership—and provide them with the opportunities to advance at their own pace to more challenging activities. Not a little of my concern was derived from my own experience at the Frederic Burk grammar school I had attended in San Francisco, where each student was able to progress at his or her own rate and was given individual attention and encouragement.*

I was also a great proponent of the Head Start program, which gave early extra training to financially disadvantaged children, many of whom did not have helpful environments at home. This program produced dramatic results. I saw firsthand the difference it could make when I visited a poor area of Kentucky and saw how much more confident and eager to learn were the children enrolled in Head Start. Opponents said it worked *too* well—it gave these children a great boost that would only turn to disappointment when the standard public education system failed them. I argued that with Head Start at least some students would succeed against the odds.

Improving each individual's chances of success was also at the heart of my approach to welfare reform.

By the time I came to HEW, the welfare system, if it can be called a system, was a mess. It had exploded in the 1960s, partially, I think, due to pressure from special-interest groups that believed their influence would be increased if they had more people—clients, as they called them—participating in as many government programs as

---

* John Dewey, an educator at Columbia University and a leader in the "progressive movement," was a pioneer in this approach.

possible. So "outreach" to recruit more "clients" was their constant endeavor. This outreach idea was enthusiastically embraced by those who administered the programs. Instead of concentrating on helping people get off welfare, the whole system was geared to getting people *on* welfare. By the end of that decade, there were second-generation welfare families.

It was not until Governor Reagan's State Welfare Reform Act of 1971 that that trend was challenged. Robert Carleson, chief architect of the governor's welfare plan in California, explained it well: "Key elements were a work requirement, intensified scrutiny to determine initial and continuing eligibility, and stiff new laws under which welfare payments to a family that has been deserted by the father constitute a civil debt that the father owes to county welfare agencies. Savings realized from these reforms made possible a 27 percent increase in the size of cash grants to those genuinely in need."

Shame used to be associated with being "on the dole" in England, but that was not as prevalent in the United States (nor is it much in evidence in England now). To Americans welfare had become an entitlement. Many, of course, genuinely needed temporary assistance. Unfortunately, federal welfare programs in the early 1970s—such as Aid to Families with Dependent Children (AFDC), Food Stamps, Medicaid, and housing assistance—provided little or no incentive to get off the rolls and find work.

On the contrary, there were built-in inducements to stay on welfare: benefits increased the more children a family had; there was no real effort, by state or federal governments, to make absent fathers pay child support; and a recipient's benefits were slashed if he or she actually worked to earn income.

President Nixon wanted to find better ways of helping people. Sometimes he took a liberal direction. In early 1969 he expanded the Food Stamp program and increased individual benefits. Then, in August 1969, he proposed an interesting innovation—the Family

Assistance Plan (FAP). It offered a direct cash assistance grant to replace the many piecemeal welfare programs for poor families with children. I felt that it was a good idea to cut bureaucracy but that it did not go far enough. For one thing, it did not have a strong work requirement. And once Congress got hold of it, it would become yet another perpetual categorical grant. FAP twice passed in the House, the second time weighted down with congressional provisions and additions. Both times, FAP failed to reach the Senate floor for a vote. Critics killed it by saying that poor people would spend cash granted on liquor or lottery tickets; only bureaucrats could spend the money properly—a low opinion of poor people that I thought was thoroughly unjustified.

At about the same time, in the fall of 1972, another measure—the Supplemental Security Income (SSI) program—was cavalierly dumped into a Social Security bill near midnight and passed with no hearings. I strongly opposed this legislation, but, supported as it was by vigorous lobbies and members of both parties attached to traditional welfare, it became law anyway. The president could not be persuaded to veto a Social Security bill, particularly in an election year.

Basically, the SSI program required the conversion to a single *federal* system of the more than 1,150 then-existing state and county welfare programs of cash assistance to the aged, blind, and disabled. This task was assigned to HEW, and it had to be accomplished in only fourteen months. The SSI program was designed to ensure that people who cannot work have enough to eat, a place to live, and other essentials of living—certainly worthy goals, but this legislation, I felt, was poorly and hastily developed, with no hearings or opportunity for amendment, and its provisions were ill-defined. And of course, it required a great deal more money and a whole new layer of bureaucracy to administer it. These features ran counter to all of my core beliefs, as did shifting control of welfare away from states and counties—those closest to the problem—and giving it to the federal government. By extraordinary efforts on the part of many skilled people, we in the department did get SSI up and running in the required fourteen months.

On another front we had a presidential directive to find a way to reform welfare. I concluded—after more than a year of study—that a negative income tax, as proposed by Nobel Prize–winning economist Milton Friedman, was the best plan to limit government programs, slash bureaucracy, and give people more control over their lives.

The plan I proposed became known as the Income Supplement Program, or ISP. I preferred to call it "Welfare Replacement." Under this plan, the major categorical, means-tested programs—AFDC, the new SSI program, and Food Stamps—would be eliminated and superseded by a simple, universal cash transfer for families that fell below a certain level of income. The single cash payment would be reduced as a family's other income rose, until the combined total exceeded a predetermined break-even point. After that, even with a tax liability, a family earning more than the break-even amount would still have a higher net income than if it were receiving government assistance under the programs I wanted to abolish. The ISP would be integrated with the tax system and would provide work incentives because benefits would be reduced by only half of increased earnings. At the same time, those physically unable to work would be taken care of with a guaranteed minimum income.

I felt strongly that the ISP should be administered by the IRS rather than HEW or other departments experienced only in welfare. Coordinating the welfare and tax systems, as I wanted to do, was based on the fact that both have the same mechanical function—a cash transfer between the individual and the government—and the same rationale for computing the amount of the transfer: the ability to pay (or, negatively phrased, inability to pay) or need. And no new bureaucracy would be necessary.

Another major benefit in the ISP proposal was that it gave poor people what they needed most: money. Again, there was the argument, mostly from social workers, government bureaucrats, and other conventional-wisdom followers, that poor people do not know how to spend their money "properly"—an assumption I thought demeaning and wrong.

In general, liberals were concerned that ISP's benefits would be inadequate, conservatives were concerned about increasing the number of recipients, and the entrenched welfare bureaucracies were simply opposed to change.

Of course, we anticipated difficulties with Congress. First of all, jurisdiction over our proposal would cut across many committees, and this would threaten both Congress's own power and the categorical programs it loved so dearly. Second, I was sure it would have been sorely tempted to add benefits without eliminating any of the existing programs, such as Food Stamps.

Unfortunately, our Welfare Replacement plan never even reached Congress for consideration. President Nixon's highest priority became surviving the Watergate scandal, so our legislative agenda fell by the wayside, and President Ford, although favorably inclined, again deferred action until he could be elected president.

Another problem under my purview was health care costs, which were shooting upward in the early 1970s—not only for citizens trying to handle medical bills themselves but also for government programs such as Medicaid and Medicare. When President Johnson signed the Medicare program into law in 1965, he pledged that the doctors would be paid for whatever services they performed and that they would not have to get government approval ahead of time. Not surprisingly, costs skyrocketed. By late 1973, Medicare and Medicaid together were costing the government nearly $17 billion a year. The lifting of price controls, when President Nixon's Economic Stabilization Act expired on April 30, 1974, only exacerbated the problem.* Within two months, medical care costs exceeded other consumer costs by as much as 70 percent.

The administration tried to rein in these runaway health care costs in a number of ways. President Nixon advocated the concept of health maintenance organizations (HMOs), and in late 1973 he signed the Health Maintenance Organization Act, which authorized the federal government to test some HMO pilot projects around the country. The basic idea was to keep costs down by emphasizing *preventive* medicine. I felt that this was generally a good approach, but the structure of an HMO plan—requiring that only government-approved physicians be used—kept many people from choosing their own doctor, which remains one of the big problems with HMOs today, nearly thirty years later.

To avoid undue government interference in health care, I encouraged peer reviews—that is, other *doctors, not* Uncle Sam, would advise on proper treatments and various cost-saving proposals, such as how long to keep a woman in the hospital after childbirth. This was achieved by the formation of PSROs, or Professional Standards Review Organizations, and at first that did bring costs down. But technology, and its concomitant expense, was advancing rapidly and quickly overtook any gains realized from the PSROs.

President Nixon wanted a more comprehensive solution to skyrocketing health care and health insurance costs. In February 1971, he had introduced the National Health Insurance Partnership Act, which was seen as a good, middle-ground position between a complete federal takeover of the health insurance industry, as proposed by Senator Edward Kennedy, and minor changes in the insurance and delivery

---

* President Nixon and the Cost of Living Council voted to end price controls in all areas *except* health care because it was clear that medical costs were ready to explode. But Congress did not approve that exception, so all controls were allowed to expire.

systems, as proposed by others. The National Health Insurance Partnership Act required employers to provide health insurance for, and share the costs with, their employees, and it would augment or replace Medicaid assistance for poor families.

But during early debate on these issues, while I was at OMB, a number of deficiencies in the administration's bill became evident. It was widely criticized for its lack of universal coverage: low-income single people and childless couples were excluded. Democrats also objected that it did not provide for sufficient benefits, and Republicans and fiscal conservatives maintained that patients' cost-sharing requirements were not high enough, so the government's costs would go up.

This first administration attempt at health insurance reform was not enacted. When I came to HEW in early 1973, I began a thorough analysis of the entire problem, with all relevant staff involved. We worked diligently for most of that year, and by November we had developed a "new and improved" proposal designed to correct those deficiencies while maintaining the basic structure of the original plan.

As with the first plan, the crux of our new proposal was the requirement that all companies procure private insurance for their employees. The government's role was primarily to provide assurances that insurance companies were solvent, their policies comprehensive, their costs reasonable, and that all businesses had at least a minimum program to provide their employees with coverage. I felt it was important that the government only set standards and certainly not be so involved in the details of health care that it was virtually practicing medicine. An additional benefit of emphasizing private insurance was that premiums would go down as competition was fostered among insurance companies for the new big market for insurance.

This part of the proposal was called the Employer Plan, and employers would pay a percentage of the premiums. For employees who were not low-income, we proposed a higher deductible than was included in the previous bill. A fundamental principle that we followed was that higher cost-sharing with more comprehensive benefits was preferable to narrower coverage with lower cost-sharing. Also, we felt that a relatively high deductible would discourage overuse of services, which, in turn, would keep the cost of such services down. We did, however, include a maximum annual liability feature, which provided protection in case of lengthy illness and a guarantee to protect people from having to pay for catastrophic medical care costs.

The second major component of our new proposal was the Government Plan. Under this part, the federal government would arrange with the states, which would be expected to share roughly 25 percent of the costs, for the states to offer coverage by private insurance companies to all low-income people, as well as those with high-risk medical problems who were unable to obtain private coverage at affordable rates. The major group covered would be low-income people without steady employment. However, even people who were employed but had a total family income under $7,500 could choose to enter the Government Plan rather than the Employer Plan.

Both plans would cover a wide range of services, including hospital and physician services, outpatient and inpatient prescription drugs, preventive care, mental health services (very controversial then), and extended care.

A user-friendly feature that we included was a "Healthcard"—a credit card individuals could use to facilitate billing. So instead of going into the hospital and being required to write out a check when you are on a stretcher, you would simply present the card and be billed later. The card would also contain vital medical information about the holder.

Medicare would be retained but adapted to conform with the new plan, and Medicaid, for the most part, would be terminated. We estimated that the federal government's costs for the new proposal would be just under $6 billion a year—only about one-third what it was spending annually for Medicare and Medicaid.

I felt that our new health insurance plan would be particularly appealing, providing universal access to affordable insurance and using public financing only where private financing was not available.

Our Comprehensive Health Insurance Plan, or CHIP, as it was called, was introduced in Congress in February 1974, accompanied by the president's health message, in which he outlined the measures in the plan that were "designed to contain costs, improve the efficiency of the system, and assure quality health care."

Health insurance was a hot topic at that time, and Congress was awash with a great many competing bills on the subject during most of Nixon's presidency. In the Ninety-third Congress (1973 and 1974), over twenty-two separate bills were introduced to establish a national health insurance policy.

Late in 1973, Senators Long and Ribicoff put forward a bill that had fairly wide political appeal. One of its features called for substantial reform of Medicaid. There was no question it was a very inefficient and inequitable system, but I felt that simply tinkering with the existing structure or tacking further convoluted provisions onto it would not go far enough; it needed to be entirely replaced. The Long-Ribicoff bill also proposed measures designed to protect all citizens from the crippling costs of prolonged medical care (catastrophic illness), a goal that we shared. We differed mainly on how best to accomplish that.

Many liberals—led by Senator Edward Kennedy, who also introduced a bill in the Ninety-third Congress—favored the single-payer plan, the single payer of course being the government. Under this system, modeled on Canada's program, the government would pay *everyone's* health bills, which of course would mean that the government could tell doctors what they could and could not do, and there would be nothing to keep doctors from charging as much as they wanted. And patients had no incentive not to go to the doctor every time they had a hangnail. With no incentive to reduce costs or to stay

well, medical costs would inevitably grow higher and higher. Social-
ized medicine is a huge drain on any government, and citizens are
not afforded the best care. Senator Kennedy's cradle-to-grave coverage of every American citizen had strong backing from organized
labor, but fortunately his bill did not even get out of committee.

The administration's bill made some promising progress, but it
ultimately did not fare well either. By late summer of 1974, after
substantial missionary work by many of us in the department, the
insurance industry had come to support it, and even labor was starting to come around. We were able to get the powerful House Ways
and Means Committee chairman, Wilbur Mills, on our side. He was
determined to get a health insurance bill enacted that year, and he
apparently felt that he could work with ours.

When President Ford took office in August, he strongly endorsed
CHIP and authorized me to negotiate with Mills to try to reach an
acceptable compromise, which we did later that month. Mills objected
primarily to any deductibles or copayment provisions, but after many
hours of our reasoning together, he eventually accepted them. So we
were able to keep the main elements of our plan—health insurance
provided by private companies and paid for by workers and employers, and, in case of genuine need, the government.

The major change from CHIP in the compromise was to provide
catastrophic coverage financed by a payroll tax. Mills believed this
would be necessary in order to secure some liberal support. I had
always opposed a payroll tax because of my dislike of more taxes and
particularly those with revenues dedicated to a specific purpose.
Also, I thought more payroll taxes would discourage more employment. But we felt we could accept it since so much of our original
plan would be retained.

Representative Mills told me he had almost convinced Senator
Kennedy to go along with our compromise, despite labor union opposition, when events conspired to prevent it. In October, Mills became

otherwise occupied at the Tidal Basin, which quickly diminished his influence.* Fanne Fox did far more damage than she knew.

Then, even more damaging, in January 1975, in response to worsening economic conditions, President Ford announced a moratorium on new federal spending programs other than those related to national security or energy. Administration spokesmen expressed the hope of introducing a bill similar to CHIP once the economic climate improved, but the momentum was already lost. For many years thereafter, there were no comparable health insurance plans or indeed anything that even came close to securing the support that our compromise bill had won.

Throughout my tenure at HEW, most of my efforts in the health area centered around pushing for a viable health insurance program. In addition, there were a couple of other health issues in which I had a personal interest.

One of those developed after I came to HEW. As secretary, I visited a number of abused children at hospitals, and the scars they bore, physical and emotional, were horrifying to see. I had had no idea of the extent to which this went on and how little was apparently being done to address the problem. The lack of intervention exacerbated the situation: I was appalled to learn that most of these children I saw would simply be sent back to the same homes. There was apparently no legal way to separate them from the abusive parents. This only perpetuated the cycle—studies showed that those who were abused as children were more likely to abuse their own children. Almost as bad was abuse of women, and again we found that, after treatment, most abused wives returned to their husbands.

---

* When Washington police stopped Mills's car on one occasion, out jumped Fanne Fox, a stripper who somehow ended up in the Tidal Basin. This was quite a scandal at the time, and it proved to be somewhat of a pattern with Mills, who later admitted that an alcohol problem had contributed to his fall from grace.

As soon as I became aware of the severity of the problem, I initiated a child abuse prevention program, which funded studies on how to prevent, stop, and treat this tragic wrong to children. Child abuse has not been eradicated by any means, but I hope that increased penalties, more research, publicity, better treatments, and family counseling have significantly reduced its incidence and helped many children escape from abusive parents.

I was also interested in early child health screening, not only as a preventive, cost-saving tool but also based on my own early experiences. In classes at my grammar school in San Francisco, we were seated alphabetically, which meant that I was usually near the back of the room. Some children that far back could not see the board or hear as well as they should. These problems often went unnoticed and untreated, and it was generally assumed that the child was either unintelligent or just not trying hard enough. The Frederic Burk School I had attended was fairly progressive for its time, and the school nurse gave annual physicals of a sort for many pupils. As secretary of HEW, I realized that many children were not being properly tested for such basic things as vision and hearing or susceptibility to hereditary or other diseases. Therefore I pushed for early screening, so that deficiencies could be identified and treated as early as possible before they hindered a child's scholastic progress.

Another problem I learned about, unfortunately more from personal experience than from my work at the department, was the deplorable condition of some nursing homes and the incompetence of some in-home caregivers.

We had brought my mother with us to Washington, as her health was declining. Initially she lived with us in our small Capitol Hill home, and we tried to make her as comfortable as possible. We even rigged up a music system in her room, but for the first time in her life she expressed no interest in music.

We hired a series of nurses to help, but most proved uninterested in or incapable of giving her the attention she needed. One even failed to come at all when Jane and I were away on an official trip.

On a number of occasions we had to take her to the hospital. We concluded that it would be best if she had round-the-clock care in a nursing home. We tried several in the city, each one worse than the one before. Finally we found quite a good converted private home.

I visited her as often as I could, and I think she also enjoyed the outings we took her on—to see the Fourth of July fireworks from the Capitol, to view the cherry blossoms, or often just to walk in a nearby park. Once, while we were away at a conference, her doctor told us she was now quite ill. We hurried home and put her in the hospital.

On June 24, 1975, my wife called to tell me that Mother had died. The news was difficult but not a surprise. When I had seen her the night before, she had lapsed into a coma after a series of small strokes or cerebral hemorrhages. The doctor had said there was no way she could regain consciousness, and it was just a matter of hours until her body would shut down completely.

We had a private service for her—only my wife and I attended—and then, at her long-standing request, she was cremated and her ashes buried next to my father's grave in San Francisco.

The demands of my job did not afford me much time to grieve, but the appalling conditions I had seen in some of the nursing homes compelled me to work more actively to improve the standards of quality in such facilities, even without legislation.

The secretary of a major department, especially one as people-oriented as HEW, can do a lot to advocate causes by personally visiting institutions, programs, hospitals, and schools, and then stressing publicly the conditions that need improvement. This can focus attention on issues that are of personal interest to the secretary and can be especially helpful when funding is bogged down in

Congress. Such visits and speeches can also instill a fear of legislation which in itself can be helpful. I did a great deal of this, and I enjoyed having the opportunity to meet people all over the country and to learn firsthand what their concerns were and what was working and what was not.

Also at HEW, I took my first substantive overseas trip as an American cabinet official. I found I was becoming more interested in foreign and defense affairs, perhaps influenced by President Nixon's inclinations and activities in that direction. This interest was also stimulated by various security briefings I had received. I was always conscious of how global and interdependent the world was becoming. Of course, HEW was primarily concerned with domestic matters, so its international activities were comparatively small, but I felt that there would be some useful lessons in studying firsthand how other countries handled difficult issues such as welfare and health care. For some time, I was quite fascinated by England's cradle-to-grave health care program, which was completely government-run and tax-funded. I wasn't interested in doing it that way; I was interested in *not* doing it that way. Finding out what England's experience had been was most useful in my trying to discourage this "single-payer" system.

My first major trip as secretary was to Poland and the Soviet Union in the late summer of 1973, the period of détente, when the administration was trying to thaw Cold War relations and get to know our Communist adversaries. My visit was basically a gesture of goodwill, demonstrating cooperation on health issues and medical research; indeed, we set up with Moscow a sort of "health hotline"—a telex by which we could exchange research results on things like heart disease and vaccination effectiveness. This was all part of implementing a joint overall agreement with the Soviet Union, signed by President Nixon in Moscow the year before.

My wife and several of my staff accompanied me on the two-week trip. We went first to Poland, where, to my surprise, we were most enthusiastically received. The Poles openly expressed their unhappiness with Moscow's domination and their love for the counterexample of America. The Polish health minister and other officials told me they wanted to cooperate with the United States in exchanging research data and arranging reciprocal doctor visits but were blocked by the Soviets. (When I mentioned this to the Soviets later, they simply looked blank.) Polish foreign minister Stefan Olszowski even had on his wall, right beside the requisite photo of Leonid Brezhnev, a picture of President Nixon. When I commented favorably on seeing our president's photo, the minister said with an ironic smile, "Oh yes, we have friends all over, but he [gesturing to Brezhnev] is a much *closer* friend."

We traveled next to the Soviet Union, where we concentrated primarily on health issues. The Soviet minister of health, Boris Petrovsky, was a Santa Claus type—a short, rotund, ruddy-cheeked fellow—and a Red Army surgeon. He and his wife were very friendly, but in general, at least in Moscow, people were not as warm as in Poland. We were received correctly and politely, but with a strong undercurrent of suspicion. Direct contact with Americans was a relatively new thing, and we suspected the Soviet security forces taped all of our conversations.

Conviviality was, however, in evidence when it came time to eat and drink; indeed, drinking was a high priority. At our first dinner, the deputy minister of health explained the Russian custom of the first toast: the vodka (it was always vodka) had to be drunk completely and at once. To show that their glasses were empty, our hosts held them upside-down over their heads. If I had done that, I would have gotten some vodka shampoos. I generally did not drink except for a little wine, and I was concerned that our hosts would be offended. Fortunately, they did not mind if you only sipped subsequent toasts, of which there were many.

We were grandly entertained throughout our visit. We were treated to opening night of the Bolshoi Ballet, performing *Swan Lake* at a modern glass and aluminum Palace of the Congresses in the Kremlin;

a reception with the city council at a lovely dacha; a private tour of the Diamond Fund to see the czar's crown jewels; a tour of the Kremlin, including Lenin's apartment—spartan but with several English-language books behind an old-fashioned glass case; and a reciprocal dinner at our own embassy, Spaso House.

I was most interested in every aspect of our trip, taking photographs at every opportunity. I was also quite fascinated with what was one of my first experiences riding in a motorcade. The Chekka was a very square, uncompromising-looking car, sort of a cross between a London taxicab and a 1940 Dodge or Pontiac. It was a seven-passenger car, but it did not appear to be this long from the outside. It was very comfortable and there was an oriental rug in the backseat because, as it was explained to me, they try to make them as much like their homes as possible. In front of the motorcade, a yellow police car rode with a flashing blue light on top and a loudspeaker system, which constantly ordered drivers in the way to get to the right. The result was that we made astonishing time and quite frequently ran through the middle lane, or even off into the left-hand land, and gave only the slightest token concession to red lights.

Our days in Moscow were occupied mostly with visiting numerous health facilities: the Institute of Oncology, the Myasnikov Institute of Cardiology, the Soviet Academy of Medical Sciences, and Dr. Petrovsky's own First Moscow Medical Institute. Our stop at "Hospital Number 67" made a particular impression on me. We found a very large hospital, with approximately 1,200 beds, with a lady doctor as the director. This woman appeared extremely forbidding and disapproving at the beginning, and she was built along the general lines of a Russian tank, but she had extraordinarily fashionable platform shoes with very high heels that must have made the immense amount of walking she had to do up and down the corridors of that hospital extremely difficult. Despite the initial impression she made, she warmed up considerably as our tour continued, and she became downright friendly when we asked some questions indicating a real interest in the hospital. She also served a rather substantial spread, including some meat-filled rolls she had made herself, and had some very nice gifts for the party at the end.

I also vividly recall the brief trip we made to the then-Soviet republic of Uzbekistan aboard an Aeroflot plane that epitomized Communist backwardness. It was dirty, noisy, drafty, uncomfortable, and filled with people in various stages of disrepair. The plane took off in a long, shuddering roll. It seemed as if every bolt in the fuselage was coming out and rattling around on the floor. Eventually the plane took off, but the drafts were extreme (there was actually a hole in the plane's ceiling, which had been "repaired" by stuffing newspaper in it). The normal creature comforts were totally nonexistent. About three hours later we flew over Tashkent, then for some reason circled around the city for several hours before landing. For me, the major advantage of Tashkent—aside from its desert climate, a welcome relief from the cold rain of Moscow—was the equally welcome absence of vodka, a holdover from the Muslim roots of the area.

From Tashkent, we flew to Bukhara for a brief visit. As we were leaving, I noticed that a local band was playing, apparently for us. Soon a very large ring of people was there. Before I knew it, the deputy local mayor, a lady of about sixty who, it had been earlier reported to me, was feeling somewhat aggrieved because she had been photographed with me only about ninety-nine instead of a hundred times, appeared and motioned for me to dance. The dance was similar to high school dances of a few years earlier, with much gesturing of the hands and feet. I engaged as well as I could, telling them it was an ancient California dance. They seemed absolutely delighted, and I left with assurances that I could be elected to the council in Bukhara.

We returned to Moscow and then were taken to the airport for our return flight to the United States. In my travel book that I had kept during the trip, I recorded my general impressions:

> *September 9:* The sense of relief even on getting onto a Swedish air-line is unmistakable, although in a sense, this is unfair because our hosts could not have been more cordial, or more anxious to please us. Many of them are thoroughly delightful people, particularly Minister Petrovsky and his wife. The uniform impression you get from walking along the streets of Moscow is one of drabness. Women are extremely unfashionably dressed and most men are also. Public transportation is crowded, but very available and comes with great regularity and rapid-ity. They are a very proud people—almost totally unaware that anything is wrong, both as a matter of their pride and, I suspect, they're afraid of being reported as dissidents if they do complain or criticize. There's a noticeable contrast with the Poles. The Poles seem much more basically friendly and very anxious to be far more closely allied to us than Russia. They're deeply aware of the armored divisions on their border, and of what happened to Czechoslovakia and Hungary, and they know per-fectly well that any revolt by them would not be supported by anyone else and would be crushed instantaneously.... But the Poles are extremely friendly and warm, and I thought it very significant that in my interview with [First Secretary] Gierek, he said to me, "You know, your people should not be so suspicious of us. We do truly want to be your friends and you should let us be."

The secretaryship of HEW brought with it not only several other opportunities for foreign travel but also a great increase in other pub-lic and official appearances. The department's public affairs office gave me an interesting summary of my activities in just the first nine months I was there: I had taken forty-six out-of-town trips; visited twenty-four states; visited all ten regional offices (for many, the first by any secretary); made sixty-four major addresses to local, state, and national organizations; held thirty-six news conferences; made twenty-nine major television appearances; and been interviewed on eleven radio programs. All of this was a marked change from any of the federal positions I had held previously, but I thought it was necessary to inform the public about the new direction we were taking in welfare, health, and education. All of this was demanding, but at the same time, I found it exhilarating.

Although I often brought work home in the evenings, Jane and I also tried to attend as many social events as we could, particularly embassy events, because failure to appear at some of these was considered an affront by some ambassadors. It seemed a glittering age of entertaining, with grand parties in the company of such Washington fixtures as the *Post's* Kay Graham, society writer Betty Beale, columnist Joe Alsop and Susan Mary Alsop, and philanthropist Brooke Astor, who frequently came down from New York. Social occasions also offered an opportunity to meet with congressmen and senators and help persuade them of the rightness of our agendas.

Unfortunately, when President Carter came in a few years later, he made a determined effort to be informal and what he called "folksy." The trouble was, he was so anxious not to be stuffy that he forgot to be dignified. He made quite a show, for example, of carrying his own bag (usually empty). President Reagan, thankfully, brought back much of the grace and style that had characterized the Nixon and Ford days—brightened by his own spirit of sunny conviviality.

I have to say, though, that being a cabinet officer often reminded me of the old anecdote about an aged senator at a party studying a small index card. His hostess asked if he was looking for his next appointment. "No, madam," he replied, "I am trying to find where I am now."

At HEW, there were numerous ex officio positions that went along with the secretaryship, so many that you could spend the whole time just on those. Every day I seemed to have enough meetings, briefings, hearings, and appointments to cover at least two days. As was my usual practice, I wanted to see and answer all the correspondence that I could,* so I requested that it be brought to my office. I dismissed staff warnings that I'd find it impossibly large. I received an object lesson when they brought in box after box after box; the secretary's office received something like six thousand letters a day. So I deferred to the staff, who drafted responses. But I still tried to read as many of the letters as I could, particularly congressional correspondence. I also felt it especially important to maintain direct communication with the media to prevent slanted reporting or stories that often seemed based on groundless speculation. Unfortunately, many of the things reported about some other members of the administration turned out to be true.

In the late summer of 1973, I heard rumors that Vice President Agnew would be indicted for bribery. Although I had not known Agnew before he took office, I simply could not believe that this was true. But then, when I was in the middle of a speech a couple of months later in Virginia, I was handed a note saying he had resigned. I tried not to break the flow of what I was talking about, but it was a great shock.

Two days later, on the evening of October 12, I, along with many other administration officials and press, gathered in the East Room of the White House for President Nixon's announcement of his choice to replace Agnew. As we waited for the president, longtime Soviet ambassador Anatoly Dobrynin came bounding in, beaming and shaking everyone's hands. One reporter said to another, "My God, you don't suppose. . . ." That would be the ultimate in détente.

Of course, Nixon chose Gerald Ford—congressman from Michigan, House minority leader, supporter of our agenda, and vocal

---

* Ironically, I recently came across a letter I had written home from college in which I admonished my mother not to try to answer every Christmas card they received.

defender of the president. Ford's nomination was somewhat of a surprise because Nixon had come to regard Congress as his adversary. At a cabinet meeting, he told us, "The Congress is going to continue to be difficult, and if, at the end of some hearing, the committee chairman tells you that 'you have been helpful,' you have failed."

Actually, the president seemed increasingly wary of everyone, and he grew withdrawn and private, even with his closest advisers. President Nixon appeared to regard cabinet meetings as a nuisance. He used them mostly to announce policies and report on trips. He did not regard the cabinet as a decision-making body.

Our cabinet meetings were not on a regular schedule; they were usually called quite suddenly, which made it difficult for everybody. I always felt that this practice probably stemmed from the eagerness of the White House staff to keep a close hold on the reins of power and not disperse any of it to the cabinet or anyone else.*

Bob Haldeman and John Ehrlichman resigned in the spring of 1973, which meant less White House interference with the departments. I also have notes from a cabinet meeting on May 1, 1973, that their departure was meant as a warning:

> [The president] also said everyone should feel quite humble because there but for the grace of God might go anyone. He then said somewhat puzzlingly, "From time to time, I have defended all of the cabinet members who may have been under attack."

---

* The British have trouble understanding this random and rather informal nature of American cabinet meetings. Even in President Reagan's administration, cabinet meetings were not always on a regular schedule, and I remember one instance when this caused Prime Minister Margaret Thatcher puzzlement and not a little alarm. I was late to meet her at the Pentagon because of an impromptu cabinet meeting. When I finally arrived, I found that they had held her motorcade so I could arrive first and formally welcome her. When I apologized and explained that I had not known about the cabinet meeting very far ahead of time, she assumed that there must be some kind of crisis. That was not the case, but in her government, the cabinet was her chief decision-making body, and of course it met on a regular basis.

Perhaps this was an oblique call for us to stand by him come what may. I certainly urged my own department to concentrate on doing our work, concluding that if the Watergate "scandal" were permitted to cripple our constructive energies, that would be the greatest scandal of all. I thought Nixon was right to remove anyone from the administration who was even suspected of wrongdoing, and I continued to defend the president (as did my wife and several other cabinet wives), not so much because he might have expected it but simply because it was incomprehensible to me that he would have ordered the break-in at the Democratic headquarters; I attributed the incident to an overzealous staff and felt that the story was fueled and blown out of proportion by a hostile press corps. I even publicly called Watergate an "ephemeral" matter, which sent several reporters off to try to find out what ephemeral meant. But, of course, I was wrong. Watergate was far from ephemeral. It dominated everything and pushed other issues and policy to the shadows.

As the scandal continued to unfold and become more public, President Nixon became more defensive and angry, though he tried to maintain a business-as-usual facade. In one cabinet meeting fairly late in the game, then-chairman of the Republican National Committee George Bush, who sometimes attended cabinet meetings, ventured a question we had all been wrestling with. We have to be realistic, he told the president—we need to know how to respond when we're asked about Watergate. The president did not care much for that, and he replied curtly that it was not necessary for us to deal with it.

He was anxious to appear outwardly as if it were not necessary for him to deal with the growing scandal, but it was clear to those of us who had direct contact with the president that it was taking a heavy toll. I had a private meeting with him in the Oval Office, arranged entirely by the White House and designed to try to get the press to write about something else. The subject was federal scholarships for college students, and I was to confer with him about it and then come out and brief the press. But the president was totally uninterested in discussing the matter. He had spent the earlier part of the morning listening to tapes, and was probably going to spend the rest of the morning doing the same, so he was anxious to get our meeting over with as quickly as possible. As predicted, when I emerged, all the press wanted to know about was the president's mood and demeanor; they were not the least bit interested in student scholarships either.

I recall that at an August 1974 cabinet meeting when Mr. Nixon himself raised the question of resignation, the president said he had found no evidence of any impeachable offense. If there were, he said, he would not stay in office one more minute. He explained at greater length that the president is not in the position of an ordinary citizen. The Constitution says the president is to be impeached by the House and tried by the Senate. It was his view that he should not take a step, resignation, that changes the Constitution and sets a precedent that resignation should instead be the method. That would introduce a parliamentary system, and that precedent should not be set or even thought of. Any action of the president that may have been illegal should be handled, he said, as provided in the Constitution, not by resignation.

Only two days later—faced with collapsing congressional support and the Supreme Court decision that all of the White House tapes must be turned over to the special prosecutor—the president changed his mind. The day President Nixon announced his resignation, our Chilean housekeeper came to me trembling and frightened. "Oh, Mr. Weinberger, when will the National Guard come?" She was the widow of a Chilean army officer, and she assumed the military would assassinate everyone in the government and "take over."

My driver, Sarge, was also quite shaken and upset about the news of the president's resignation, so much so that he had a small accident driving me to a speaking engagement at the National Institutes of Health. (I ended up hitching a ride with a kind motorist.)

The next day—August 9, 1974—was a sad day for the country and wrenching for all of us in the Nixon administration. My wife and I and other cabinet members and White House staff filled the East Room, where we had been summoned to hear the president's farewell address. We were acutely aware that we were present at a historic event. As the president began, it felt as if we were collectively holding our breath— as though that would prevent the inevitable from happening. But through the apprehension, incredulity, and even grief that hung heavy in the air, a beaten president delivered a long, rambling talk in which he constantly mentioned his mother but never once made mention of his wife, who had stood by him and supported him throughout the whole ordeal, indeed through his entire career. This omission was noted by many, and I thought it was particularly unfortunate.

Shortly after Nixon departed from the White House by helicopter, Vice President Ford was sworn in as our thirty-eighth president. He then made a splendid short speech, beginning with, "My fellow Americans, our long national nightmare is over. Our Constitution works." He said exactly the right things, striking a perfect balance between compassion for Nixon and the importance that the country move on. The mood in the room improved palpably as he spoke. I tried to carry that feeling of hope to my own department, calling a meeting of all HEW employees, at which I encouraged them to seize this new beginning with President Ford. And it was a new beginning. Only two days later, I appeared on *Meet the Press* to discuss health insurance, and for the first time in months I actually was allowed to talk about policy rather than Watergate.

Even though President Ford knew public opinion was against it, he made the courageous decision to pardon President Nixon in order to put Watergate behind us. I believe it was the right thing to do because Nixon had already suffered far more intense personal anguish than any trial or jail sentence could have imposed; also, it was important that the country move forward.

Unlike President Nixon after his reelection, President Ford asked everyone to stay on. As I wrote of his first cabinet meeting, on August 10, 1974:

> The president said, "I don't want any resignations submitted to me." He said without reflecting on anyone or implying any criticism, "I thought the wholesale resignation called for after the 1972 election was just terrible."

Nevertheless, I offered to resign if President Ford had his own candidate for my job, but he kindly asked me to stay. President Ford told us in that first cabinet meeting:*

> "Everybody's style is different and mine will be different than President Nixon's. I like to see people. I am a better listener than I am a reader. I want you to come in. I also like to get business done and over with. I don't like a lot of chitchat, that isn't my style. Your time and mine is precious, and I want to observe that and protect it."
>
> I told him I thought this was a much better system than the one that had been in effect before, when not only was it impossible to get our memoranda through, but it was virtually impossible to get an appointment. He smiled sympathetically.

Unlike Nixon, President Ford sought advice from his cabinet members, including our recommendations for vice presidential candidates. The people I suggested were the same ones whose names I had submitted (unsolicited) to President Nixon when Agnew resigned: Nelson Rockefeller and Ronald Reagan. Both men, I felt, were superb governors, and either one would bring great strength to the ticket if President Ford decided to run for the presidency in 1976.

---

* The quote may not be exact; this is how I recorded it in my notes.

Governor Rockefeller was usually seen as a liberal, even though he often spoke of his admiration for Governor Reagan's conservative policies. Rockefeller himself did not worry about labels; he was an enthusiastic "idea man," vigorously supporting those he believed in, whether the ideas happened to be liberal or conservative.

When President Ford nominated Governor Rockefeller to be his vice president, he was confirmed, but only after long and disagreeable confirmation hearings marked by far more questions about the Rockefeller family wealth than anything substantive.

As I admired Nelson Rockefeller for his openness to ideas, I also admired President Ford because I found my meetings with him were far more substantive and productive than were my meetings with Nixon. As I wrote after one such meeting in May 1975:

> These working meetings in which the president actually makes decisions and follows closely domestic policy and has been well briefed in advance and is willing to have various others from the departments present... are a great improvement from his predecessor, and we all remarked on it following the meeting.

After two depressing years in Washington, I felt that the clouds had finally rolled away. Once again, I enjoyed government service.

But by April 1975, with my mother's health deteriorating, and with my wife suffering from arthritis and eager to return to California, I informed President Ford that I must reluctantly resign office as soon as he could find a successor. He said he was disappointed but understood my reasons.

I felt it was too bad to have to leave before I had completed everything I had set out to do, but I was proud of what we had been able to accomplish in my two years at HEW. We had put into effect some programs that had just been handed to me, such as the Title IX regulations and the whole SSI program. We had also succeeded in at least shifting the public debate from a concentration on huge federal government programs more toward individuals, even if we were not able to get all of our specific proposals through Congress. Unfortunately, though, Congress had often passed measures over administration protests, resulting in several increases in Social Security and Medicare payments which pushed HEW's budget up nearly 55 percent just in the time I was there. It was a huge, unwieldy department, but one that provided many exciting challenges and the opportunity to try to change things for the better.

In a meeting with the president to say good-bye, I suggested Frank Carlucci (then undersecretary of HEW), former treasury secretary John Connally, or Governor Reagan to succeed me, but he ultimately chose Dr. Forrest David Mathews. Mathews was a professional educator who had made some innovative changes at the University of Alabama, where he was then president.

The date set for Dr. Mathews to take over was August 8, nearly one year to the day since President Nixon had left office.

A number of people I had come to know during my five-and-a-half years in Washington gave some lovely farewell parties for us. One that was particularly special to me was a testimonial dinner given not only by my staff at HEW but also by those with whom I had worked at OMB and the Federal Trade Commission.

I also hosted a party (at Camp David, which President Ford was kind enough to let me use one weekend) for the HEW staff and their families to show my appreciation and gratitude for their great support of the work we had tried to do. I would venture that no other agency of government had such a diversity of professions and skills as those required to operate the roughly three hundred (at that time) programs of HEW efficiently. We had physicians, researchers, lawyers, educators, social workers, economists, actuaries, typists, the maintenance force—and all of them were dedicated to doing their jobs well and serving the many Americans who relied on them.

On the morning of August 8, my last day in office, I attended Dr. Mathews's swearing-in ceremony in the departmental auditorium. That afternoon, I went to a cabinet meeting and said good-bye to my colleagues and the president, who was very kind and generous in his comments.

I considered this the end of my government career. The main contribution I expected to make to the government from then on was to pay a large income tax. My wife and I loaded our dog into the car and literally drove off into the sunset.

CHAPTER 14

RETIREMENT FROM PUBLIC LIFE — OR SO I THOUGHT

*T*he day after my resignation from HEW, I experienced a very peculiar sensation. It was the first time that I had been in Washington with nothing official to do. There were no meetings to get to, no press conferences, no congressional hearings, nothing to prepare for. At first, it left me feeling almost lost.

So we became sightseers. My wife and I spent a couple of days enjoying the beauty of Washington and then embarked on a cross-country journey. We drove northeast to Maine, where, two years later, we bought a house near Jane's childhood home, at the head of a meadow running down to Somes Sound, a long fjord flowing in from the sea on Mount Desert Island.

In that summer of 1975, we drove from Maine to Toronto to see Arlin, then back into the United States and down to California. We liked to get up early each day and start driving by six so that we would reach our overnight destination by early afternoon. That gave us some time to look around the towns or swim in the motel pools. I had not made such a trip since my college days, and then I was more interested in getting "there," wherever that happened to be, than in appreciating the scenery or resting anywhere.

Our new home was in Hillsborough, California, about twenty miles south of San Francisco. We decided on a lovely, old, white, Tudor-style house in the same neighborhood as our previous California home.

Everything about our new house was on a large and old-fashioned scale. It had spacious rooms, including a ballroom and a library. There were a couple of splendid redwood trees in an old garden (a garden much improved later by Jane) and room for a swimming pool, which we put in. All that new space worked out well when Cap Jr. and his wife and daughter lived there with us for a few years.

We had some remodeling done on the house, work that Bechtel, my new firm, kindly supervised before we arrived. They also put in gates and a fence for security.

Our first night in our new home was September 11, 1975. The next morning, I drove into San Francisco to begin work for Bechtel.

As early as June, Bechtel, a global construction firm based in San Francisco, had begun efforts to recruit me. My former colleague George Shultz was already there, and I had known some other Bechtel executives when I had practiced law at Heller, Ehrman, including Bill Slusser, Bechtel's general counsel. The company had a sterling reputation and track record. Warren Bechtel started the business in 1898 when he bought a team of mules and contracted to lay railroad tracks across what is now Oklahoma. By the 1970s, Bechtel was a huge firm involved in heavy construction of tunnels, pipelines, nuclear and other power plants, refineries, building complexes, transportation systems, and a number of civic projects of substantial size, which meant that our customers were often foreign governments. Bechtel would provide broad and varied work—not just legal work—and that and the overseas aspect particularly appealed to me.

The recruiting process had been flatteringly intense. Bill Slusser wanted to retire, and wanted very much for me to succeed him. Bill was a thoroughly charming, delightful, and persuasive man whom I had known for many years, through the Bohemian Club and elsewhere. Ultimately, I met with Steve Bechtel Jr., who had recently succeeded his father as the company's chief executive.

Steve was an extraordinarily effective leader, who benefited from having served in virtually every job—from beginning laborer—on the construction side of the firm. He and his delightful wife, Betty, had lived in construction trailers on sites in inhospitable climates all over the world. Steve was a native Californian, enjoyed intense outdoor activities, and lived for the success of the company.

I accepted his offer to join Bechtel as a vice president, a director, and special counsel, which, if all went well, would lead to the general counsel's position after Bill Slusser actually retired. Steve wanted me to avoid political activities—indeed, *all* outside activities—at least for the first year of my employment. I said that would be difficult because I had already had offers—in which I was interested—to sit on various corporate boards. I thought the experience to be gained there would be most helpful, particularly as many of the offers had come from corporations that had international operations, as Bechtel did. Eventually, Steve relaxed the requirement a bit and offered generous compensation which included valuable shares of Bechtel stock. I accepted the offer.

My other concern, which I expressed frankly to Steve, was that I hoped my responsibilities would encompass much more than strictly legal work. I wanted to visit construction sites, learn all about the actual work of the company, and serve, if I could, on some of the corporate-wide committees that had other duties besides legal work. I was assured that that would be the case.

I received Steve's offer while he, Bill Slusser, and I drove up together to attend the annual encampment of the club at Bohemian Grove, north of San Francisco. I had been a member of the Bohemian Club since 1973. Bohemian Club members, as is the case with most private clubs, are expected to maintain what we called at Harvard a "decent reticence" about its matters.

What we can say is that the club was started in 1872, basically as a fraternity of artists, writers, and musicians, with a few philistines who, if not artists themselves, enjoyed and appreciated those who were. Since then, the club's membership has shifted more toward prominent businessmen, industry titans, and political leaders.

Over the years, the club had acquired about 2,700 acres of an extraordinarily beautiful and secluded portion of the ancient redwood forest north and west of San Francisco, within which were various campfires, tents, dining facilities, and other gathering places. Each camp was unique, and I was particularly fortunate that both Bill Slusser and Ted Meyer, my original sponsors, had paved the way for me to be taken into one of the oldest, the Isle of Aves, named for a mythical island in a poem by Charles Kingsley. Other members of the Isle of Aves included my old friend Bill Clark, former governor and Chief Justice of the United States Earl Warren, the presidents of Stanford and the University of California, and many other San Franciscans.

I gave a few of the so-called Lakeside lectures, which were generally held in the afternoons of the two-and-a-half weeks of the summer encampment. Lakeside talks were a lot of fun but a real challenge to any speaker. The audience consisted of up to a couple thousand people, most of whom were very well known, and most of whom had heard far better speakers from all over the world, because these were the people who were attracted as guests to the Grove. There was one further challenge: it was necessary when speaking to compete with one or two large and very ancient frogs, who competed with very throaty noises during most of the speeches. The crowd also fully expected to be entertained, and if a little instruction or governmental views went along with it, that was acceptable, but it was essential that one be both amusing and effective.

The club was a very happy part of my life at that time, and I enjoyed my membership thoroughly. The artistic talent that had started the club was still an important requirement, and new members particularly were expected to participate in one way or another in the plays or other entertainments that were a part of the Grove's summer encampments. My thespian experience at the club was limited to a Grove play which involved Noah's ark. My role was the somewhat narrow and not particularly demanding one of holding up a portion of the rainbow which appeared after the flood. This required the skills of a college football card stunt, and I like to think that my quadrant of the rainbow appeared at the right time and in the proper sequence.

All of these antics—indeed, the whole idea of a grown men's camp-out—may seem rather puerile to outsiders, but having a brief retreat like this in such wondrous surroundings is salutary. It provides a temporary release from the pressures of leadership and responsibility, both of which weigh heavily on most members, by virtue of their positions in life and work. I know I found the summer encampments to be a welcome respite and always a help to regain perspective and balance.

The food at the Grove was extraordinarily good—plain, hearty fare, served on great camp tables in one of the most splendid of all redwood groves. The sight of 1,500 to 2,500 people all dining in those glorious surroundings has provided most happy and satisfying memories. It was, of course, not the first time I had spent time in the redwoods, because many of our summer vacations years before, with the children, had been in some of the earliest of the California state redwood parks. So the majesty and glory of these great trees were already well known to me.

I attended my first Bechtel directors' meeting nearly a month after I accepted Bechtel's offer. The company owned one twenty-three-story building in San Francisco's financial district and two others nearby. Steve Bechtel Jr. would walk all the way up to his twenty-second floor office every morning, a feat that I could not emulate then and certainly not now. I had a large, corner office on the twenty-first floor with a splendid view of the bay and much of the city.

There was no such thing as a "typical" workday at Bechtel, which was one of the things I liked most about the job; and, unlike the slower-moving government, you could actually see progress being made.

Though the company was enormous, it retained a personal touch. For many years, Steve Bechtel Sr. knew the first names and family facts of every Bechtel employee. He was admired and respected by everyone who knew him. And he was a man of vision. Once when he was in Saudi Arabia to negotiate a contract for an oil refinery, he said, "What you *really* need is a new city." The Saudis agreed, and Bechtel built Jubail for them. In fact, so expansive became their plans that the Saudis concluded they needed two cities, and they created the Royal Commission for Jubail and Yanbu. Each became a successful industrial site and a full-scale city. Jubail had been a small, remote fishing village; it is now a thriving city of several hundred thousand people.

Along with Bill Slusser and Steve Bechtel Jr., I was delighted to work again with Virginia Duncan, my friend and former colleague from KQED, who became my executive assistant. She had just left KQED, having been elected to a California bank board, and later was appointed to the board of the Corporation of Public Broadcasting. She said she wanted to gain more business experience, which worked out perfectly for me as well, because I needed an executive assistant who was good at managing the many nonlegal details involved in administering the legal and insurance departments. Insurance had been part of the general counsel's duties for some time, and that was another set of new responsibilities I had to learn. Virginia had skillfully handled many important details at KQED, so she came to Bechtel and did the same for me there.

George Shultz had joined Bechtel about a year before I did. As seemed to be the case every time we worked together (before and since Bechtel), we often had differing viewpoints. This was most evident when lawsuits were brought against the company, particularly large class-action suits. The arguments for settling them to avoid trial might be strong, but agreeing to huge settlements could set precedents that might encourage future suits, some of which would be virtually legal blackmail. So generally I would recommend that we fight rather than yield, but invariably George would want to settle. Later, when we both served in the Reagan administration, George was sometimes more eager to send in troops than I was.

I served on Bechtel's personnel and finance committees, which oversaw things like training programs, compensation packages, and health insurance plans, of which Bechtel offered one of the best.

I spent the first few months familiarizing myself with the contracts and projects in progress and the people working on them. This, of course, involved visiting many project sites, which I loved to do because it was a great education. In early October, I toured a number of Bechtel's Stateside projects, including the San Onofre nuclear power plant in southern California and the tunnel for Washington, D.C.'s Metro subway system.

In the fall of 1975, Bill Slusser took Jane and me to meet the staff in our London office, and then to Saudi Arabia and Kuwait. I was fascinated by the Mideast and the Arab cultures, and Bechtel veterans were well versed in the behavior expected in these countries. I learned, for example, that one should never show the soles of one's shoes (as when crossing one's legs), as Arabs deem this a great insult. The new city of Jubail was a huge single construction zone, including a new port, an industrial complex, highways, apartment buildings,

hotels, hospitals, schools, and all utilities. At the same time, we were
beginning on a new airport for Riyadh.

As we traveled throughout the region, I wrote a number of impressions and observations, some important, some trifling.

> *8 November 1975:* Flew from Kuwait to Riyadh. The baggage formalities at the Riyadh airport took some time although they have a very new, modern machine for bringing the baggage up from the ground floor, and for the first time in my entire career of travel one of my bags came out first.
>
> *9 November 1975:* Parenthetically, I should note that it is always interesting to see how many different viewpoints you get. From the people who are in the operating divisions there is usually a very substantial optimism. From the people who have to coordinate all of the company activities there is a kind of controlled pessimism and worry.
>
> Riyadh reminds me very much of some of the Philippine towns I saw during the war. Parts of the streets are paved, the center dividing strip is sand, and the wind blows a lot of dust around. Even though it is November, it is excessively hot, and dust is in most of the buildings. There seems to be very little central air conditioning although there is a vast number of air conditioning units.

We were received very cordially by Saudi and Kuwaiti officials, many of whom had been educated in the United States or England, but a sensitive issue caused some legal and business problems. As today, most Arab countries boycotted companies that did business with Israel—a practice that both Bechtel and the U.S. government agreed amounted to economic sanctions, which were illegal. A great deal of legal work was required to make sure that we did not violate U.S. law *or* jeopardize our dealings with *any* country. Fortunately, many high-ranking Arabs did not support the boycott anyway.

As usual, keeping up with the myriad responsibilities of the general counsel's post did not satisfy my need to branch out into other activities. So I pushed hard for Bechtel's approval—which was reluctantly given—to sit on the boards of PepsiCo and Quaker Oats.

PepsiCo is a huge, innovative conglomerate, and Don Kendall—then CEO and chairman of the board of PepsiCo, and a longtime friend—was quite impressive himself, as a 1977 article in *ARCOspark*, the magazine of Atlantic-Richfield, pointed out:

> In 1947, [Kendall] heard by chance that Pepsi had an opening for a fountain syrup salesman. PepsiCo is the only company he's ever worked for. After super-selling his way into the international VP job at Pepsi, he talked management into funding a Pepsi exhibit at the 1959 Moscow trade show. Under pressure to justify the endeavor, Kendall persuaded then-vice president Nixon to bring Khrushchev by the Pepsi booth for an introduction. What happened was the famous "kitchen debate" between Nixon and the Russian Premier.
>
> "It was a hot day and I was there passing out Pepsis," Kendall recalls. "Khrushchev ended up drinking eight and he passed them out to his aides. Pictures of Khrushchev with Pepsis in his hand appeared in newspapers around the world."
>
> Kendall—who took over Pepsi in 1963—has always believed in trade with Eastern Europe. And the kitchen debate paved the way for Pepsi in Russia. In 1972, Pepsi became the first American firm to make a consumer product in Russia. Pepsi has two plants in Russia with three more on the drawing boards. Kendall today oversees a $2.3 billion sales empire which includes North American Van Lines, Wilson Sporting Goods, Monsieur Henri Wines, Ltd., and Frito-Lay.

I went with Don Kendall and the rest of the board to the Soviet Union in the fall of 1979 to open new Pepsi bottling plants, and I observed firsthand the impact Pepsi had there. There were long lines at the Pepsi kiosks in the city squares, and it was gratifying to realize that in the Soviet Union, popular American products were playing such a large role—which was mostly because the people had so little of any quality that they could buy.

The Soviet Union was also benefiting from an arrangement with PepsiCo: the Soviets would buy Pepsi and pay for it by giving us Stolichnaya vodka to sell in the United States. The problem with this for Pepsi came later, when the Soviets invaded Afghanistan and many Americans refused to buy any Soviet products.

Other aspects of that trip were not quite so impressive—such as the night train from Moscow to Leningrad. It was supposed to be a marvel, but I was incautious enough to brush my teeth with the water on board—not a wise thing to do.

My return (which I made alone, as I had to get back for a Bechtel meeting) had problems as well—this time, at the Moscow airport. A large dragon lady in charge of customs asked what one of my bags was, and without thinking I identified my shaving kit as my "drug kit." Huge mistake. My answer delayed me by almost three hours (just enough time to miss my plane) while officials examined every single article I had in each of my bags. Unsuccessful in my attempts to explain the misunderstanding, I tried to call the health officials I had met when I was there as secretary of HEW, hoping they could help. But they were no longer in office.

I joined the board of Quaker Oats in 1977, after being recruited by the company chairman, Bob Stuart. I had known Bob for many years, as he had been active in Republican politics. He is a thorough gentleman, is an excellent businessman and diplomat, and has a delightful, quiet manner. Quaker, although a large conglomerate, seemed like more of a small family business. The Quaker meetings were held every other month at Chicago's Merchandise Mart, and I would usually fly in and back on the same day.

I managed to fill available fragments of time with other endeavors. I resumed my involvement with the Episcopal Church, a nearly life-long interest kindled by my mother that had only grown over the years. Now back in the Bay Area, we attended regular services at St. Luke's, and in the summer of 1977 I was appointed treasurer of the Episcopal Diocese of California. It seemed I was destined always to be responsible for balancing someone's budget.

I was also asked to write a few book reviews for the *Riverside Press-Enterprise* and the *Wall Street Journal*, which I was glad to do because it revived an old interest begun as a reviewer for the *San Francisco Chronicle* years before.

However, as always, my real and deepest interest was not in the boardroom or the church but in the ever changing rough and tumble of government and politics. Unfortunately, Bechtel frowned on political activities, particularly by former government officials, and Steve Bechtel worried that I was not fully dissociated from the public sector. I am afraid he was absolutely right. By the time I had been with Bechtel a year or so, I think Steve was pretty well resigned to the fact that I was always going to have other interests. In any event, he gradually eased his objections and allowed me to take part in some governmental activities, including serving on President Ford's Committee on Science and Technology and, in 1980, even working with Ronald Reagan's campaign.

In 1977 I accepted an invitation to join the Trilateral Commission, an organization whose origins stemmed from President Nixon's diplomatic overtures to China. Many American business leaders and former government officials were alarmed that our allies had not been consulted when the president made his China visit. I agreed that new relations with traditional adversaries should not be pursued at the expense of our relationships with our allies, particularly Western Europe and Japan. So the Trilateral Commission was formed with representatives from the United States, Europe, and Japan. It was an attempt to keep everyone informed through an extragovernmental consultative body that provided a forum for addressing common concerns and possible solutions. It was not a policy-making body, though it included a number of former and future government leaders, such as President Carter, Vice President Walter Mondale, Secretary of State Cyrus Vance, Defense Secretary Harold Brown, and National Security Adviser Zbigniew Brzezinski. When all these men took office with Mr. Carter in January 1977, they resigned from the commission but, fortunately, kept the trilateral U.S.–Western Europe–Japan relationship as the centerpiece of their foreign policy.

I know some right-wing zealots feared that the commission was a conspiracy to create a world government. David Rockefeller, whom I have known since Harvard days and who was basically the founder of the commission, was particularly suspect by the farthest of the far right, as well as by many far leftists. In reality, he was scarcely a revolutionary figure. But since he was part of the East Coast foreign policy establishment, to some people that automatically spelled a sinister conspiracy.

I did not agree with every report of the task forces of the Trilateral Commission—indeed, I thought some of the reports took a weak line on so-called Euro-Communism—but the commission was examining important issues and helped to strengthen our alliances, and we needed all the help we could get.

In the summer of 1978, I was offered another opportunity to indulge my love of public policy—this time by a Democrat. California governor Jerry Brown appointed me to his Commission on Government Reform, which he established in response to the passage of Proposition 13. The voters of the state had overwhelmingly passed the measure, which drastically reduced property taxes (by 67 percent, or approximately $7 billion) and limited future increases to 2 percent of property value. California was the first state to roll back the property tax so radically.* It was a great example of the power of the people and the use of the initiative to bring about changes that were inconceivable under the ordinary legislative process. Indeed, it was viewed with absolute horror by longtime state and local government people because the property tax had been one of the best sources of revenue.

Governor Brown and others considered the passage of Proposition 13 an emergency about which something had to be done. Never mind that it was the will of the people or that the repudiated property tax had been particularly onerous—given that property taxes rose with property value rather than income or ability to pay.

The fourteen-member commission was fairly evenly divided between Republicans and Democrats, and, as such, predictably, it did not reach a consensus about how the state and local governments could reform the way they taxed and spent. At least it gave me a platform to air many of my own long-standing ideas for tax and spending limitations, but I also suspect Governor Brown thought of the commission as bipartisan cover for enacting tax increases. He knew he could not survive politically if he recommended them, so he wanted to have a commission of experts say they was necessary.

Until serving on this commission I had not been active in political matters since returning to the private sector. It was not the most encouraging time to be a Republican. The party had been badly beaten in 1974—in Congress as well as in governorships and local elections, no doubt due to what today might be called "Watergate fatigue."

---

* California led a nationwide tax rebellion. According to *California and the American Tax Revolt: Proposition 13 Five Years Later*, edited by Terry Schwadron, "Between 1978 and 1980 . . . fully 43 states adopted new limitations on local property taxes or new property tax relief plans, either on official initiative or as a result of the electorate's decision."

Then, in 1976, we lost the White House. I believe one reason was that the party was divided. Governor Reagan challenged incumbent President Ford, which I thought was a great mistake. Rifts remained even though Governor Reagan made a gracious concession speech at the convention and supported President Ford after narrowly losing on the convention's first ballot. Stiff nomination fights generally spell doom for Republicans.

By 1980, after nearly four years of economic and foreign policy defeats under President Carter, Americans were ready to take another look at Republican candidates—and Governor Reagan was ready to make another run for president. When he began his campaign in late 1979, he was given little chance of winning. Moderate Republicans considered him a right-wing nut who could never win, and many party loyalists resented him because they felt he was at least partly responsible for President Ford's defeat in 1976. Primarily, however, they feared his challenge to the conventional wisdom. Even foreigners were wary of him, concerned about an actor's ability to run the country. People I knew in London were horrified at the prospect of Ronald Reagan as president, and they felt that it could not possibly happen. (I reminded them of that several years later, and they were extremely grateful that they had been wrong. President Reagan turned out to be nearly as popular abroad as he was at home.)

Governor Reagan's campaign message resonated with the American people: he advocated a 10 percent across-the-board tax cut to boost our economy, pull us out of inflation, and put people back to work, and he supported the usually unpopular idea of rebuilding our hollowed-out military (which ultimately brought the Soviets to the bargaining table on arms control). All of this, and the hope he held out of a better America, rather than a country mired in "malaise," made him a most attractive alternative to a haggard and ineffectual President Carter.

My good friend Bill Clark was active in Governor Reagan's campaign from its early stages, and at his suggestion I began doing some informal consulting and speaking for the campaign in mid-1979. At first it was fairly limited, but gradually I became more involved, and by the summer of 1980 I was an at-large delegate from California to the Republican National Convention in Detroit.

Former president Ford was also running, but he could not match Governor Reagan's popularity. A number of Ford's people were still bitter about Governor Reagan's challenge in 1976, and they could not imagine that Reagan was up to the job. "Reagan," they liked to say, "knows nothing about foreign policy."

So, after the governor won the nomination at the convention, a number of President Ford's people began pushing for what would essentially be a "joint presidency": Ford would be Reagan's vice president but would do all the substantive work—in effect, operating like a prime minister, while Reagan's duties as president would be strictly ceremonial. It was a perfect plan, they thought. Reagan had all of the charisma and vote-drawing ability, but Ford would be there to serve as president in all but name.

Governor Reagan, as the party nominee, of course did not agree to such an absurd arrangement, but he was rather amused by the rumors. When he jokingly asked me about the idea, I pointed out that there was one minor problem: it was totally and completely unconstitutional—and that was just to begin with.

But the machinations and rumors continued, and leaks of this "dream ticket" spread like wildfire, reaching fever pitch when it was actually reported that the deal was done. Finally, Governor Reagan told a group of his supporters in his hotel suite, "This has gone far enough. Get me George Bush."

George Bush was the obvious choice, and a good one, for a running mate, since he had finished second in many primaries. I think Bush was surprised to be asked, but the press was completely astounded. They kept asking me (and anyone else they believed had Reagan's confidence) what had changed the governor's mind. I pointed out that he never had agreed to the "joint presidency" idea. "You've got it all wrong," I told them. "*Nobody* but the press thought this thing was all settled. Nobody ever bothered to consult Ronald Reagan."

In the following months leading up to the election, I continued consulting with Governor Reagan and his campaign staff. We all became increasingly enthusiastic as his candidacy continued to build momentum. Many of us had long known of the governor's leadership abilities and solid conservative values, and it was tremendously gratifying to see the rest of America getting to know him and beginning to recognize the many assets he could bring to leading the nation.

CHAPTER 15

In the Arena Again

onald Reagan's disposition and the weather in Los Angeles were equally and typically sunny when Jane and I arrived at the Century Plaza Hotel, Reagan's favorite hotel in the city, on November 4, 1980. As soon as we got to our hotel room, somewhere between 5 P.M. and 6 P.M., I turned on the television to see President Carter already conceding. We went to the headquarters suite, where a familiar coterie was gathered: Bill Clark, Ed Meese, Mike Deaver, Bill French Smith, Bill Casey, and various other aides and friends. The rest of the evening was a jubilant blur: meeting with hundreds of Reagan supporters, doing many quick radio and television interviews, and attending the president-elect's gracious speech acknowledging his remarkable victory. Almost as exciting was that the new Senate would have a GOP majority.

Carter's early concession infuriated the Democrats because the polls were still to be open for three more hours in the whole western part of the country, and they feared that his early concession would discourage many Democrats from voting at all. But Carter had

guessed right; the results were clearly tilting in Reagan's favor.*
Weary of high inflation and unemployment, the energy crisis, and
the inability to gain freedom for fifty-two citizens held for over a year
in Iran, Americans were ready for strong leadership and watershed
changes in policies.

Change was in the offing for me personally as well, although I did
not know, or even think about, that then.

I returned to San Francisco and my job with Bechtel, but soon
after Election Day President-elect Reagan appointed me to head his
task force on reducing federal spending. I recommended a two-track
approach of deep spending and tax cuts (directly contrary to the
Keynesian theories) as the only effective way of both slowing federal
budget growth and stimulating the economy. I also recommended
that Reagan have his own budget ready to submit to Congress as
soon as possible; he would *not* want to govern on the basis of
President Carter's last budget.

In addition to heading the economic task force, I was asked, and
enthusiastically agreed, to serve on the president-elect's Task Force
on National Security. Rebuilding America's defense was as important
to Ronald Reagan as was restoring America's economy. Reagan keenly
understood the importance of military strength. In his acceptance
speech at the Republican convention in 1980, he said, "We know
only too well that war comes not when the forces of freedom are
strong, but when they are weak. It is then that tyrants are tempted."
President-elect Reagan and I agreed that America's national security
took precedence over every other policy priority.

The core decision-making group during the transition was Reagan's
"kitchen cabinet"—essentially his longtime backers and advisers,

---

* Reagan ended up winning forty-four states and 489 electoral votes—only to garner
even more impressive results in his reelection race four years later: forty-nine states
and 525 electoral votes.

such as Holmes Tuttle, Justin Dart, and Henry Salvatori. A number of us who had served in the president-elect's gubernatorial administration were also included.

This group held frequent meetings, usually in the big conference room at Bill French Smith's law firm in Los Angeles. Bill had been Reagan's personal attorney for many years. Whenever one of us was suggested as an appointee, that person was asked to leave the room. So I took it as something of a compliment that I had to leave the conference room several times. I was apparently suggested for OMB, Treasury, attorney general, State, and Defense. I definitely did not want to run OMB again; two-and-a-half years of virtually continuous budget cutting there had been enough. I was ambivalent about the Treasury post; I suppose my inclination at that time was to get away from exclusively budgetary or financial matters and concentrate more on other issues, preferably relating to foreign and security policy. The attorney general post would have allowed that to a greater degree, but I knew that Bill Smith was Reagan's choice, and I strongly supported that. Frankly, if I were to be involved at all in the new administration, I was most interested in the State or Defense Departments. When Ronald Reagan called, in late November 1980, he said, "I know you have a very full, comfortable, and probably rich life, and now I want to spoil the whole thing by asking you to serve as my secretary of defense." Although accepting would mean another major upheaval in our lives and a significant loss of income, I knew immediately that I wanted to serve the president and execute his plans for regaining America's military strength.

I called my wife, who, as an army nurse commissioned early in the war, had outranked me when we both served in the army during World War II. So I took great delight in saying, "Lieutenant Dalton, now *you* may salute." I must report that she was not terribly enthusiastic about the prospect of uprooting and moving once again to Washington and living under public scrutiny to an even greater extent than before. But, as she had done so many times, she recognized that I felt this was something we should do, and as always she agreed and began the enormous task of organizing and carrying out our move to Washington.

My appointment was announced on what would have been my father's ninety-fourth birthday—December 1, 1980. I like to think that he would have been especially proud that day. I was the only cabinet member confirmed on the first day of the Reagan administration. I was approved by the Senate by a vote of 97 to 2,* the two opposing votes cast by North Carolina Republican senators Jesse Helms and John East, who thought I would not pursue a sufficiently hard line against the USSR and would not spend enough on defense. Senator East died early in the Reagan administration, but not before he had apologized to me for misjudging what I would do at Defense. Senator Helms later was kind enough to tell me he greatly admired my work, and we became good friends.

So many things happened at once, and so many priorities needed to be addressed as soon as I took office, that trying to recall those first days brings to memory only a vast blur of meetings, briefings, interviews, and paperwork. I immersed myself to learn not only large policy matters but also esoteric details, which I knew would come up at congressional hearings, though sometimes I didn't appreciate quite how detailed my knowledge would have to be. At one of my first budget hearings as secretary, a congressman asked me why the Defense Department had decided to contract out the laundry service at Eglin Air Force Base to a private firm. I had spent many, many hours preparing for this hearing, working with a vast number of staff and military people, trying to anticipate committee questions. This one we hadn't anticipated.

---

* Senator Sam Nunn abstained.

Of tremendous help to me in acclimating myself to my new position—and indeed, throughout my tenure at Defense—were two outstanding assistants, Thelma Stubbs and Kay Leisz.

Thelma knew everything about the office, having served as personal assistant to seven secretaries of defense before me. From composing letters for my signature to knowing whom to let in and whom to keep out, Thelma was the one to see.

Kay was recruited by Will Taft during the transition to be my executive assistant. A native of North Dakota, she had been secretary to a North Dakota senator who was retiring. She proved extremely competent and loyal, and she has stayed with me even since I left government. I think it is fair to say that I could not have accomplished what I did at Defense, and what I have since, without Kay at my side.*

The hugeness of the job manifested itself in many ways, particularly in the early days and weeks of the administration. I was pursued by a lot of forwarded mail, and there was one letter from Dun & Bradstreet, following up on a report that I had changed my business. It was addressed to "C. Weinberger, Secretary," and they wanted some information on the new firm. A form letter asked if it was correct that I had three million full-time employees but no sales, no profits, and no net worth. I had to admit that that was what the accountants would say, but I insisted that the Defense Department had a huge net worth. I never did find out what our credit rating was.

There were more important issues to be dealt with than laundry service and filling out forms. I was already aware of the general deterioration of our military during the Carter years, but as I began

---

* After we left Defense, Kay did all the tasks for me that had been performed by five or six people in the department: making schedules; keeping me on schedule; handling travel, speech, and invitation acceptances and regrets; preparing briefing books for meetings; and so on, ad infinitum.

receiving the classified data on our capabilities, I found that it was even worse than I had thought. It was truly appalling. Our nuclear deterrent was in serious need of modernization. Our conventional forces were underbudgeted and undersupplied, with limited funds for training exercises, which meant, in short, they were unready. Steaming time for the navy had been cut back, yet operational tempo and overseas tours had been increased; flight hours for air force crews and field maneuvers for the army had been curtailed. And we were woefully short on training funds for the National Guard and reserves. Morale among military personnel was miserable, and early retirements rivaled the number of new volunteers.

Almost as bad, my briefings revealed that we were losing the respect and support of our allies because of the Carter administration's erratic policies. Moreover, both our allies and the Soviets suspected we lacked the conventional military strength—and perhaps the will—to prevent a Soviet advance into Western Europe.

In view of my reputation from California and my OMB days as a zealous budget cutter, many may have thought it odd that the president-elect would ask me to conduct and lead the great military buildup that we both knew was necessary. I had always felt that we needed to maintain a strong defense at all times. I had recognized this back in 1972, when I was director of the budget, and I made no secret of my opinion.

In a talk to the American Enterprise Institute,* I concluded my opening statement by saying, "If our defense budget is inadequate, nothing else will be of much moment, and we will only know it when it is too late."

* "The Defense Budget," *American Enterprise Institute: A Town Hall Meeting*, October 17, 1972, p. 19.

In a *U.S. News & World Report* interview that same year, I elaborated: "...none of the domestic programs we've been talking about has the slightest meaning if our borders aren't secure.

"There's another factor in defense spending that is unique. In education, in health, in welfare, and in almost every other field, what the federal government doesn't do, other levels of government or the private sector will attempt to do. The only unit of government that pays for defense is the federal government. What we don't do in defense at the national level doesn't get done."

A strong military force seemed to me even more necessary in 1980, after a decade of neglect in a hostile world.

President Reagan was also deeply concerned about America's standing in the world—and what the increasing impotence of our hollowed-out military was doing to that standing. Reagan keenly understood the importance both of military strength and of having strong, supportive allies. He said frequently to me that if it ever came down to a choice between balancing the budget and spending enough to regain and keep our military strength, he would always come down on the side of the latter.

The gap in strength between the Soviets' and our capabilities, and between the Warsaw Pact's and NATO's, had widened enormously, and that gap was still growing. The Soviets had made major increases in a decade when we had made major reductions. Beyond just the differences in numbers, I was struck by the differences between our governmental systems. In the USSR, three or four men in the Kremlin made all the decisions on allocation of all their resources, on how much they would raise and spend on their military. They were not concerned about public opinion because none was permitted in the USSR. That had given them an enormous military advantage, which we needed to recognize, and they had used it to acquire vast stores of new weapons, such as high-tech missiles, and to draft and equip huge numbers of divisions, air wings, and so forth, despite the generally wretched quality of life suffered by the Russian people. The government needed no debates and no congressional hearings, nor any votes to acquire this weaponry—only the decision of a few men responsible to no one but themselves.

All of this caused me—and President Reagan—more than a little alarm. When we took office, the first thing we did was to add $32 billion to the Carter administration's Defense budget requests for fiscal years 1981 and 1982. We were criticized for this spending, but in truth it wasn't nearly enough. We had to modernize all three legs of the strategic triad at once: our sea-based, air-based, and ground-based nuclear missiles.

I knew too that we would have to rebuild our conventional strength, including finally deploying a new and effective main battle tank, the M-1, after years of design, redesign, and indecision. We also needed additional and improved helicopters, spare parts for everything, equipment for the Rapid Deployment Force, enhanced electronic warfare capabilities, and improved intelligence capabilities. All of this and much more had to be done and done quickly. Even basic maintenance at our bases had been deferred, and deferred maintenance is one of the worst ways to reduce costs.

In addition, we had to convince our allies that we had every intention of regaining our strength and that it would be not only safe but also very much in their interest to stay with us rather than to become neutral or slide over to the other side. That would take a great deal of cultivation of all of our NATO allies, of Japan and Korea, and of our friends in the Mideast. Korea was particularly nervous because President Carter had talked about removing our troops from there. There were other countries, too, whose strength and support we would need and who would in turn need our strength.

The crucial element in this recovery of strength was people. So our most urgent task would be to address the needs of our uniformed men and women and to improve morale, thereby strengthening the volunteer system, which was failing badly. I had been told many times during my confirmation hearings that we had to have a draft. But I knew how the draft had pulled the country apart and ripped the whole social fabric during the Vietnam War. I was convinced that the volunteer system could work if we treated the men and women fairly. We had begun to get a decent salary and benefits package for military personnel through Congress, but there was more to the equation than that. People do not join the military to make money. A sense of pride had to be restored—pride in the work they were doing and in the uniforms they wore. They also had to know that they were needed and that their government and its leaders respected and admired them.[*]

Hand in hand with this, we needed to change the public image of the military, as a profession and as individuals. I began thinking of a message to all the troops, and this ultimately became my first message as secretary: "Our new president and I share a deep appreciation of the sacrifices you make and the skills with which you serve and defend all the people. One of my major priorities is to be sure that our country fully recognizes and honors your great service at home and all over the world."

The president exercised vital leadership here, making numerous appearances at military events and posts, praising, with his characteristic warmth and patriotism, the men and women in uniform who are willing to sacrifice their lives for their country. This helped enormously in changing the public's perception of our armed forces into

---

[*] One minor change that I made within the Pentagon that I believe furthered this end was to reinstate the requirement that all military personnel, regardless of rank, wear uniforms while on duty. The Carter administration, apparently not wanting to seem too militaristic, had discouraged this basic practice, thus further eroding the spirit and pride of those in the military.

one of deep appreciation and respect. It also helped raise the morale
of the troops themselves, and that improved recruiting.

Our military buildup during the Reagan administration would be
the most important part of our foreign policy, which had essentially
four major goals. The most basic, of course, was to protect our national
security—our physical borders, our citizens, and our interests abroad.

Protecting our allies was essentially an extension of this policy, as
peace-loving nations contribute to regional and global stability. We
would always need to convince our friends and allies that our interests
were mutual and that we were reliable partners.

Taking this strategy one step further, our third goal was to encourage countries trying to get out from under the yoke of Soviet
Communism.

Our fourth major policy goal, about which President Reagan felt
passionate, was to bring the Soviets to the bargaining table and
achieve real nuclear arms reductions. Our major military buildup was
instrumental in making that happen. This seemed paradoxical to
some, but if we did not have real strength, the Soviets would never
even talk to us. For peace can come only to those who are strong and
determined enough to fight for it.

The president and I rejected détente, which argued that we should
accept the Soviet Union as merely having a different political out-
look. I thought President Reagan's definition of détente was more
accurate: "a French word the Russians had interpreted as a freedom
to pursue whatever policies of subversion, aggression, and expan-
sionism they wanted anywhere in the world."* The president and I
wanted to *roll back* Communism so that the people of Eastern Europe
and elsewhere could breathe free.

Poland's Solidarity movement provided the first opportunity to do
this in the new administration. As President Reagan wrote in his

* Ronald Reagan, *An American Life* (New York: Simon & Schuster, 1990), 265.

autobiography, "We were witnessing the first fraying of the Iron Curtain, a disenchantment with Soviet Communism in Poland, not realizing then that it was a harbinger of great and historic events to come in Eastern Europe."*

At a preinaugural meeting, we reviewed the Polish situation. Since the early 1970s, there had been stirrings for freedom within Poland, which only grew stronger when John Paul II—a fervently anti-Communist Polish cardinal—was named pope in 1978, the first Polish pope. By 1981, Polish factory and shipyard workers, led by Lech Walesa, were beginning to organize trade unions to ensure basic workers' rights. But any kind of individual rights, and any form of power or authority other than the government dictatorship, was anathema to Soviet interests. The Soviets reacted predictably, with threats of brutal repression. They could not tolerate the idea of free labor unions or anyone being free of government domination.

When Poland's puppet civilian Communist leaders did not take a sufficiently hard line against Lech Walesa's Solidarity movement, the Soviets quickly replaced the civilians with a military regime. At the same time, the Soviets massed tanks and troops along the border of Poland, ready to reinforce their two resident divisions. This obvious threat of Soviet invasion I called "invasion by osmosis."

We in the Reagan administration supported Solidarity in as many ways as we could—including sharing information with the Vatican. In addition, President Reagan directly warned Soviet general secretary Leonid Brezhnev of harsh economic sanctions if Moscow intervened militarily.

On December 13, 1981, the puppet government in Poland, now headed by General Wojciech Jaruzelski (whom I called a "Soviet general in a Polish uniform"), arrested Solidarity leaders and imposed martial law in an operation orchestrated by the Soviets.

* Ibid., 301.

President Reagan imposed sanctions on Poland and the Soviet Union, but he also ordered that financial and material assistance be sent to the Solidarity movement. We also gave them information, communicated largely through Radio Free Europe and the Voice of America. We even provided equipment and support for the publication of a small underground newspaper and encouraged labor organizations in the United States to support Solidarity.

I recalled that at that first meeting on Poland, I had told the president that while our conclusions were correct, he should know that we could not stop the Soviets by threats or strong messages, much less by any military maneuvering, if they insisted on going ahead against Poland. He had said, "Cap, I know that, and we must never be in this position again. We must regain our military strength quickly if we want to secure any kind of peace."

President Reagan's strategy worked and proved crucial in the eventual collapse of the Iron Curtain. The sanctions squeezed Poland's economy to the point where the Polish government, fearing for its very survival, capitulated to U.S. demands, released its political prisoners, and agreed to allow Solidarity to exist and grow without interference or retribution.* This was the beginning of the end of Soviet-dominated Eastern Europe.

All of the great results of President Reagan's foreign policy initiatives went far beyond what any of us had imagined when we took office back on that cold January day in 1981. Supporting democratic movements in Eastern Europe, while at the same time applying economic pressure on the countries' Communist leaders, was not the only effective aspect of his foreign policy. Securing real reductions in nuclear arms was another unique accomplishment.

It was clear that President Reagan understood that weak nations have no influence at the negotiating table and that any agreement

---

* Sanctions were lifted in January 1987.

reached from a position of weakness would provide an illusory kind of security at best. Any effective arms reduction agreement would now have to include reductions in real forces and capabilities, and not just be an agreement that resulted in nothing more than a photo opportunity. As the president said many times, he believed in peace through strength, not peace through a piece of paper. It was all the more imperative that we regain a deterrent capability, no matter how long it would take and no matter how unpopular. Thereby we would let the Soviets (and any other potential aggressors) know that a nuclear war could not be won and must never be fought.

For most of the 1980s, Soviet Communism constituted a very real—and indeed our greatest—threat, militarily and morally. Those who were anxious to sign any kind of agreement labeled "arms control" viewed our efforts as overly dire, alarmist, and simplistic. But it seemed crystal clear to me that the USSR was bent on world domination, as evidenced by its writings, doctrines, and actions, particularly its acquisition of a huge military capability designed to achieve that domination.

That such Soviet plans existed was made quite explicit by a speech Mikhail Gorbachev delivered at Vladivostok in 1986, in which he spoke of the Soviet Union's determination to be a major player in the whole Pacific region. That speech was largely ignored by those who regarded Gorbachev as a great peacemaker and who still felt we could easily coexist with the Soviets. Gorbachev's speech had been preceded by the huge expansions the USSR made to the base we had built at Cam Ranh Bay during the Vietnam War, its acquisition of so-called fishing rights far south in the Pacific, and a number of other actions that indicated that its permanent goal was a continued increase in both its nuclear and conventional arms far beyond anything needed for what its apologists called its understandable fear of having its homeland attacked. The Soviets were plainly arming and preparing for aggressive action. If you move out with forward "defenses" so far that on one side you encompass, for example, most of the Pacific, or a good bit of Europe on the other side, then you are clearly not simply trying to protect your border.

This approach ran counter to the image many Americans had at that time of Mr. Gorbachev, the Soviet Union's new leader. Indeed, he was more dynamic and visible and familiar with our media than the old, stodgy apparatchiks to whom we were accustomed, but his outward persona belied his real intentions, which were steeped in traditional Communist doctrines and goals that he has never repudiated.

By the end of my service in 1987, I had seen his many attempts to capture a favorable world opinion. This was new. The Soviets had never worried about that before. But a public relations campaign is a long way from changing fundamental behavior or ultimate goals. I did not believe that they were becoming a kinder, gentler country that we could trust, as many people hoped and wanted to believe.

This worry about whether the Soviets could be trusted—indeed our worry about the whole concept of the unverifiable Anti-ballistic Missile (ABM) Treaty, with its reliance on philosophical assumptions about Soviet behavior rather than on actual defenses—was one of the major factors that led the president to embrace the concept of strategic defense. This concept was, essentially, a shield that could destroy incoming missiles in their ascent phase or before they reentered the earth's atmosphere or reached their targets. The president announced his Strategic Defense Initiative, or SDI, in March 1983. This change of strategy offered mankind the hope of deterring a nuclear attack by military defenses rather than by relying on guesses as to what the Soviets might think or do.

When we signed the ABM Treaty in 1972, we gave up any hope of being able to destroy or defend against Soviet missiles. But the Soviets themselves pursued their own strategic defense program for nearly two decades, starting right after they signed that treaty, without any regard to the fact that their actions violated it.

We, on the other hand, complied with the ABM Treaty, doing nothing to acquire any effective defenses until 1983. After President Reagan's proposal and the beginning of our research, a large amount of time was spent debating whether *any* attempt to defend ourselves and our allies was permitted under the treaty. We could easily use Article XV of the ABM Treaty to end our participation in it and change the defenseless position we had been in ever since 1972. Most of this debate, led by the largely Democratic Congress, was an attempt to block us from proceeding with SDI, even though, as I noted, the Soviets had been working on a similar system for years.

The president began winning nuclear weapon reductions with the Intermediate Nuclear Forces (INF) Treaty signed in December 1987. We secured that because we were patient about it and because we negotiated from renewed strength. The treaty had its roots in the so-called zero option that I had proposed to the president, with which he had wholeheartedly agreed, in the fall of 1981. It was a simple proposal: if the Soviets would take out their SS-20 missiles, which could hit any target in Europe and many in Asia, we would not deploy our Pershing IIs, which could reach targets inside the Soviet Union.

What had changed between the time of our original zero-option proposal in 1981 and the INF agreement reached in 1987? By 1987, we had deployed the Pershing IIs and ground-launched cruise missiles in Europe, and we were negotiating from a vastly stronger conventional military position. Despite fierce Soviet opposition to our missile deployment, NATO had held firm. And we had continued to modernize our strategic nuclear forces and to work on SDI. Throughout six years of negotiating, President Reagan never grew desperate for "an arms control agreement" to decorate his presidency. He wanted the right agreement and refused to bargain away SDI, which was the keystone of his strategic vision.

Despite our internal division and the strong, bitter opposition from many followers of the old conventional wisdom both inside and outside of the administration, I also was convinced that SDI was a key factor in negotiating arms reductions and, indeed, in securing peace and freedom. I was particularly concerned with the Soviets' evident desire to force us to give up SDI so that they could keep their monopoly. I was very concerned that we might give in on SDI in return for some sort of chimerical arms reduction agreement, which the Soviets—or even our own State Department—might be able to persuade the president to go along with. These views led to the impression that I opposed all arms reduction agreements, whereas my position was that I wanted a good one, not just any agreement such as the Strategic Arms Limitation Treaty (SALT), which actually permitted an *increase* in strategic arms. I was perfectly willing to walk away from negotiations, as the president also proved to be, unless we achieved the kind of agreement we wanted.

Ironically, many saw my resignation in November 1987, just before the INF Treaty was signed, as a protest against the agreement.* Hardly anyone seemed to remember that I was the one who had proposed its general provisions in the first place in 1981 and that virtually everyone else in the media, think tanks, and government had opposed the idea.

There is no better example of the importance of negotiating from strength than the INF Treaty; there is no better argument for President Reagan's defense policies than the signing of that treaty.

The lesson of the INF Treaty is that we can secure our own modest agenda, which is simply peace and freedom for ourselves and our allies, only if we are militarily strong. Further, we needed to be militarily secure enough to resist aggression from the Soviets, or now from other sources, which could flame into action quickly.

---

* The only reason I left office when I did was because of my wife's health.

The INF Treaty should, and I think will, stand as a monument to President Reagan's determination to regain our military strength and to put his desire for a treaty that is in American interests far ahead of the political clamor for an agreement no matter what it may provide.

Our military buildup had an economic impact as well. The Soviets' desperate attempts to keep ahead of our greatly improved military capability added to their already serious economic woes. Indeed, some of the earliest intelligence briefings we received after we took office indicated that, even at that point, the Soviet economy was in deep trouble. Following his instincts, which were supported by many of his national security advisers, including myself, President Reagan determined to take advantage of Communism's inherent weaknesses—chief among them the lack of free-market incentives. As President Reagan wrote in his autobiography, "You had to wonder how long the Soviets could keep their empire intact. If they didn't make some changes, it seemed clear to me that in time Communism would collapse of its own weight, and I wondered how we as a nation could use these cracks in the Soviet system to accelerate the process of collapse."*

To that end, we and some of our allies squeezed credit to the Soviets; we restricted the transfer of militarily useful technology; and among our Solidarity sanctions against Moscow was an embargo on equipment the Soviets needed to build their trans-Siberian natural gas pipeline. President Reagan also, of course, used the bully pulpit of the Voice of America, Radio Liberty, Radio Free Europe, and the U.S. Information Agency to launch an ideological assault on Communism and to promote the democratic aspirations of the people of Eastern Europe.

From the earliest days of his administration, President Reagan made a concerted effort, as part of a coherent overall strategy, to win the

---

* *An American Life,* 238.

Cold War and consign the Soviet system to "the ash heap of history." His many critics thought this was an impossibility. And indeed, without Ronald Reagan's strategic clarity, moral courage, firmness, and determination, it might very well have proved impossible. Luckily, Reagan was there, and I was proud to be at his side.

CHAPTER 16

DAY-TO-DAY IN THE DOD

*S*uch was the grand strategy and greatest foreign policy accomplishment of the Reagan administration. But my day-to-day work as secretary of defense covered much else besides. It was arduous but immensely fulfilling work. The physical office of the secretary was imposing in its spaciousness and simplicity. A large desk dominated the room; all of the other furnishings were modest in comparison—mahogany, upholstered chairs; a small round conference table; a formal couch. Behind the desk was a large table on which rested the massive telephone console, and above that loomed a dour portrait of James Forrestal, the first secretary of defense. He looked almost destined for his tragic end, when he took his own life at Bethesda Naval Hospital. So on almost my first day in office, I had his portrait removed and replaced it (courtesy of my friend Carter Brown, head of the National Gallery of Art) with a richly colored Titian portrait of a cardinal gracefully bestowing a beneficence. I found him much more agreeable and soothing to the soul, and the colors were a continuing inspiration. Most of the other walls were blank and it took time to add pictures of my own choice.*

The whole atmosphere became more comfortable as I settled in and added some of my own items. Proud specimens from my elephant collection lined the front of my desk. From the service museums, I borrowed quite an impressive fleet of model airplanes and ships, which occupied the windowsills and back table. I also obtained a bust of General Douglas MacArthur and one of a typical infantryman, both of which I found reminiscent and inspiring. I also wanted to make it clear that our administration was not worried about being thought of as "too militaristic."

Some features of my new job took a bit of getting used to. For one thing, I had never seen, much less used, such an elaborate telephone board. There were numerous outside lines, as well as lines that connected directly to my executive assistants, the deputy secretary and undersecretaries of defense, the Joint Chiefs, the service secretaries, the major commands, and the White House, and even the proverbial red phone—a hotline to the president himself. All of these were secure, presumably untappable lines to prevent eavesdropping or interception, possibilities to which I had never given much thought, except for a brief, unpleasant time during the days of the White House plumbers when I was at OMB.

The importance of genuine security was emphasized to a much greater degree at Defense than in any of my previous positions. I certainly understood and vigorously advocated the need to safeguard military information, be it in the form of intelligence, operational plans,

---

* Each president is permitted to borrow pieces from the National Gallery of Art with which to decorate the White House during his tenure. I am not sure if this privilege officially extended to cabinet members, but Carter was a good friend, and he generously allowed the Titian to reside in my Pentagon office all seven years I was there. A magazine story about my office did not quite get it right: "Behind his desk hangs the famous picture 'Titian and Associate.'"

technical data, or any other aspect. What was difficult for me to get used to was that my personal safety—I "knew too much" to be allowed to be kidnapped—was also a major concern. I had never felt that I was in any kind of danger, and my lack of fear—or perhaps lack of common sense—more than once agitated the fine Defense Department security agents who had the unenviable task of protecting me.

I was often criticized, particularly in budget arguments, for using an air force plane when I traveled, especially to my home in Maine. That was necessary for exactly the same reasons: as the second person in the national military chain of command, I had to have access to secure communications at all times, day or night, wherever I was. Also, being the repository of so many of the nation's secrets, I was told early on how important it was that I not be taken hostage from a commercial plane, or from my home, or while out walking, or anywhere.

On one early trip to Bonn, West German officials suggested that it would be safer if I were taken to a secluded area in the countryside for my daily jog. My security detail agreed, but I thought the idea absurd—a waste of time, gas, and personnel—when I could easily jog around the neighborhood near my hotel. I was overruled, and so we jogged through a lovely forest. (Perhaps the Germans simply wanted me to go elsewhere because my jogging suit was considered too old and clearly not chic.)

On another European stop, I caused considerable panic among my security contingent when I instinctively jumped out of my limousine in a motorcade to help a police officer who had been knocked off his motorcycle in a minor traffic accident. We succeeded in freeing him from his fallen motorcycle, but I was immediately hustled back into the car.

Even in the United States, spontaneity was precluded by security requirements. Such normal activities as visiting an art gallery or bookstore, or grocery shopping, could not be done without extensive preparations: not only did agents have to accompany me, they also had to check out the route and destination ahead of time, sometimes even sending dogs in to sniff out the place.

It took some time for me to get used to all of these restrictions and precautions, but I know they were necessary, particularly when various threats were received through foreign intelligence sources. I knew that all of the men and women whose job it was to protect me did so in exemplary fashion, undoubtedly making ineffective any threats, potential and real, and I did not want to add to their problems by being "difficult."

I soon settled into a regular schedule—that is, as regular a schedule as it is possible to have when you are working with ever changing situations and fluid events. I would generally arrive at the office around 7 A.M., where a CIA courier would brief me with the President's Daily Briefing. As the name suggests, this was a summary of the most sensitive intelligence that was compiled every night for the president. The briefing was shown to only a handful of officials involved in national security, and it was always first on the agenda. The actual document was never left with anyone—the briefer read or summarized the report and I was able to look it over every morning while the high-ranking courier waited and expanded on various parts of the PDB, as it was called. It was a very valuable, excellently written and edited group of concise intelligence reports, and a summary analyzing important developing situations. I always received the briefing no matter where I was. I have been told that Mr. Clinton did not bother with it, designating the national security adviser or someone else to receive it.

Then, at 8 A.M., I would have a staff meeting, which was held in my office and generally included the deputy secretary of defense, the undersecretaries, and the department spokesman, as well as the assistant secretary for legislative affairs, the assistant secretaries for policy and international affairs, and of course the military assistant to the secretary. The purpose of these meetings was essentially to prepare for the day's activities and to discuss the status of ongoing projects and any late developments or crises. This was the only formal staff meeting scheduled each day, but I would consult with the deputy secretary, in person or on the phone, ten, twelve, maybe fifteen times throughout the course of the day; the physical layout of the offices lent itself to that sort of thing.

I felt that the deputy secretary was an alter ego to the secretary and that both should be fully engaged in all aspects of the department, not responsible for separate sets of issues. A true deputy is a person who is able to take over when the secretary is out of town, ill, or disabled, without any break-in period or major change in duties.

I was fortunate to have some very fine people serving in this position, particularly Frank Carlucci and, later, Will Taft. I had worked with both of them in the Nixon administration,* and I recruited both to come with me to Defense. They were completely dedicated, extremely able public servants and very good friends.

There was some difficulty getting Frank confirmed. Many conservatives in Congress, and some in the White House, were wary of him simply because he had served in the CIA as deputy director during the Carter administration. Although he had been appointed by Carter, his was not a political position. But despite this, and notwithstanding that he had also served most effectively in posts under Presidents Nixon and Ford, a few Republicans tended to view him as one whose loyalty to President Reagan was questionable. Some also were concerned (as they had been with me) that Frank would not take a strong enough stand for defense. The vote, and even the debate, on

---

* Frank had been my deputy at OMB and undersecretary at HEW. Will Taft had been one of my first law clerks at the FTC and my executive assistant at OMB and HEW.

his nomination was held up for weeks, and many tried to persuade me to drop the effort. Both because I wanted Frank for the deputy and because it would be a very bad start to give in, I stayed firm, as, of course, did the president.

At the same time, some strict conservatives in the White House felt that Will Taft was also too liberal and that if he were to be appointed as general counsel, as I was insisting, he had to be balanced by an appointment of the former director of the Arms Control and Disarmament Agency, Fred Iklé, who was considered a true-blue conservative.

Finally, after some persuasive calls from President Reagan and some get-acquainted meetings with Frank and Will, the vote was allowed to proceed. They were confirmed in early February 1981 (as was Iklé). They all performed extraordinarily well. Frank and Will both had the tremendous capacity and willingness to work endless hours, and both were able to grasp quickly all of the policy issues, as well as the more arcane technical and procedural aspects involved in whatever post they were assigned. Fred Iklé was both conservative and extremely knowledgeable about all the details of our international responsibilities. He too became a good and most loyal and able friend.

Also at Defense, I had the privilege of knowing and working with Richard Armitage, who had absolutely encyclopedic knowledge of many of the foreign countries we dealt with, as well as longtime friendships with many of the governmental leaders and ambassadors of those countries. Of equal significance was his complete appreciation of the importance of these relationships and alliances to the United States—something that many of his colleagues at Defense and, particularly, the State Department never seemed to share. From time to time, on my visits abroad, I was complimented on my knowledge of some of these countries, their history, and our long-term relationships with them. If any of these compliments was deserved, it was owed entirely to my patient and extraordinarily able tutor, Rich

Armitage. In his present post as deputy secretary of state, Rich is, I am sure, giving the same extremely skilled and brilliant advice to Secretary Colin Powell.

Most days, after the regular staff meeting, I met with the chairman of the Joint Chiefs of Staff. No one attained this position without excellent credentials and distinguished performance in a long military career. Three extremely competent men served as chairman during my tenure, and I feel that I worked very well with each of them.

General David Jones, of the air force, was a holdover from the previous administration, but even before I took office or knew him, I recommended that he be allowed to serve out his term, and the president agreed. I thought it might appear that we were politicizing this most important position in our military if the new president changed chairmen as his first act. Jones was an able man, but I never felt that he was quite as comfortable with me as his successors were.

General Jack Vessey, who became chairman in the summer of 1982, was a fellow army man who had served in World War II. We shared several bonds like that, and he was a delightful, warm human being and a great soldier. I have rarely worked with anyone for whom I had greater respect and admiration. General Vessey was a National Guard sergeant from Minnesota. He was given a rare battlefield commission for extreme bravery and skill on Anzio Beach.

I had known Jack Vessey's successor, Admiral Bill Crowe, for many years, from the time he was our commander in chief in the Pacific, and felt completely at ease with him. I was pleased that he was chairman for my last two years at the Pentagon. I know that he felt we should make more of an effort at rapprochement with the Soviets than I did, but he was loyal to my policies.

I met with all of the Joint Chiefs together at least once a week in their conference room on the first floor, which was called the Tank. That is also where we met with the president when he came to the Pentagon to meet with the chiefs.

I feel that General Colin Powell deserves mention here, even though he did not chair the Joint Chiefs until the Bush administration, after I had left government. Of course, most people are familiar with him from his invaluable leadership during the Gulf War, but I was impressed with him long before that. When I was at HEW, I helped in selecting him to be a White House fellow, and he was my military assistant when I was at Defense. In both cases, I saw that one of his principal assets was that he clearly knew more about the subject matter of almost any meeting than did any of the other participants. He also knew exactly what had to be accomplished at each meeting, and as a result he was able to participate in the most effective way possible. His subsequent career is so well known that it requires no additional elaboration from me. Suffice it to say that his appointment as secretary of state by President George W. Bush was, I think, quite properly received with universal acclaim and immediate confirmation.

Every Tuesday, I received a full military intelligence briefing in the National Military Command Center (NMCC). The NMCC was a large, two-story room with a semicircular table and places for each participant. There were elaborate phones at each console and several large display screens for the various slides used in presentations. This briefing was particularly valuable, covering, as it did, the world.

In addition, I met every Thursday with the service secretaries. I do not know if my predecessors or successors followed this pattern, but these meetings ensured that I had regular input from each branch of the military and that they all had the opportunity to bring their views and concerns to me directly. They also allowed me to make better informed program and procurement decisions based on the overall picture. Some critics said that I blindly signed off on everything the services requested, but as I am sure all the services would confirm, this was simply not the case. I made every effort to minimize redundancy in weapons systems or missions, while always bearing in mind

our constant goal of securing as quickly as possible a strong and unified military force that could fight effectively and win on at least two
fronts simultaneously if necessary.

One service secretary who particularly impressed me was Jim
Webb—a marine through and through, with a stellar record of service in the Vietnam War. I strongly recommended to President
Reagan that he appoint Jim as secretary of the navy, which he did in
1987. Jim has always been, even more than I, sickened by the contempt with which Vietnam veterans were treated when they returned
home from that war. We both feel that combat in service to one's
country should be honored, and Jim does not have much tolerance
for critics who have not been in the military themselves. His understanding of the navy and his recognition of the support the military
deserves and needs from its leaders served him well in the Pentagon
and impressed me in our meetings. He is also a superb writer; his
Fields of Fire is one of the great novels of the Vietnam War.

Often, while listening to presentations and discussions in these
various meetings, I would, as had long been my habit, close my eyes
because I find that I think and concentrate better with my eyes
closed. Early on, some of the briefing presenters and other participants were disconcerted by this, unsure if they should continue talking while, as they feared, I might be asleep. But when they found that
I was hearing everything they were saying and I could ask relevant
follow-up questions, they learned to proceed with confidence, if not
a little amusement.

Of course, on rare occasions, I actually was asleep, an inevitable
by-product of frequent eighteen-hour workdays. Some attributed this
to jet lag, but I really do not think I have ever experienced jet lag.
I can sleep through a meeting whether I've been flying or not.
President Reagan was fond of telling the story of the time when we
were viewing an exhibit of weapons captured during our rescue invasion into Grenada. The president remarked that it was eye-opening

to see all of this, and as the news camera zoomed in on me—sound asleep—the commentator said, "Except, apparently, to Secretary Weinberger."

Another weekly meeting I established was a breakfast with Bill Casey, director of central intelligence. Bill was much underestimated by his critics. He had a quick and penetrating mind and great intellectual interests, and was an avid and encyclopedic reader. He even wrote a very competent history of the American Revolution. He was also skilled in the ways of Washington and in dealing with large bureaucracies and numerous presidential aides. He was deeply conservative and constantly aware of the Soviet threat to freedom. He was no appeaser. He and I worked very well together for all the years he was in Washington, starting with his leadership of the Export-Import Bank when I was at HEW. He had also, of course, performed yeoman service as manager of President Reagan's campaign for the presidency.

Every Wednesday when we were both in town, I would have a working breakfast with the secretary of state—first Al Haig, then George Shultz. We alternated these breakfasts between the State Department and the Pentagon. The two departments were probably in agreement more often than most people have been led to believe. The policy matters on which we differed—whether we should have been back in Beirut, whether we should be more conciliatory with the Soviets, when to use military force, and things of that kind—were played up and emphasized more than the many issues on which we concurred.

There are of course some inherent differences between Foggy Bottom and the Pentagon. I think that the State Department generally, and George Shultz in particular, felt that there was value in any American military presence, whether it was capable of winning any battles or not, or whether there were any battles to be fought. So State was much more ready than we were to deploy our troops. It is probably easier for people to advocate using military forces if they do not have the responsibility for the care and safety of the troops, as I did. I also felt keenly that we should not wander into any situation or conflict unless we felt it was important enough to win. We should define our mission carefully—and then go in with overwhelming force to ensure victory.

I also advocated bringing massive strength to bear on a narrow front in policy as well as in military terms. I did not feel that we should enter into any arms reduction agreement just to secure an agreement. I thought it was much more important to have a good agreement, and I was not sympathetic to the cry that we did not care about arms control because we had not signed an agreement during our first years. When we did sign the INF agreement with the Soviets in 1987—after patiently sitting out the criticisms, protests, and public demands—it eliminated an entire category of deadly weapons: the intermediate-range nuclear forces.

I had known George Shultz for a long time and had worked with him many times, and in spite of our differences of opinion, we both did our best to carry out the president's desires. We had quite different styles but I think we were sincerely trying to secure good long-run objectives.

Personality differences were most apparent when Al Haig was secretary of state early in the administration. From day one, he made his presence known. On January 20, 1981, while the inaugural parade was still going on, he attempted to get my approval for a sweeping set of procedures under which the State Department would preside at practically every intergovernmental meeting. He was very conscious of his time in the Nixon White House, when he had participated in taking duties away from the State Department. Now he wanted to get them back. Similarly, though he had been a powerful White House staff member, now he regularly fought against a powerful White House staff, presumably because he saw how that undercut cabinet secretaries. He had had a most impressive military career and had been a fine Supreme Allied commander in Europe; it was apparent he wanted to be a "supreme" cabinet member as well.

This apparent desire for power eventually caused him a bit of a public relations problem on the day of the assassination attempt against President Reagan. The first intimation I received that something was seriously amiss was when I was meeting in my office about 2:30 P.M. with Bobby Inman, then deputy director of central intelligence, who was giving me a general briefing. Kay Leisz gave me a message to hurry to the White House Situation Room as soon as possible. My driver had been given the afternoon off since I had no other scheduled appointments, so Bobby offered to drive me over. When we located his rather ancient car in the parking lot, we picked up what we could on the radio. Later it struck me as quite ironic that two people with major responsibilities in the security area received their information about this most vital happening in the new administration in this rather archaic way. When we reached the White House and convinced the various sentries to admit this rather "unofficial" car, I went to the Situation Room. I looked up at the TV monitor and wondered aloud why it was showing old clips of an Al Haig press conference. "Those aren't old clips," someone said. "That's Al. He's up there." He was trying to reassure the American people that because he was in charge while we waited for news about the president, the ship of state was not adrift. When Al came back downstairs to the Situation Room, he challenged my telling the chairman of the Joint Chiefs of Staff to have strategic air crews moved from their alert quarters to the planes themselves. I mentioned that Ed Meese, calling from the hospital, had confirmed that the "national command authority" rested with me as secretary of defense and that the orders to Al Haig were to "calm other governments." Al kept insisting that I should "read the Constitution." I believe he was relying on an older order of succession—president, vice president, secretary of state— that had been in effect as a law (but not in the Constitution itself) until 1947. Al was seemingly unaware that the secretary of state was not in fact next in the chain of succession after the vice president.*

In any event, and conceding the strains of that day, it should be said that Al was a dynamic and colorful member of the administration, and one who made many valuable contributions to it.

He was strong, ambitious, and knowledgeable, but he also could be quite abrasive, and he fiercely opposed anyone else's discussing foreign policy matters before the president. The president, on the other hand, just as when he was governor, liked his cabinet members to talk freely, even on issues outside their specific responsibilities.

My own relations with the White House were, for the most part, less dramatic than Al's. I frequently discussed matters with the national security adviser and asked to have my views presented, but if I wanted to go to the president directly, I did. Yet I did not feel I had to meet with the president every day just to demonstrate that I could.

When Dick Allen, Bill Clark, and, later, Frank Carlucci headed the National Security Council, this arrangement worked well. Unfortunately, that was not the case with Robert McFarlane, who did not want my input to the president to interfere with his own agenda. It was that agenda which sadly led to the so-called Iran-contra debacle. More on that unhappy tale later.

From the beginning of the administration, I decided that the best way to keep the president apprised of Defense Department activities without monopolizing his time or relying on intermediaries to pass my thoughts along was to send him regular summaries. So began my practice of writing weekly reports to the president. These were a slightly expanded version of the mini-memos that had worked so

---

* See Richard Allen's "The Day Reagan Was Shot" in the *Atlantic Monthly*, April 2001, pages 64 to 68, for the best account of that whole episode. Allen's article is based on the only tape recording made at the time and is an invaluable bit of history.

well in his gubernatorial days: two or three pages covering eight to ten issues—everything from training exercises and performance reviews on new weapons, to the status of our budget in Congress, to my trips and meetings with foreign officials. A staff man was assigned to select major topics to be included, but in large part I wrote (and always edited) these reports myself, because I wanted the president to have my unvarnished views.

Besides keeping the president informed, I felt it was also important, as much as possible, to let the American people know what we were trying to do and why we had to do it. It is the natural instinct of most people in a democracy, save in wartime, not to want their tax dollars spent on the military. Consequently, I gave far more speeches and appeared on television far more often than I wanted to. I preferred the most direct way to reach the public because I could express our policy objectives with a minimum of editorial screening. Press conferences and press interviews, in contrast, frequently passed through the filter of the reporter's own opinion. Still, plenty of press conferences had to be given. Sometimes one of the Pentagon press secretaries, Henry Catto, followed these by announcing, "What the secretary *meant* to say was. . . ." So my press conferences sometimes went through a double filter. I often joked that I had to read the *Washington Post* to see what I was thinking that day.

I admit that in those speeches for which formal texts had been released, I often wandered from what was written, preferring a more off-the-cuff approach, but the basic content, and certainly the facts, remained unchanged. Still, I gained the reputation among reporters of being a "textual deviate."

Much of my time was spent testifying before congressional committees—and I spent even more time preparing for them. The intense "practice" sessions, in which my staff would grill me (often in a rather hostile manner, for maximum realism), were somewhat appropriately called "murder boards." They covered everything from weapons systems to strategy to the line items in our budget request. It was the same preparation I had used at both OMB and HEW, and that preparation was, for me, a vital part of every hearing.

Dealing with Congress was, unfortunately, often contentious—especially because having a credible deterrent and the capability of defending American interests around the world is expensive, and military spending in a democracy is never popular. As every writer since Montesquieu has noted, people in democracies generally have pacific natures and are not interested in—and in many cases are repelled by—subjects such as weapons capabilities, military strategy, and the like. Besides, they would rather have their funds spent on something else, or preferably not spent at all.

The real problem, as I repeatedly said, is that if we want to remain at peace, we have to be able to deter any attack that might be made against us or our allies. The potential attacker must *know* that we have that ability. With respect to nuclear weapons, I never subscribed to the theory embodied in the ABM Treaty—essentially, that the only way to be completely safe from nuclear attack is to be completely vulnerable. A credible deterrent is essential for us to be truly protected.

Having a defensive strategy, with no plan to attack anybody, is a much heavier burden to carry before Congress than having an offensive strategy. A defensive strategy has to cede to the other side the time, place, and manner of attack and, ultimately, the battle. That puts a higher premium on preparedness and on acquiring the tools necessary to deter or defeat *any* kind of attack. This was often difficult to get across to some members of Congress.* Fortunately, enough of them knew the importance of rebuilding our military capabilities to enable us to pull ourselves up out of the danger zone after a few years of vastly increased spending. I am convinced that if we had had

* I was once chided by a senator for "coming back here and asking for more when we were not attacked last year."

a mere 2 percent annual real increase in military spending during the 1970s, we would not have had the herculean rebuilding job we had to do in the 1980s to regain a credible deterrent.

All of the varied activities I have described thus far represent only a fraction of my responsibilities as secretary of defense. There were also cabinet meetings, National Security Council meetings, budget discussions, visits to various military units and installations at home and abroad, presentations of awards, and foreign visitors to be received, negotiated with, and entertained, to say nothing of dealing with crises that presented themselves without the slightest regard for schedules or plans. Perhaps the best way to convey how many different kinds of things went on, on any given day, is to show entries for a few sample days from the daily summaries that I wrote (complete with my own "shorthand," explained in brackets, and some editing for a more general understanding):*

July 30, 1982
Driven to CIA

Saw CIA courier at CIA

Breakfast with Bill Casey, Frank Carlucci, Jack McMahon

Saw Frank Carlucci re budget and pay caps for military and [Richard] Perle's travels

In office 9 A.M.–12:45 P.M.
Called Dr. Taylor re sore heel and blood test

Presided at staff meeting

Bob Gray and Barrett of USO in office [re health appointments]

---

* I began keeping such notes during my early law office days, when we were required to account for our time so clients could be properly billed. Keeping these summaries became such a fully ingrained habit that I scarcely remembered doing it—of which more later.

[Military Assistant] Carl Smith in office re ceremony for astronauts

[Protocol officer] COL Tiplady in office re same

Astronauts on shuttle flights in office for photographs

Presented medals to astronauts at ceremony

Saw Marybel Batjer re health appointment & USO request

Saw COL Tiplady re dinner for George Shultz & swearing-in ceremonies for General Gabriel & Admiral Watkins

Called Sen. Domenici in Albuquerque—out, lw [left word]

Called Carl Smith to get data for Sen. Schmitt

General Vessey, Carl Smith, Frank in office—re possible USSR reading of our signals from SAC exercises; also re Honduran-Nicaragua air maneuvers; departure of Winston Lord

Iran still being thrown back by Iraqi Army; our intelligence reports & Gulf of Sidra exercise—I want it to go forward despite Libyan threats

John Tower—wants to meet with me before conference—agreed— he doesn't know why Baker & Domenici are mad about President sticking to his original '84 & '85 Defense figures [Apparently they were under the impression that the president had told them we would not seek increases in 1984–85. But this was clearly not true.]

Called Bob Michel—out, lw

Called Del Latta—out; lw

Rich Armitage in office re preparation for meeting with President & Cong. GOP leadership on Taiwan

Attended Int'l Economic Policy Group on pipeline in USSR and related issues—in WH—Don Regan [there]

Attended meeting of President & GOP Senators & Congressmen— on Taiwan—no change either in our policy or our obligation to maintain Taiwan's defense qualitatively & quantitatively

In office 2:30 P.M.–7:20 P.M.

Met with Jack Marsh, Frank Carlucci, Shy Meyer, Korb, etc. re women in Army—no quotas—no combat for women

Met with new Ambassador from Philippines Romauldez—President
Marcos visit in Sept still on

Army doctors in office—for new blood pressure tests & my sore heel

Cong. Latta rmc [returning my call]—from Ohio—says he agrees no
bad faith on President's part in staying with his '84 & '85 Defense budget

Sen. Domenici from Albuquerque—rmc—same

Called Bill Clark—re Gandhi dinner—GPS [Shultz] Dinner Aug 9—
he can't come; my letter to John Nott [U.K. minister of defence]; my
visit to Israel & meeting with Shamir; VP to swear in General Gabriel &
Admiral Watkins

Ginny Duncan from SF (2)—re Corporation for Public Broadcasting post

Called RJ [my wife—Rebecca Jane] in Somesville

Carl Smith in office (2) re Weekly Report to President

Fred Iklé—to get report on pipeline meeting

Attended dinner of Mrs. Gandhi's for VP Geo Bush—[attendees:]
Mrs. Gandhi's son Rajiv, George Shultz, Kay Graham, etc. Saw Bob
Michel—he agrees there was no misleading by President in retaining his
'84 & '85 Defense budget

Called Arlin in SF

Called RJ in Somesville

April 10, 1984

In office 7:05 A.M.–3:35 P.M.

Saw Colin Powell re [Nestor Sanchez and] continuing stories that we
have contingency plans to put troops into Cent. Am.

CIA courier in office

Attended Intelligence Operations briefing in NMCC [National
Military Command Center]

Presided at staff meeting

Called Colin Powell re General Chain going to State—will speak to
General Gabriel & Jack Vessey

Secure conf. call—Bud McFarlane, Shultz, Bill Casey—McFarlane wants to put out joint statement to stop false stories on "plans" to put troops in Cent. Am. & mining of harbors in Nicaragua

Held Press Conf.—in PA [Public Affairs] studios on release of *Soviet Military Power*

Held satellite Press Conf. with Brussels & European press corps in PA studios re same

Called Bud McFarlane—out; lw

Saw Colin Powell—re [Nestor Sanchez's] stmt's that we do have contingency plans for Cent. Am.

Full Honors ceremony for Sheik Salem al Sabah—MOD [Minister of Defense] of Kuwait

Met with him in office

Gave lunch for Sheik al Sabah

Richard Goldman—SF—in office—he has joined AIPAC [American Israel Public Affairs Committee]—wants me to make talks to Jewish groups

Herb Klein in office—wants me to see Sidle report on press relations and the military & put recommendations into effect—told him we had a Media Advisory Group to review that. [This was a group I appointed to make recommendations for our press relations, including forming a small pool of reporters when military situations did not permit mass coverage of combat, etc.] Also he hopes no action will be taken v. [against] Capt of Rangers

Met with Joint Chiefs in Tank—re our ability to monitor Soviet missile tests—not good—we can't break encryption yet

Taped interview with Steve Bell at ABC—for *Nightline*—on *Soviet Military Power* & Cent. Am.

Attended signing ceremony in Oval Office by President of Bill Archer's tax bill for deceased soldiers

Saw Bud McFarlane—approved joint statement on Nicaragua & El Salvador

In office 5:10 P.M.–6:35 P.M.

Colin Powell in office (2) re Bernie Rogers' objections to WH desire for plane for Poindexter group. Told him we had to follow WH; also re keeping records on search for Vietnam Unknown—most agreed no need to keep records

Shultz—wants General Chain

General Chain in office—he wants to take State job

Attended reception for Defense Minister of Kuwait at Kuwait Embassy

Attended dinner at British Embassy for 1st Sea Lord—[attendees:] Sen. Warner, Cong. Sam Stratton & John Whitehead, etc.

A full honors ceremony is quite an impressive event. It not only is a sign of respect for an ally, but it also provides an opportunity to demonstrate the fine military forces of the United States. Such a ceremony is tendered to visiting foreign ministers, ministers of defense, and heads of state.

The basic protocol dictated that I meet the visiting dignitary—in this case, Sheik al Sabah—when he arrived in his limousine in front of the Pentagon. From there, we would proceed to the parade ground just across the road, where I would introduce him to my senior staff and the Joint Chiefs. We would then stand together on the platform while a military band marched past, playing first the visiting country's national anthem, then ours. Then, the commander of the guard would invite the visiting dignitary to inspect the honor guard and review the troops. At that point, a detachment of each of the four services would march past. When this concluded, the visiting dignitary would thank the commander, and the ceremony would be officially over.

Music would continue to play as we proceeded to the Pentagon and to my office, where we would usually have a one-on-one meeting and, quite often, a lunch given in his honor (or a formal dinner would be given later in the visit).

Soviet Military Power was an annual assessment of just that, published by the Pentagon. It helped us measure and adjust our own forces and capabilities in relation to the Soviets'—an ongoing exercise that was crucial for realistic planning and budgeting. It was also most useful in persuading some of our allies that they needed to increase their defense efforts.

November 28, 1984
In office 7:05 A.M.–11 A.M.

Saw Colin Powell re NSC proposed changes in my speech today to Press Club

Called Bud McFarlane re above

CIA courier in office to brief both Shultz & me

Breakfast with George Shultz—he wants to have regular meetings of himself, Bill Casey, Bud, and me to talk things out & try to get agreements. I told him I thought they should be with President too. Also told him I thought we had to sell F-15s to Saudis—& also that I was making Press Club speech

Called Bud McFarlane—re meeting with Shultz & further changes in speech—also that our budget is under attack

Presided at staff meeting

Attended DRB [Defense Resources Board, an internal body that reviewed our budget] meeting with CINCs [Commanders in Chief of the Unified & Specified Commands]

Ed Meese—"core group" will be presenting recommendations on cutting Defense budget at 11

Attended "core group" session in Cabinet Room with President—[OMB director] Stockman presented recommendations on cutting budget including ours

Spoke to National Press Club on "Uses of Military Power" [saw there:] Jim Fogerty of *SF Chronicle*, also a reporter for *Cleveland Plain Dealer*

Met with [Republican congressman/ranking Republican on House Armed Services Committee] Bill Dickinson in his office—with Russ Rourke—Dickinson mad he wasn't consulted last year on our budget plan

<u>In office 3:10 P.M.–7:25 P.M.</u>

Saw Colin Powell re JCS meeting

Met with DRB & CINCs

Paul Robinson in office—our amb. to Canada—he wants to be Secretary of Navy

Honduran delegation—COL Gansleer in office—general courtesy call

Jack Vessey in office re keeping helicopter ship off Lebanon but letting [carrier USS] *Eisenhower* go on regular, previously planned trip

Called Mike Burch (2) re reaction to my speech & re *LA Times* article that my speech was just to get back at Shultz—told him no

Called Ginny Duncan in SF re speech & her son John

Dick DeLauer in office—ceremonial call prior to his leaving

Spoke at farewell dinner for Dick DeLauer

Attended GOP Senators dinner—at Library of Congress

It was customary to submit to the national security adviser any speeches I planned to make, more for his information than to get his okay. Of course, changes were often suggested and sometimes were adopted.

This particular address to the National Press Club, on the uses of military power, I wrote myself because I felt that forum was an important one in which to present a synthesis of a number of ideas I had formulated over a period of time, starting with my strong disapproval of our policy in Vietnam to commit large numbers of our forces to a war we did not intend to win. In my Press Club speech, I outlined six major criteria to be weighed before committing our combat forces abroad.

First: The United States should not commit forces to combat over-seas unless the particular mission is deemed vital to our national interest or that of our allies. Our actions in Grenada and Libya while I was in office were practical examples of missions vital to our national interest.

In the early 1980s, Grenada, a small island country in the Carib-bean, became essentially a satellite of the Soviet Union and Cuba, using their help to build its military capabilities, including a huge new airfield. This in itself presented ample reason for us to be concerned, since Grenada was now basically an enemy outpost near our own borders. The political situation in Grenada deteriorated further in 1983, when an even more radical Marxist faction overthrew the gov-ernment and held a violent grip on the tiny country. This clearly threatened the safety of Americans inside Grenada* as well as the security of neighboring Caribbean nations who were friendly with the United States and were begging us to intervene.† All of these factors made it quite clearly a matter vital to our national interest.

As a result of our intervention, we successfully rescued the American medical students, captured the airport, and drove out all Cuban and other resistance.

In the case of our bombing of Libya in 1986, we were responding to indisputable evidence that Libyan terrorists had been responsible for the bombing of a West Berlin discotheque that killed and injured American military personnel. It was certainly in our national interest to demonstrate that we would not tolerate deliberate attacks on our citizens inspired, and paid for, by any other country. The United States had engaged Libya militarily on a couple of previous occasions, when

---

* Including many American students attending a U.S.-owned medical school.

† Mrs. Eugenia Charles, prime minister of Dominica, made a particularly eloquent plea to President Reagan, pointing out the very real threat Grenada's radical govern-ment (by then virtually an anarchy) posed to all of the outer Caribbean states.

Libya challenged our right to conduct regular maneuvers in the Gulf of Sidra. The Libyans claimed that this part of the Mediterranean belonged to them, when of course, it is recognized under international law as international waters. It was imperative not only that our pilots defend themselves when fired upon, but also that no country be allowed to deny any other country passage through international waters. This has been part of our policy since at least 1812.

The determination of national interest is not always as clear-cut. It is the first decision that must be made before military action is taken, because not everything we may dislike or feel is wrong amounts to a violation of our national interest serious enough to warrant the use of our troops abroad.

The *second* consideration that I laid out in my Press Club speech was that, if we decide that it is necessary to put combat troops into a given situation, we should do so wholeheartedly and with the clear intention of achieving a decisive victory. If we are unwilling to commit the forces or resources necessary to achieve our objectives, we should not commit them at all. We should never ask our people to go into battle and risk their lives for an issue that the country does not think is important enough to win—or, indeed, specifically intends *not* to win, as was the case in Vietnam. In that conflict, we went in with no particular goals or firm resolve. We committed a thousand troops one week and ten thousand the next week, and soon we were up to 565,000 with still no real plan for total victory. In fact, our government continually emphasized that our objective was never to win the war decisively, but only to "contain Communism." Containing Communism is roughly like trying to contain quicksilver by simply pushing in at the margins of the quicksilver pool.

Some question whether "winning" is a meaningful term in the nuclear age. Certainly, a nuclear war cannot be won and must never be fought, but we can win wars in the sense of convincing an opponent that he should not attempt a nuclear strike. In the Cold War, we won every day that the USSR or any other nuclear power did not launch an attack.

Third: If we do decide to commit forces to combat overseas, we should have clearly defined political and military objectives. We should know precisely how our forces can accomplish those objectives, and we should send forces capable of achieving them. Otherwise, there will be no real measure for sizing and equipping and maintaining our forces until we do win. Also, it should be an equally vital part of our policy to withdraw when—but only when—we have secured our objectives.

The importance of this criterion was demonstrated by our experiences in Lebanon in 1982 and 1983. The United States was part of the first multinational force (MNF), along with France and Italy, which supervised the departure of the Palestinian Liberation Organization (PLO) army from Beirut. This objective was mandated in an arrangement negotiated by our special envoy, Philip Habib, and agreed upon by the Lebanese government and the other various factions in the area. It was a clear mission, which was accomplished successfully, and our forces were then promptly withdrawn.

The next year, however, after Lebanon's president-elect was assassinated and Israeli forces reentered Beirut (as Ambassador Habib had assured the departing PLO forces they would not do), many people began urging President Reagan to send in another MNF. The State Department and some members of the National Security Council staff were particularly vocal in pushing this idea, eager to establish an American military "presence" in Lebanon to facilitate the withdrawal of warring armies.

Having a buffer between such forces is quite reasonable, as each side would be deeply suspicious of the other and vulnerable to violations of any withdrawal agreement by the other side. The problem in this case was that there was no agreement, by any party, to withdraw from its position. So American troops and those of any country that was persuaded to join the second MNF would be vulnerable, precariously inserted between countries that had no intention of stopping their fighting. Our mission would be nebulous at best, with no way to tell when it was completed.

Although I made these arguments repeatedly and forcefully, the president, unfortunately, concluded otherwise and sent a second, lightly armed contingent to join an MNF in Lebanon. My greatest fears were realized when, on October 23, 1983, our marine barracks and another building occupied by French forces were bombed, resulting in the deaths of 241 American and 56 French servicemen.

I have never overcome the feeling that I somehow should have been more persuasive in urging the president not to engage in such a flawed policy. The whole episode ingrained even more deeply in me the conviction that we should never commit troops into situations where the goals we give them are not clear and where the equipment we give them is not sufficient at least for self-defense.

The *fourth* point I listed in my speech was that, once we have committed military forces, we must continually reassess the situation. Every conflict is fluid, and circumstances may very well alter our objectives or dictate changes in the size or type of forces needed.

The *fifth* important factor to consider is that we must have reasonable assurance—*before* we commit combat forces abroad—that both our mission and our troops will have the support of the American people and their elected representatives in Congress. This emphatically does not mean that we should take a Gallup poll or consult some focus group before we do anything, but we cannot fight a war that the American people oppose. That was one of the major lessons of Vietnam. I believe that the necessary support cannot be achieved unless we are candid in making clear the threats we face and that support cannot be sustained without close and continuing consultation with Congress and the people. That is called leadership, and I fear we were woefully lacking in that in the Clinton years.

I did not touch on it in my press club speech, but this point can be carried a step further. Ideally, Congress should be completely in agreement with the administration on the need for the contemplated military action *before* troops are sent abroad. Often, the march of events cannot wait for the concurrence of such a large deliberative body. Inevitably, Congress is rankled when a president commits troops to action, and the lawmakers are often too eager to exercise their authority under the War Powers Resolution, which says that the military forces must come out within ninety days unless Congress gives its approval to their remaining in action. This act puts major and, I think, unconstitutional restraints on the president, as commander in chief, to use American forces when and where they might be necessary. It also can render those forces ineffective at best, or put them in greater danger at worst, since any enemy knows that he has only to suspend his objectionable actions until our forces are withdrawn, or to conduct even more hostile attacks against us in an effort to negatively influence American public—and thereby congressional—opinion.

The *sixth* and final criterion was that the commitment of troops should always be a last resort. I firmly believe that diplomatic efforts should be completely exhausted before we turn to the troops. But diplomatic efforts frequently fail, or they can succeed only by our giving up vital principles and objectives, so those efforts must never be seen as a permanent alternative to military action.

These six tests were intended to sound a note of caution, which is not only prudent but also morally required of a secretary of defense. Some thought it incongruous that I did so much to build up our defenses but was reluctant to commit forces abroad. It was not incongruous at all. I did not arm to attack. "We armed to parley," as Churchill always said. We armed so that we could negotiate from strength, defend freedom, and make war *less* likely. I never wanted to risk the lives of Americans in uniform unless it was necessary and my criteria were met.

Another few days' entries from my notes give a good sense of what some of my travels as secretary were like:

February 26, 1984

Shopped at Safeway

Spoke to National Governors' Association at Hyatt Regency, Capitol Hill. Gov. Robb, George Deukmejian, Gov. Orr (Indiana), etc.

Saw Colin Powell & Mike Burch—Marines are finally all out of Lebanon

Held brief press interview in lobby of hotel re above

Called Arlin in SF

Colin Powell re NSDD [National Security Decision Directive] on Lebanon—OK

Will Taft—re same & NSC meetings on E-W relations

Called Cap Jr. at home

Flew to London 8:05 P.M. (ET)–7:55 A.M. (GMT) 2/27

February 27, 1984

Arrived in London at 7:55 A.M.—met by Charles Price, our amb.

Driven to Churchill Hotel

Saw Colin Powell with PDB [President's Daily Briefing]

Met with Prime Minister Margaret Thatcher at #10 Downing Street—with ambassador

Driven to American Embassy residence—Winfield House

Met with Lord Peter Carrington re NATO issues—at Winfield House. He offered a very good quote:

"You Americans care too much what your critics say about you—when we were running things, we did not much care."*

---

* This would have been even better advice for President Carter. His great fear of our being criticized for practicing "colonialism" led him to give up the Panama Canal and two nearby military bases.

Lunch at Winfield House—[with] Peter Carrington, [Defense Minister] Michael Heseltine, [Foreign Minister] Francis Pym

Driven to Churchill Hotel

Colin Powell in office with video tape of earlier Oxford Union debates

Driven to Oxford

Attended reception & dinner at Oxford Union; undergraduate president [of the Union] Andrew Sullivan [who had originally invited me to do the debate]; former president of the Union [and later prime minister of Pakistan] Miss Benazir Bhutto [daughter of former prime minister of Pakistan who was killed by his political opponents]; Nemon (sculptor [of Churchill]), etc.

Called RJ in Washington

Debated Professor E.P. Thompson and others in Oxford Union building on "Resolved: there is no moral difference between foreign policies of US & USSR"

Driven back to London

Saw Colin Powell re call from Sam Pierce

Called Sam Pierce in Washington—rhc [returning his call]—n/a [no answer]

February 28, 1984

In London

Call from Mrs. Thatcher that I won debate at Oxford Union last night, 272-240

Breakfast with Michael Heseltine at Admiralty House

Met with Michael Heseltine at Ministry of Defence

Mrs. Thatcher—congratulations on winning debate

Met with Geoffrey Howe at Foreign Office

To Churchill Hotel

Called Sam Pierce in Washington—rhc—wants me to see Treasury Bond people for sales drive

Called RJ in SF

Visited & toured BBC—Langhorne Place

Called Colin Powell (2) re messages & tonight's agenda

Driven from BBC to Churchill Hotel

Charles Price—he will be coming to airport

Met with Archbishops of Canterbury & York, & Bishop of London—at Church House [Anglican headquarters] re nuclear & military issues

Spoke to Oxford & Cambridge Club after reception there

Saw Colin Powell re tomorrow's schedule, reporting cables back to President, Defense & State Departments re my meetings with British officials

February 29, 1984

In London

Colin Powell in room with PDB, today's schedule in Lebanon, etc.

Driven to Heathrow

Flew to Cyprus 7:05 A.M. (GMT)–1:20 P.M. (CT)

Met by Cypriot Defense Minister Veniamin & our Admiral Martin

Met with Defense Minister at airport

By helicopter to USS *Guam* 1:35 P.M.–2:30 P.M.

Spoke to *Guam* sailors & part of MAU [Marine Amphibious Unit] brought out from Beirut

Awarded them Navy commendation citation

Press briefing on ship

By helicopter to Beirut

Met by Ambassador Reg Bartholomew & toured Embassy compound—met with Marine General Joy

Joy had met with Ambassador & Gemayel in Damascus—may sign accord today

Toured Marine positions

Flew to USS *Trenton* by helicopter

Spoke to troops on *Trenton* & presented them with citation

Visited with troops on *Trenton*

By helicopter to Larnaca, 4:30 P.M.–6:20 P.M. (CT)

Flew from Larnaca to Shannon 6:30 P.M. (CT)–10 P.M. (GMT)

[Surprise] celebration aboard plane for debate victory

Saw Colin Powell re reporting cables & tomorrow's schedule

Flew from Shannon to Andrews [Air Force Base] 11:10 P.M. (GMT)–12:55 A.M. (ET)

Visiting our men and women in the military was one of my favorite activities. To see firsthand the pride they exuded in what they were doing and to hear their concerns directly was very satisfying, and I always encouraged them to ask any questions they wanted. I found it helped to break the ice if I recalled a few incidents and differences from my own enlisted service.

Some of the troops I visited were sailors in the engine rooms of our ships. This required going down innumerable stairs to the lowest decks—areas, I was told, that were rarely visited by assorted dignitaries. They seemed to appreciate my talking with them. I was also happy to talk to the marines who had been given the thankless job of serving as a buffer between warring factions in Lebanon. After the tragic barracks bombing, many of the marines thought they were being viewed at home as having failed. I told them they had done their duty superbly under very difficult circumstances, and I think I dispelled their notions of failure.

The original purpose of this trip, and its main event, was to participate in the Oxford debate. I had accepted the young Mr. Sullivan's* invitation without hesitation, but some in the administration—

---

* I found out later that he was a self-professed Marxist, but the job he did of presiding seemed to me to be admirably fair. He may even be a conservative now with all the changes that have happened.

mostly in the State Department, and even a few within the Defense Department—were wary about my participation. Their primary concern seemed to be that if I were to lose, as an official of the United States, it would undermine our ability to hold anti-Communist allies together. I thought this a specious argument, and besides, I did not intend to lose. I was quite eager to point out all the reasons why democracy was much superior to the Soviet system and how our foreign policy objectives were far more benevolent than theirs. In addition, I saw this as an opportunity finally to visit Oxford, having foolishly passed up the chance to study at Cambridge after college. Still, it was over some protest at home that I went. I suspect that part of it was not only the fear that I would lose, which would be a big story, but also the feeling that if it were going to be done at all, it ought to be by a trained diplomat.

As on my other trips to England, our group—which generally consisted of Will Taft, Colin Powell, Kay Leisz, Thelma Stubbs, a press aide, and the necessary security agents—was put up at the Churchill Hotel. It would have been delightful to stay at Winfield House, the beautiful American Embassy residence, and our ambassadors always invited us, but I knew what a major disruption it would be for them to have me as a houseguest, with our large number and special security and communications requirements. Besides, the Churchill was a perfectly nice and comfortable hotel, and it was already wired for our special needs.

After a reception and dinner at the Oxford Union on the night of the debate, I entered a large room that was set up much like the House of Commons, so that you face your opponent. It was incredibly hot from dozens of bright television lights, and the situation was not helped by being in a dinner coat. I had been told that black tie was the dress code, and the officers of the Union were in white tie. But my opponent, Professor E. P. Thompson, wore an old sports coat and sweater. He said he had never believed in black tie, that it was just a mark of class distinction. I remarked that, on the contrary, my father always said it was the most democratic of all costumes because everybody wore exactly the same thing. Thompson, an admitted Marxist, was not terribly amused.

Before our debate began, three or four student speakers—including a young Indian woman who was viciously anti-American—debated on the same question: "Resolved: There is no moral difference between the foreign policies of the U.S. and the USSR." This trendy view was called "moral equivalence." It rested on the idea that the Soviets' foreign policy was based only on their national interest and that the United States was wrong to worry about their acquiring a lot of other countries because it was simply to protect their borders by creating a buffer zone.

Then Andrew Sullivan, president of the Union, introduced me and Professor Thompson, and we began our debate. Thompson went first, and I responded—all of which took well over two hours, mostly because the rules of procedure were much like those in the House of Commons. If an opponent wants to question you, he just stands up and interrupts, and you have to sit down while he puts his question. There is apparently no limit to the number of times a person can be interrupted, so the evening can become quite prolonged.

Mr. Thompson spent the large part of his time denouncing the arms race and, more specifically, America's military power and our military presence in a number of countries. In fact, he spent a good deal more of his time lambasting the United States than he did addressing the original question. So much so that when it was my turn to speak, I began by saying that I thought perhaps I had come on the wrong evening, because before the debate began, one of the student officers announced that next week's debate would be on the question "Resolved: Christopher Columbus went too far."

In my attempt to disprove the resolution actually before the Union, I made essentially three points. First, the Soviet Union's policy was to promote Communism, while the United States sought to promote freedom. Second, they were in other countries by force; we were in other countries by invitation. And, last, whatever our respective policies might be, the Soviet people had absolutely no control over government policy, whereas if Americans were not satisfied with U.S. policy, they could, through a free political process, change it. I think these excerpts from my talk express my views best:

> The Soviet definition has always been that moral policy is what advances the Soviet state. That moral policy is what helps the cause of Communism.... It is a moral system which turns the definition of the word "moral" upside-down as far as we are concerned. Our view of morality is basically that a policy is moral if it advances certain basic principles and rights—something that we mentioned to you in a letter that we sent about two hundred years ago and which says that we hold these truths to be self-evident: that all men are created equal and that they are endowed by their creator with certain unalienable rights and that among these are life, liberty, and the pursuit of happiness.
>
> We've never used our power to try to conquer. We have used our power to try to help others.... Now we've heard a fair amount tonight about the American troops who have been here thirty-nine years.... The ... other important difference between these troops and the troops in the Warsaw Pact is the fact that the troops here are here by invitation of NATO and by invitation of the host country... [and] are here for a very specific purpose of ... join[ing] with people to protect and preserve their own freedoms because they have been invited by the regularly chosen, legitimate governments of these countries to do that.... If you told us to take our soldiers out of Great Britain, they would be gone within a day or two.... There's quite a difference between that and the Warsaw Pact troops, who are there because they are imposed on those countries.

We think you can't have a moral foreign policy if the people cannot control it—if the people cannot change it. We've heard many instances tonight of the problems that individuals have with individual aspects of American foreign policy. I had a lot of problems with our foreign policy four years ago and I expressed those views very vigorously and I was not jailed. I was able to do that and I was able also to be of some help in assembling a group of people who turned out ultimately to be a majority, and those foreign policies were changed, a great many of them.... You have the freedom of choice and you can make a difference.... Tonight you'll exercise that freedom—you'll make a choice and I rest my case on your liberty to walk out either door and not have anything happen thereafter. There will be no intimidation, no threats, no arrests. I ask you to consider whether in the other system you and your families could have been here, or if you felt it was safe for your family to come here tonight and express things on either side.... So I urge your opposition to this motion so that you can come again.

At the conclusion of the debate, a vote was taken—not by a show of hands or roll call but by the same famous division used in the House of Commons: "Ayes to the right, Noes to the left." The Union members present then exited either to the "Aye" lobby or to the "No" lobby.

It had been a long evening and I was tired, so I went back to the hotel before the vote was counted. I felt that I had done reasonably well, but I also knew that Professor Thompson was very popular with the students who composed the Union. So I really cannot say I was expecting the victory, of which I learned the next morning. Those in the British Foreign Office and Defence Ministry, as well as Mrs. Thatcher, were extremely pleased, as, needless to say, was I.

When I finally decided to resign as secretary of defense, it was because of my wife's health. She had been suffering with arthritis for several years, then had a bout with cancer, developed osteoporosis, and broke two vertebrae. I needed to fulfill my obligations to her. Not only had she been in tremendous pain for some time, but she had never been especially enthusiastic about moving back to Washington in the first place; indeed, she had wanted me to leave office after President Reagan's first term. At that time, I did not feel that I had completed the mandate he had given me—to rebuild our military strength—and it was too crucial a goal to leave unfinished. But with only a year left in his second term, I concluded that I had done what I could, and I needed to redirect my attention to my wife.

Helping in this decision was my assumption, at least my hope, that Will Taft, my deputy of three-and-a-half years, would succeed me. I knew that he could be counted on to carry on my vigorous advocacy of the Strategic Defense Initiative and that he knew the Pentagon— and Washington—inside and out.

The president was agreeable to naming Will, but Howard Baker, then White House chief of staff, and others persuaded the president that the post required someone of more "stature." They decided on Frank Carlucci, who was serving ably as national security adviser. Frank was, indeed, extremely competent and knowledgeable, but I was sorry that Will did not get the opportunity to move up. Will continued to evidence his great loyalty and selflessness by agreeing to continue as deputy secretary of defense under Carlucci. He never expressed any bitterness. Later, the president appointed him to be our ambassador to NATO, where again he performed superbly. President George W. Bush also recognized Will's great worth by appointing him chief legal counsel to the State Department in February 2001.

Prior to my departure, an impressive military parade and a nineteen-gun salute were held in my honor on the Pentagon parade ground. A display of honor guards passing in review, along with military marches and even flyovers of aircraft from each service, culminated in the president's presenting me with the Presidential Medal of Freedom, a most splendid accolade in itself, and a great surprise to me. Something that

I considered an even greater honor was the tribute the president paid me at a most moving Rose Garden ceremony later that week:

> Today, just about any enlisted man or woman will tell you that Cap is a defense secretary who cares about the troops. And maybe that's because Cap had seen firsthand that the backbone, the sinew, the soul and spirit of our armed forces are the men and women who dig the trenches and swab the decks, fix the engines, drive the tanks, fly the planes, and face the enemy for all of us. He knows of the truth of what his old commander, General Douglas MacArthur, once said—that in the field, morale would quickly wither and die if soldiers come to believe themselves the victims of indifference or injustice on the part of their government.

My nearly seven years as secretary of defense, while stressful and demanding, were some of the most fulfilling of my life. I felt that I was able to make a difference and perhaps help set our nation on a more stable, secure course than it had previously been following. Sadly, much of what President Reagan and I worked so hard for was severely cut and compromised by the Clinton administration in its eagerness to do whatever seemed most popular at the moment and to follow whatever course it thought might enable it to avoid criticism. The defense of our country and its citizens is much too important ever to take a backseat to political expediency.

CHAPTER 17

THE DANGERS WE STILL FACE

*W*hile the final victory over Soviet Communism was not fully realized when President Reagan left office in January of 1989, the momentum he had started was unstoppable. That year saw breathtaking changes in Eastern Europe, as those nations began the difficult but welcome process of liberating themselves after more than four decades of harsh and brutal Soviet domination and repression.

In January, Hungary allowed pluralistic political parties and open demonstrations, and Estonia made its own language the official language, as did Lithuania.

In February, the Communist government of Czechoslovakia jailed a dissident and brilliant playwright named Vaclav Havel and others for participating in rallies opposed to the Communist regime. But by the end of the year, Havel had not only been released, but he had been elected president of Czechoslovakia. I will always remember how he began his speech to a joint session of our Congress when he made his first state visit here in early 1990. He said, "While I know most people begin a speech by saying how glad they are to be here, I really mean it. Only a few days ago, I was in jail!"

In March, the Soviet people, in the first national election since 1917, overwhelmingly defeated several high-ranking official Communist candidates, and Boris Yeltsin, Gorbachev's leading opponent, won by a landslide.

By August, Poland formally named a Solidarity leader, Tadeusz Mazowiecki, prime minister, and Lithuania took major strides toward its own independence, which it formally declared in March 1990.

In September, the most dramatic events of the decade began when East Germans poured into Hungary, which allowed them free passage to West Germany.

In October, Erich Honecker, Communist leader of East Germany for eighteen years, was ousted, and over 300,000 East Germans demonstrated for democracy.

In November, the East German government resigned, and all travel restrictions were lifted. No one who saw it, in person or on television, will ever forget the extraordinarily inspiring sight of the Berlin Wall tumbling down piece by piece while jubilant masses poured over and through it. Today, a section of the wall stands at the Reagan Presidential Library as a lasting reminder of the repression he ended, the millions of people he freed.

That same November, Czechoslovakia's Communist government resigned after huge demonstrations demanding democracy continued for eight days. Next, Hungarians voted in their first free election in forty-two years. But harsh Soviet measures of repression against Lithuania were imposed this month, including deploying Soviet tanks used to intimidate the Lithuanian parliament and shutting off promised oil and energy shipments—all because of Lithuania's statements of independence. Yet this dying gasp of Communism ultimately failed. Lithuania, today, is free and independent.

December of that sunrise year of 1989 brought East Germany's decision to have free elections, Havel's election as president in Czechoslovakia, and the overthrow and execution of Nicolae Ceausescu, the ruthless and particularly brutal dictator of Romania. East Germany ceased to be a separate Communist nation, and the newly unified Germany entered the new decade under the conservative government of Chancellor Helmut Kohl.

Of course, the transition of the former Eastern bloc countries to full-fledged independent nations did not happen overnight. Their growing pains continued over several years and, in some ways, are still going on. All are vastly better off because they now have the freedom to realize their own destinies.

How did all this happen? What caused this virtually complete collapse of Communism in Russia and Eastern Europe?

In short, how and why did we win the Cold War?

Clearly many causes and factors were involved—but I always felt there was one major turning point that led inexorably to the winning of the Cold War.

That was the moment when we decided we were going to win the Cold War. And that was when President Reagan, in perhaps his most major violation of the conventional wisdom, blatantly told the world that Communism was an Evil Empire. With this, he ended the years of national indecision about the nature of Communism. With that single stroke, we gave up "containment," "détente," "moral equivalence," and the idea that Communism and freedom were simply two different but compatible systems.

On March 8, 1983, in a speech in Orlando, Florida, President Reagan asked for prayers for the "salvation of all of those who were in that totalitarian darkness.... Let us be aware that ... they are the focus of evil in the modern world."

He urged his audience to beware of the "temptation of blatantly declaring yourselves above it all and label[ing] both sides equally at fault, [and the temptation] to ignore the facts of history and the aggressive impulses of an Evil Empire."

Ronald Reagan felt so strongly about it that with this speech he overrode his "moderate" advisers and restored those phrases, which had twice been cut from his draft of a major speech that he gave in 1982 to the British Parliament. Otherwise the world would have heard his call half a year earlier.*

Predictably, the president's calling the Soviets and Communism the "Evil Empire" and its victims the "focus of evil" horrified all those who believed we could, by appeasement or accommodation or other means, persuade the Soviet Union to stop being the Soviet Union so that we could live in peace together.

Reagan would have none of it. He was willing to negotiate reductions in nuclear arms, but he warned against calling "the arms race a giant misunderstanding and thereby removing yourself from the struggle between right and wrong and good and evil."

Typical of the storm of protest that followed the president's openly voiced determination to win the Cold War was the reaction of Anthony Lewis of the *New York Times*, who said the president's speech was "primitive and dangerous." Lewis went on to ask, "What must Soviet leaders think? However one detests their system, the world's survival depends on mutual restraint."[†]

"Mutual restraint" had never characterized the Soviet Union, nor had containment contained or détente slowed its ever increasing military strength.[‡]

---

* See a fascinating article in the Allentown, Pennsylvania, *Morning Call* on March 5, 2000, by Frank Allen, based on his thorough research in the Reagan Archives and Library.

† See the *New York Times*, March 9, 1983.

‡ *Soviet Military Power*, Volumes 1–9 (Washington, DC: The Pentagon, 1983–99).

What else, besides President Reagan's determination to win the Cold War, won it?

First: Our military buildup, designed not to give us superiority, but only to regain a credible enough deterrent to make it clear to the Soviets that they could never win a war against us. President Reagan never wavered in his determination to regain that degree of strength in our armed forces. And his administration carried out his policies with ceaseless advocacy.

Second: Our determination to construct and deploy an effective defense against ballistic missiles. This was another of the great violations of the conventional wisdom, involving the ultimate repudiation of the ABM Treaty and the Mutual Assured Destruction theory.

Third: The repair and strengthening of our strategic alliances, particularly in NATO and also in the Pacific, the Mideast, and Asia.

Many credit Gorbachev with helping end the Cold War. I do not. He did recognize that the Soviets could not win a war with the United States and NATO, but he never repudiated Communism, and despite all his rhetoric, he remains dedicated to Communism in theory and in practice.

The winning of the Cold War also enabled Poland, Hungary, and the Czech Republic to decouple themselves from the Soviet Union and then to seek to join the NATO alliance—a step that seemed unbelievable just a few months before. These countries made great strides in establishing democratic and comparatively free-market regimes. So to me, this was a natural fit: NATO was the quickest and safest way for these newly free countries to seal their fledgling friendships with the United States and the West, and NATO needed the additional defensive strength they could provide to discourage a western thrust from an unstable Russia. Imperial-minded Russians were furious at the prospect of their old "colonies" joining NATO. So were the usual common scolds of the West who wrote and chattered endlessly about "provoking" Russia by guaranteeing Eastern European freedom under NATO.

It was then that we saw the beginning of President Clinton's repeated attempts to appease the unappeasable Russians. Clinton and his strongly pro-Russian deputy secretary of state, Strobe Talbott, delayed by several years the official entry into NATO of Poland, the Czech Republic, and Hungary. The Clinton administration was determined to back Russia but, typically, tried to please everyone and offend no one. So it proposed the usual fuzzy compromise. This one was called the Partnership for Peace, launched in late 1993, as a substitute for the NATO membership the three former Warsaw Pact nations really wanted. This "partnership" invited Russia and the other fourteen republics of the former Soviet Union, as well as the former Warsaw Pact countries, to join together for "peacekeeping, crisis management, search-and-rescue missions, and disaster relief." They could "consult with NATO"; maybe later some could actually join; but the reality was that the willingness of those nations to share in the burdens of NATO was being summarily rejected by us when we should have eagerly embraced all three. It is one thing to extend help to Russia; it is quite another to spurn refugees from the Warsaw Pact who wish to join NATO.

Russian opposition should have been ignored, and we should have made clear to them that while we were prepared to help them economically, they could not control or influence us to ignore our best interests and the urgent needs of Soviet victims. It is our duty, and very much in our best interest, to help freedom-loving countries. How many of our allies will remain allies if we turn our backs on nations that want to be free and if we violate years of our historic attachment to such countries? To do so simply because we do not want to offend Russia just adds salt to the wound. To support the aggressor and oppose the oppressed was both irresponsible and incomprehensible behavior for the champion of democracy and the world's only remaining superpower.

In March 1999, Poland, Hungary, and the Czech Republic were admitted to NATO, but only after we made so many concessions to Russia's ego that NATO was unnecessarily and substantially weakened. The Clinton administration promised, implicitly or explicitly, that we would not admit any other nations to NATO; we invited Russia to sit on a NATO council; and we basically allowed Russia to claim a veto over NATO missions. We also promised that no NATO troops or weapons would be deployed in the new members' territories. We even offered to put Russian observers in all major NATO posts, rendering NATO potentially impotent and making its three new members feel like second-class members.

The Baltic states were treated even less well by the Clinton administration, which offered them a lukewarm compromise—the Charter of Partnership. The charter recognized that NATO membership was a "goal" for these nations but said they must wait until they were "ready"—a term not defined.

We never required Spain to be found "ready" when we were begging that country to join NATO in 1982. And we certainly never asked Russia then for its opinion or permission.

Our tepid response to countries trying to join NATO was part of a pattern demonstrating Clinton's overriding fear of displeasing Russia. To give Russia what amounts to a veto power over our decisions regarding our alliances—or, for that matter, over our entire foreign policy—is not why we fought and won the Cold War.

Some argue that since we have triumphed over the Soviet Union, there is no longer a need for NATO at all. This is a dangerous assumption. Russia still has a vast arsenal of nuclear warheads, a potentially unstable government, and, in Vladimir Putin, a man who gave the KGB complete satisfaction for seventeen years. Putin now talks of restoring "Russia's greatness." He has continued a brutal war in Chechnya, seems to have a rapidly developing relationship with

China, and needs to be regarded with the same caution with which we would approach any other potentially hostile power. He also joins Russia with North Korea, Serbia, Iran, Iraq, and any other countries with which we may have disagreements.

The Russian military is low in morale, but it has a huge and growing inventory of new and ever more lethal weapons[*]—paid for largely by unsupervised and unaudited U.S. and Western aid. The Russian economy is, to put it charitably, far from strong, and the quality of life is far from enviable. Even at the beginning of the 1990s, though, many in our own government seemed to be unaware that the crumbling of the Soviet Union could conceivably end in a full return to a Stalinist dictatorship and Russian military aggression—a possibility that could arise very quickly in a country like Russia. Making drastic cuts in our military strength, as we have done, including deep cutbacks in our commitments to NATO, on the grounds that we no longer have significant foreign threats after the Cold War, is particularly imprudent. That idea should have been rudely exploded on August 2, 1990, when Saddam Hussein suddenly invaded Kuwait on his way to conquer Saudi Arabia and the United Arab Emirates and thereby gain control of about 70 percent of the world's known oil reserves.

Fortunately for the world, the United States then had the military capabilities, the leadership, and the will to block this aggression and

---

[*] As Roger W. Robinson Jr. wrote in the August 28, 1998, *Wall Street Journal*, "During this decade, even as some Russian workers were going unpaid, Moscow continued construction of a massive network of underground command and control bunkers in the Ural Mountains, deployed a new, mobile 'Topol-M2' (the SS-27) intercontinental ballistic missile, commissioned a new aircraft carrier (the *Admiral Kuzhetsov*) and nuclear cruiser (the *Peter the Great*), refitted its Typhoon Class submarines to accommodate SS-N24/26 missiles, began a stealth-fighter program (comparable to our F-22), and built a fifth-generation Borei Class ballistic missile submarine." All of this cost at least $18 billion.

organize a powerful coalition of Arab, Asian, and European nations. This coalition was not only fully capable of acting with the United States, but it was equally determined to stop Saddam Hussein's plans.

Initially, this remarkable coalition of nations and the United Nations imposed major economic sanctions against Iraq, enforced by an air and sea blockade. It became increasingly apparent, however, that because the blockade specifically excluded foods and medicines, Saddam Hussein channeled whatever he could to his military. The sanctions could not, in any reasonable amount of time, force Saddam out of Kuwait. It was also apparent that his continued occupancy of Kuwait was causing increasing hardships and misery not only to Kuwaiti citizens but also to thousands of workers and refugees who had fled Kuwait.

President Bush tried every possible diplomatic move. But when Saddam Hussein forbade his representative even to receive the president's letters, it became clear that the force authorized by virtually unanimous UN resolutions, and later by our Congress in a close but decisive vote, must be exercised. So on January 16, 1991, the allied forces unleashed air strikes of unparalleled intensity against Iraq, and the crippling of key components of Saddam's military strength began.

This was followed by ground troop insertions, which, with superior generalship, armaments of all types, and complete control of the air, overwhelmed the remaining Iraqi troops, many thousands of whom surrendered without a fight. They were weary and hungry and demoralized, and they seemed to welcome the opportunity to escape from the brutal minority Ba'ath party rule in Iraq, even if only temporarily. There was some hope that Iraqi unhappiness with the leadership of their country might lead to the overthrow of Saddam Hussein. I do not think this should have been left to hope alone.

President George Bush provided decisive leadership in this crisis. But I always felt it was imperative that we not only expel Saddam from Kuwait and restore the legitimate government (which we did) but also ensure that Saddam be deposed and punished. It was important that Iraq not be left with a military capability to reinvade Kuwait or attack other countries. We destroyed much of Saddam's military,* but, unfortunately, we allowed Saddam to remain in power, and we accepted his promises—promises that included our right to inspect his weapons sites—which he predictably broke.

Saddam Hussein has not yet tried to retake Kuwait, but his presence precludes any hope of lasting peace in the Mideast. Reliable intelligence tells us that Iraq continues to manufacture chemical and biological weapons and to shop relentlessly for nuclear weapons, despite UN sanctions.

The Clinton administration, not surprisingly, was erratic and ineffective in dealing with the problem. Our "patience ran out" several times; we sought a "diplomatic solution" with a vicious killer who does not negotiate and who can never be believed or trusted; we occasionally dropped a few bombs or chased an Iraqi fighter jet out of the no-fly zone. But our credibility with our allies and against Saddam was seriously doubted because of Clinton's deep defense cuts, the irresoluteness of American policy, and the domestic political considerations that seemed to govern Clinton's foreign policy in the area.

We wondered why Saudi Arabia would not let us use its bases to support an attack that ultimately could have protected it and others in the region from Saddam Hussein's ever increasing capabilities to destroy them. I suspect the Saudis knew that, under Clinton, we would not do more than carry out a few days of token bombing, if that, if Iraq moved again into Kuwait or elsewhere.

---

* Typically, those who were not there criticized us later for being too thorough and for not allowing armed Iraqis to escape, which would have meant potential harm to our forces.

All we sought was to reinsert UN inspectors into Iraq for a few days, with fewer restrictions placed on them, and yet Saddam continued to refuse even that. If we wanted to rid the world of the threats we faced in 1990 and 1991, we should have bombed every one of the disputed sites two or three times each, day and night, and we would have had to be prepared to ignore Saddam's inevitable lies about injured children.

Bombing alone would not oust this mass murderer, but if we were able to and did maintain a firm offensive, we could inflict enough damage to serve notice that we would not be bluffed any longer, thereby also warning other potential aggressors. We also could encourage and support opposition to Saddam inside and outside of Iraq. We should have eliminated or jailed Saddam himself—and still must do so, if we want any peace in the region.

Unfortunately, Iraq was not the only place where the Clinton administration abdicated its leadership responsibilities. Clinton's handling of the situation in Bosnia was a humiliation for the West comparable to the attempt to appease Hitler in the late 1930s.

How did this happen? When the uneasy alliance that was Yugoslavia broke apart, four nations—Croatia, Slovenia, Bosnia-Herzegovina, and Macedonia—claimed independence and were admitted to the UN. Serbia, meanwhile, embarked on its longtime goal of creating a Greater Serbia—controlling all of the former Yugoslavia of which it had also been a part. Serbia's allies in Bosnia cooperated with a shocking "ethnic cleansing" of Bosnia's Muslims, following Hitler's example.

The West's ultimate mistake was its failure to stop the Serbs at once. The problem again was the doctrine of limited objectives. Just as those who preached "containment" never intended to win the Cold War and those who sent our troops into Vietnam never planned to win, so too our approach to Serbia. We cautioned many times that we did *not* plan to defeat Serbia—only to stop its criminal atrocities.

President Clinton compounded this error when, shortly after his inauguration, he sent Warren Christopher to Europe, not to galvanize resistance to the aggression (as President Bush had done in the Gulf) but to inquire weakly what other countries would like to do. Naturally, none of them wanted to do very much, which sent a clear signal to the Serbs that they could pursue their aggression unhindered.

A routine UN arms embargo was put in place against Bosnia, but Russia continued to supply arms to the Serbs. For more than a year, UN and European "negotiators" bleated for cease-fires and "safe areas" and proposed various peace plans that awarded Serbia anywhere from 49 percent to 70 percent of Bosnia. The Serbs agreed to more than thirty cease-fire and safe-area proposals—and sometimes even kept their promises for as long as five or six hours.

The United States played an ignoble role, agreeing to giving the UN full command of the peacekeeping operation, which was manned by 23,000 lightly armed, ill-equipped troops scattered in hopelessly ineffective clusters and without effective rules of engagement. Predictably, these peacekeepers were attacked, ignored, overrun, and taken hostage, and the UN convoys of food and medicine were allowed to pass only when the Serbs gave permission.

This was the much-touted Dayton Agreement, signed in December 1995, which was supposed to create a stable, new "multiethnic Bosnian country." Instead, we accepted a partitioned Bosnia, which is what the Serbs wanted, with three parliaments (one federal, two regional), two separate armies, and two police forces, overseen by a rotating three-man presidency. Subsequent elections only emphasized that such a Rube Goldberg–like structure could not be built, let alone succeed.

Again, this demonstrated how easy it is to secure an agreement: just give up as much as the other party demands, and then we can have a big signing ceremony, proclaim ourselves peacemakers, and nominate our negotiators for the Nobel Peace Prize. Meanwhile, the victims of Serbia's aggression continue to suffer.

The United States has always been, and always should be, willing to accept the burdens of keeping peace and helping maintain freedom for ourselves and our allies. When, after two years of fatal, bumbling inaction, we cobbled together a paper agreement solving none of the conflicts that started the war, it was simply common sense to oppose deploying any soldiers, U.S. or NATO, to a mission inviting disaster—a "peacekeeping" mission where there was no peace to be kept.

Much earlier, we should have assembled a Gulf War–like coalition and told Serbia that its military targets would be mercilessly bombed by air forces under U.S. and NATO command if Serbia continued attacking civilian populations. When the brutality of Serb leader Slobodan Milosevic was again unleashed, this time in Kosovo, we ultimately did support NATO bombing, but with restrictions and restraints bound to make any operation ineffective.*

Ultimately, a new Serbian government ousted Milosevic from power. A few months later, he was turned over to the United Nations' War Crimes Tribunal, where he is now awaiting trial.

Another murderous regime sits in North Korea. It frightened the Clinton administration into another gross act of appeasement (called a "framework agreement"), initiated by our own appeaser-negotiator, former president Jimmy Carter, who told the North Koreans he would try to get American sanctions against them lifted. The sanctions were lifted in the summer of 2000.

Time and time again, the Clinton administration inexplicably made concessions to North Korea in the hope the Communist regime

---

* Targets could be bombed only after the approval of a large committee was secured.

would stop its nuclear weapons program. Under the "framework agreement," we even arranged to give the North Koreans two new nuclear reactors—ostensibly for more power, although the reactors are fully capable of producing plutonium, the very stuff of which nuclear weapons are made.

This absurd appeasement proceeded despite increasingly hostile actions by North Korea, including "test" launches over Japan of its new, long-range missiles—which can ultimately reach the United States—and thinly veiled threats against South Korea.

For example, in 1996, when the North sent a submarine with some twenty-five terrorists into South Korean waters, South Korea urged the United States to restart the valuable joint military exercises we had conducted with the South Korean armed forces from 1976 to 1994 (which we had stopped as part of the appeasement agreement we made with North Korea). But President Clinton merely urged "restraint" on both sides. Sadly, this is just one more example of the way in which the Clinton administration cavalierly disregarded and alienated our allies.

Aside from our increasingly strained relations with our allies, our own security was dangerously weakened by the inept Clinton as our commander in chief. Part of the problem was that President Clinton did not understand the military, and worse, he did not *like* the military. Moreover, he did not recognize the importance of a strong defense.

Gone was our military strength that won the Cold War. By the late 1990s, we were spending less on new weapons and equipment than at any time in the last forty years. Spending on research and development programs had been cut by nearly 60 percent.

It has been said that we fought and won the Gulf War with Cap Weinberger's forces. In a 2000 interview with Rush Limbaugh, Dick Cheney summed up the current regrettable situation well: "We had 6 percent of our GNP going for defense during the Reagan years; [we have] less than 3 percent today. We used to have eighteen army divisions; today we're down to ten. We used to have some twenty-four wings in the air force; we're down to thirteen today."

Each new administration appropriately begins with a reexamination of existing strategic policies. This process is under way with the new Bush administration, and the first result is usually a spate of rumors as to what has been decided, what new policies will be followed, and which existing policies will be changed.

There have already been many and varied reports, including that we are abandoning the "two-war" strategy and that we are offering to take out of service or destroy all of our largest and most accurate MX missiles, which were finally deployed after a major struggle with Congress and others in the 1980s.

Regardless of what our policy is called, we must have armed forces of the strength necessary to deter and conquer any threat. If two attacks, leading to two wars that must necessarily be fought nearly simultaneously, are a possible threat, we must be strong enough to fight and win those two wars.

Such a threat is at least possible. China could decide it would no longer attempt to secure its "one China" goal by treaty or negotiation. Instead it could try to take Taiwan by force. Indeed, the continued increasing deployment along China's east coast of missiles facing and aimed at Taiwan cannot be ignored.

Should China attack Taiwan, North Korea, despite all of Clinton's attempts to offer what it wants, is equipped and positioned to launch another attack on South Korea.

The so-called two-war strategy was simply a convenient term for measuring and obtaining the kind and amount of deterrent military capability we might need. So long as giving up the two-war strategy does not mean giving up the military capabilities we may well need or the defense budgets big enough to support those capabilities, we need not worry too much.

But when we look at what has happened to the matchless military strength President Clinton inherited in January 1993, it is doubtful now that we could win one of those hypothetical two wars.

From 1985 to 2000, the total active-duty military personnel in our military went down by 34 percent.[*] Yet under Clinton, our forces were asked to serve in overseas assignments far more often and for far longer than they should.[†] Few of these missions improved military training. Most were called "operations other than war," and our troops were "spending more and more time working on aging equipment at the expense of honing their important war-fighting skills."[‡]

All of this was compounded by the Clinton "procurement holiday" and substantial cuts in the research and development work that earlier had produced the weapons with which we won the Gulf War.

Thus, today, our military faces extraordinary operation and maintenance costs for military hardware and weapons systems that it would be cheaper and more effective to replace with new models. New weapons systems not only have all the performance advantages of new technology, but they are increasingly built modularly, which means that they are far cheaper and easier to repair than older

[*] See Jack Spencer's "Building and Maintaining the Strength of America's Armed Forces," Chapter 10 of *Priorities for the President* by Baker Spring and Jack Spencer (Washington, DC: The Heritage Foundation, 2001).

[†] Our forces "have been used over thirty times beyond normal training and operations since the end of the Cold War." This is compared with only ten such deployments in the preceding forty years. See Spring and Spencer, page 214. Dick Cheney also said, in his 2000 Rush Limbaugh interview: "We've given the forces a lot of assignments they didn't used to have, the so-called peacekeeping assignments. What that means is that the guys are away from home all the time. The thing you hear about is 'the birthday problem.' A guy will tell you, 'Look, I missed my kid's last three birthdays because I was away from home. So I'm leaving. I can't take it anymore.'"

[‡] General H. H. Shelton, Chairman of the Joint Chiefs of Staff, testimony to U.S. Senate Armed Services Committee, September 27, 2000.

weapons systems. While our military's operations and maintenance costs are skyrocketing because of aging weapons systems and infrastructure, our vital military research and development budgets are suffering. The result is a military whose operational capability is in serious danger of exponential decline. The Clinton administration inexcusably hollowed out our military capability and has left President Bush with the tab for making good Clinton's deficits on what should have been spent.

Not surprisingly, all of this has contributed to a loss in morale and a most worrisome difficulty in recruitment and retention of troops— something we never experienced during the Reagan buildup in the 1980s.[*]

We need to return to major increases in defense spending overall, and in particular, we need to rebuild the Reagan-era navy. Our navy today is roughly half as large as it was in the Reagan years, and yet the most immediate challenges we will likely face are naval challenges, since our most likely areas of conflict are separated from us by vast oceans. We have to be able to move our armed forces around the map, so we need a drastic upgrading of our air- and sea-lift capabilities. It takes six or seven years to build and fully deploy—with trained crews—aircraft carriers and nuclear submarines. We need to be building them now. It takes two or three years to build and deploy combat aircraft. We need to be building them now as well. After the years of Clinton neglect, we are seeing a disastrous de facto build-down—by failing to replace out-of-date ships and aircraft—of major and highly disturbing proportions.

With the election of George W. Bush, things are improving, and I expect that his commitment to our military will alleviate many of

---

[*] See Spring and Spencer, pages 217–218.

these problems. Still, it will take time and continued advocacy and determination to repair the damage wrought by eight years of the Clinton administration.

President Bush has also taken to heart the highest defense priority we should have—building a defense against intercontinental ballistic nuclear missiles and missiles with chemical or biological warheads.* Russia alone has an estimated 15,000 to 20,000 nuclear warheads.†

The Reagan administration worked for years to build a genuine, nationwide defense against these incoming intercontinental and intermediate-range missiles, but we were continually hampered by demands from Democrats and some Republicans that everything be "ABM Treaty–compliant" (read "totally ineffective"). No one in the Reagan administration was suggesting that we violate our treaty obligations. What was repeatedly urged was that we use the specific provisions of the treaty itself to get us out of it, as legally permitted, so that we can build and deploy effective defenses.

President Clinton and his State Department remained wedded to the flawed 1972 ABM Treaty, despite intelligence reports—and later, Russia's own admission—that the Soviet Union had violated the treaty almost from the beginning by deploying its giant radar at Krasnoyarsk. In September 1997, Secretary of State Madeleine Albright signed agreements designating Russia, Kazakhstan, Belarus, and Ukraine as our ABM Treaty partners in place of the collapsed USSR. Strobe Talbott, her Russophile deputy secretary, said as late as May 2000 that we meant to adhere to and strengthen the ABM Treaty. None of these new agreements, however, was ever submitted to the Senate. And now, with President Bush, thankfully they will not be;

* For the best description of the nature and size of the ballistic missile threat we face, see *The Ballistic Missile Threat Handbook* by Jack Spencer (Washington, DC: The Heritage Foundation, 2000).

† *Military Almanac* (Washington, DC: Center for Defense Information, 1999), 9.

already in his young administration, it is clear that capable, tough-minded professionals such as National Security Adviser Condoleezza Rice, Secretary of State Colin Powell, and Secretary of Defense Donald Rumsfeld have returned to putting the legitimate interests of the United States and our allies first. I have high hopes for the new administration and see it as a worthy inheritor—after the lamentable Clinton years—of the work I tried to achieve as secretary of defense for Ronald Reagan. This administration knows that peace comes through strength, that America must lead, and that nothing is more important than our national defense.

Two steps are necessary to gain any real security: we must reject any ABM succession agreements and announce that we will no longer be bound by the old ABM Treaty, and we must move ahead with the research and subsequent deployment that will give us and our allies a viable defense against nuclear, chemical, and biological weapons. The Clinton administration and its faint-hearted supporters stood in the way, and now that Senator Jim Jeffords has turned over control of the Senate to the Democrats, an effective missile defense will apparently continue to be denied to the American people.

President Clinton, inclined as he was to conduct policy by poll, should have noted that polls showed that a horrified majority of Americans were unaware that we currently have no effective defense against nuclear missile attack. Moreover, nearly 70 percent of respondents considered having a strong military to be very important and said that they were willing to pay the taxes necessary to ensure that the United States remains a global superpower.

The American people understand, if President Clinton did not, that the fact that we won the Cold War has changed—not removed—the various threats we could face.

The Bush administration has quite properly focused much time on reassessing our relationship with Communist China, and if we are to be influential in the Pacific, air power and, preeminently, naval power will be absolutely crucial to our having a convincing deterrent capability against potential aggressors.

Communist China needs to be approached with the same caution with which we should approach Russia under Vladimir Putin. Vladimir Putin was a competent spy for the KGB during the Cold War, and he likely remains a KGB operative at heart now that he runs post-Communist Russia. Like Russia, Communist China has opened up its economy to a degree—motivated by self-interest and Deng Xiaoping's vision to expand its economy—but it remains an extremely repressive and ambitious regional power. It is a disturbing scenario, but there are increasing signs that China and Russia see themselves as potential allies again—an alliance of "rogue state" supporters. This is a very hazardous, if underappreciated, situation. China has a much larger economic and population base to build on than the Soviet Union did in the Cold War—and China is rapidly expanding its military capability. In fact, China is the customer that sustains the research and development budget of Russia's military. In modernizing and improving its massive armed forces, China has focused on creating a highly trained strike force that is roughly equivalent to the size of the United States Army.

There is every reason, given the size of China and its potential threat, to revitalize the old Southeast Asia Treaty Organization, or SEATO, in a new form. A formal alliance of perhaps Taiwan, Japan, Singapore, South Korea, India, Thailand, the Philippines, Australia, New Zealand, and Vietnam would send a powerful signal to China— and to Russia—that the United States means to defend freedom in the Pacific. All of these nations—including Japan and South Korea—are at risk to Chinese pressure, because they know China has been a regional power since the dawn of Asian history. Our current allies in the Pacific cannot be allowed to doubt American resolve in the region. If we strengthen our commitment to preserving peace in the Pacific, we will find both new friends and trading partners.

Interestingly, Vietnam recently asked the Russians to leave the naval base at Cam Ranh Bay. It is time to bury our own ghosts of Vietnam. The Vietnamese, like all of China's neighbors, have every reason to be our allies today. The U.S. Navy in Cam Ranh Bay would help defend Vietnam and the other smaller Asian countries of the Pacific Rim against the awakening Chinese giant. So would American investment. So would re-creating SEATO.

A new, strong Asian alliance would help let China know that we will not shy away from rolling back Chinese Communism, any more than we shied away from rolling back Russian Communism, thereby winning the Cold War. If China threatens its neighbors, we should actively support covert operations to aid the voices of freedom against the regime in Communist China. And of course, we must carry out our treaty, legal, and moral obligations to help Taiwan preserve its own sovereignty.

Many of the views summarized here may seem uncompromising; indeed, I have been described as stubborn. Some even say that my mind closed at the age of six, and it has never opened since. However, as we have seen, the conventional wisdom is not always wise.

CHAPTER 18

THE NIGHTMARE YEAR

*T*he year 1992 was, in every way, a nightmare year for me. I suppose I had been in some danger of succumbing to the Greek condition of hubris during the nearly five years that had passed since I had left the Defense Department. If so, 1992 was to dispel any pride I might have retained.

The military was in good condition. Americans clearly felt better about their country. I saw a bit of this when many soldiers and civilians were kind enough to stop me in the street and offer their congratulations on America's "new military," and I had every confidence in my able successors in the Reagan and Bush administrations.

But, for me, things suddenly changed. On the sultry New York morning of June 16, 1992, I appeared on a television program about global business and economic conditions. At the end of the interview, I was told I had a call waiting. It was my attorney, Robert S. Bennett. "Walsh has just handed down a five-count indictment against you," he said. "They had promised me they would make no decision for a few days, but, as usual, they broke that promise and went ahead with the indictment this morning, despite all our discussions."

After five years of nearly fruitless probing, Lawrence Walsh, the independent counsel appointed in 1986 to investigate the so-called Iran-contra affair, had become increasingly frustrated and anxious to "catch a big fish." Eager to implicate President Reagan in some kind of wrongdoing, Walsh targeted Reagan's close associates. But his results did not produce the headlines he craved. Two of his previous indictments resulted in convictions that had been overturned on appeal. Several other defendants had staved off indictment by agreeing to plead guilty to misdemeanors—really a form of legal blackmail. That was Walsh's basic tactic: when he knew he could not obtain a conviction, he would threaten to indict unless his victim agreed to plead guilty to something—anything—in return for a promise of a light sentence. The very threat of an indictment can lead many to agree to anything regardless of whether or not they are guilty.

Walsh had tried this with me, repeatedly offering a "light sentence" if I would plead guilty to whatever was the flavor of the week. And, of course, I was "to be cooperative" as he continued to pursue President Reagan and Vice President Bush. I had thought that the facts we had presented to him—my steadfast refusal to plead guilty to something I had not done, and the fact that I had ardently and vocally opposed the very policy that was at the heart of the issue— would persuade him not to proceed against me.

The full story of this goes back a long way—to the plight of the American hostages being held in Iran in the mid-1980s, and my discussions about how to free them. Initially, everyone agreed that ransoming or bargaining for their release would only encourage Iranian fanatics to seize other Americans.

But on June 17, 1985, Robert McFarlane, then national security adviser, transmitted a draft National Security Decision Directive

(NSDD) to Secretary of State George Shultz and to me. In it, a number of well-known points were made about the strategic importance of Iran. Then the proposed NSDD discussed the desirability of opening a "dialogue" and making an effort to reestablish a good working relationship with Teheran—even to the extent of giving Iran arms. There was also apparently a belief that dealing with Iranian "moderates" might bring about the release of some of our hostages.

I felt that this was one of the more absurd proposals yet circulated, and so noted in the margin of my copy, adding that this would be similar to "asking Qaddafi over for a cozy chat." In my formal written reply, I said, "Under no circumstances should we now ease our restrictions on arms sales to Iran. Such a policy reversal would be seen as inexplicably inconsistent by those nations whom we have urged to refrain from such sales, and would likely lead to increased arms sales by them and a possible alteration of the strategic balance in favor of Iran while Khomeini is still the controlling influence." I argued that there were no "moderates" left in the Iranian government, because anyone with "moderate" tendencies had long since been killed by Khomeini and his forces. Secretary Shultz, in a memorandum of his own, also objected sharply to the entire proposal.

Since Secretary Shultz and I heard nothing more about the idea, we assumed it had died. I recall a White House meeting later that summer with the president, Shultz, McFarlane, Don Regan, and either Bill Casey or John McMahon, his deputy. The question of arms deals came up. Again, Secretary Shultz and I argued as forcefully as possible that the whole silly idea would completely violate our accepted policy of not ransoming hostages. I made the further point that nothing indicated any change in the virulently anti-Western attitudes of Iran's leadership. Moreover, supplying arms to Iran while urging our friends and allies to honor our arms boycott of the very same country was absurd. Finally, if the president were implicated in a secret deal, future administration policy could be blackmailed by anyone who knew. It seemed to me that the president again agreed with me.

Nonetheless, McFarlane apparently advised the Israelis that it was all right for them to sell some of their American-supplied weapons to the Iranians and that we would resupply the Israelis—this because we "hoped we could get some hostages out." Subsequent investigations have made it clear that, in Don Regan's words, the president was "upset at this news." McFarlane would later say that the Israelis had "taken it upon themselves to do this."

The president later wrote to the Tower Commission (which was conducting one of the first investigations into this issue) that he could recall nothing "whatsoever about whether I approved an Israeli sale in advance, or whether I approved replenishing of Israeli stocks around August of 1985. My answer, therefore, and the simple truth, is, 'I don't remember—period.'" I believe the president. He never approved any such plan in my presence, and I do not believe he ever did.

I did not know until much later (and I doubt the president did either) that this entire initiative had arisen from meetings McFarlane had been holding with the Israelis who thought Iran would *consider* freeing some of the hostages in exchange for arms.

My first hint of these American-Israeli-Iranian discussions came when I asked the meaning of some oddly phrased cable traffic. Our intelligence agencies told me they had made a mistake. They had received instructions *not to let me see* those messages.

I retorted that the National Security Agency was part of the Department of Defense; they had no authority to deny my access to these messages. They replied that their instructions had come from "the White House." "Buildings do not give orders," I said; I demanded that *all* intelligence traffic of any kind come to me, along with *any* instructions they had to deny me access.

After finding these cables, I demanded that all of us—McFarlane, Shultz, and all who had been present at the previous gatherings with the president—meet with the president again. Three meetings were held by the president in the late fall of 1985—long after I thought the entire Iran proposal had been killed. At the latest of these new meetings, it seemed apparent to me that the president had changed his mind—otherwise, why would we still be talking about it?

On November 30, McFarlane resigned. He never made clear why. Most reports said he was "frustrated" and "tired." I later learned that on that same day Lieutenant Colonel Oliver North of the National Security Council (NSC) staff proposed a new "arms-for-hostages" deal to McFarlane's successor, Admiral John Poindexter. When this proposal was considered by the president on December 7, George Shultz and I opposed it vehemently yet again. We also left that meeting convinced that a plan by McFarlane to deliver a message to the Iranians in London was canceled. But McFarlane, who had already resigned from the administration, went anyway.

When people ask me how the will of the secretaries of state and defense could be so easily subverted, I can say only that people with hourly access to the president, such as McFarlane, could phrase their agenda in the most favorable terms. In addition to this, they could report to the president all manner of "hopeful indications" and generally lead a busy president occupied with many other things (including preparations for the Geneva meeting with Gorbachev) to believe that "progress" was being made and that ultimately our hostages would be released.

At a January 7, 1986, meeting with the president, Secretary Shultz and I again argued against arms deals with Iran. But this time—for the first time—the president gave me the clear impression that he had approved the idea.

After the whole deal became public in November 1986, Admiral Poindexter told me that on January 17, 1986, the president had indeed approved the idea of getting four thousand TOWs (tube-launched, optically tracked, wire-guided missiles) to Iran.

When I was finally told that the president had approved the sale, I insisted that any weapons transferred from the Department of Defense go to the CIA under the terms of the Economy Act, which permitted transfers of government property from one department to another. I reminded everyone that direct transfer from the Defense Department to Iran would violate the Arms Export Control Act, and I said that I would refuse to allow such a transfer. I must record that I had hoped this added objection would slow down or possibly even stop the sale, but alas it did not.

In early November 1986, the story of apparently continuing secret negotiations by McFarlane with the Iranians broke in a Middle Eastern newspaper. McFarlane's Iranian "moderates" immediately and publicly denounced the mission. Amazingly, as I learned in December, certain administration officials continued to carry on discussions with Iran. As I wrote in a December 22, 1986, memo to Al Keel, the acting assistant to the president for national security affairs, I was appalled and outraged:

> When the President announced in late November or early December that all further arms shipments to Iran had ceased, and after it became apparent that the channels we were using to discuss hostage release, and other matters with the Iranians were, at the very least, ineffective, and, as is easily apparent now, totally counterproductive, I had assumed that we were finished with that entire Iranian episode and so testified to Congressional Committees during last week. I was astounded, therefore, to learn, on Friday, December 19, 1986, *after* my testimony, that United States "negotiators" were still meeting with the same Iranians....
>
> I must point out as strongly as I can that any attempt to conduct major activities in the security field with the deliberate exclusion of those who have some responsibility for security cannot succeed in anything but

adding to the troubles we already have. I would very much have appreciated an opportunity to present to the President arguments as to why we
should *not* continue dealing with these channels in Iran....

I think the President was entitled to have the advice of all of his security advisers, and I must strongly object that the continuation of this
practice of secrecy and attempts to exclude various advisers whose advice
it is apparently feared may not support the agenda of [certain administration officials], can only get us in more and more difficulty, and serves
the President very badly.

The president was characteristically selfless and exhibited great
political and personal courage when he later publicly admitted that
he had made a mistake. He agreed that it was not possible to negotiate or do business with the Iranians and that the advice he had been
given by McFarlane and others was not only wrong but dangerously
wrong. He also, very generously, went so far as to acknowledge that
I had been right in advising against any kind of dealings with Iran.

In the investigations that resulted from the November news leak, an
additional twist was discovered. As if the whole convoluted scheme
were not bad enough, subsequent investigations revealed that at some
stage, someone had hatched a plan to "overcharge" the Iranians (for
the weapons we should not have sold them at all) and turn over some
of the proceeds to the Nicaraguan contras, whose funding Congress
had sporadically denied. It seemed like a "neat idea" to Oliver North
and some other NSC staff members. They knew of the president's
strong desire that the contras be funded, and they regarded their
scheme as a way to support the freedom fighters without troubling
about congressional blocks—or about the legality of the action—and
without bothering to tell the president or anyone else about it. I certainly did not know of this until it became public in late 1986, and I
am convinced that the president did not know before that time either.
The contras should have been funded, but there is only one way to

secure legal spending by our government, and that is by vote of Congress, which had been denied.

In his indictment, the independent counsel charged me with two counts of perjury, two counts of making false statements (to congressional committees and to Walsh's investigators), and one count of obstructing Congress. Apparently of no importance to the independent counsel was the fact that the two chairmen of the Senate investigating committee (Senators Daniel Inouye and Warren Rudman), to whom I had allegedly lied, wrote to Bennett saying, "It is inconceivable to us that [Weinberger] would intentionally mislead or lie to Congress."

The independent counsel was intent on proving that I had deliberately lied about my knowledge of events and that I was aware of arms shipments to Iran at the time they occurred, which was simply not the case. As I have said, I did participate in several discussions of McFarlane's "Iran Initiative," but every time it came up, I vehemently opposed it. Until the January 7, 1986, meeting, I believed that the president was against it also and that, therefore, the plan would not ever be carried out.

I am entirely willing, as I was during the investigation, to acknowledge that my memory was not perfect, particularly in regard to dates, and that I had been mistaken in the chronology of some of the responses I made to various inquiries. But that is a long country mile from perjury, which requires both criminal intent to deceive and a deliberate giving of false information. There was not the slightest evidence, let alone proof, that either of these vital elements had occurred.

The obstruction count had to do with my diary notes and the charge that I intentionally withheld them from congressional investigators. The fact is that I provided to the committees everything that I thought, based on my own memory, was relevant. I also instructed the Pentagon legal department to give congressional committees whatever they requested. I assumed that anything in the files that was relevant—including some memoranda I had made of the meetings—had been produced and that the various investigating committees' questions referring to these memoranda had been answered. It did not occur to me that my notes, which were basically logs of calls, appointments, and personal matters—the type of notes I had kept for many years, long before these events—had any value or relevance for investigators.

After I left office in 1987, I deposited all of my papers from my years at Defense, including my notes, at the Library of Congress. Many years later, when investigators from the office of the independent counsel were questioning me, I told them this, and that they were free to look at anything they wished; I even gave them written authorization to do so, which is not a course to follow if one is trying to conceal anything. I also knew that all files of the department had, at my direction, been made available to them.

Walsh and his investigators failed to look at any of these papers in the Library of Congress for at least two years. Then he claimed I had "concealed" the papers, which were gathering dust in the world's most public depository and to which they had been given access by my specific written authorization. From this false premise, he tried to concoct an elaborate conspiracy theory, alleging that I was deliberately "concealing" evidence in order to "protect" the president. This was patently absurd. President Reagan was enormously proud of all the actions he had taken to try to release the hostages. He had no desire to be "protected." He told all who would listen of all he had done. In fact, when he began actually to consider some kind of deal with Iran, and some of the potential legal problems of such a course were pointed out to him, he said that he could answer charges of illegality, but he could not ever answer charges that he had passed up a chance to free the hostages.

The independent counsel was apparently not interested in the facts, only in what might support his own conspiracy theory, and in February 1992 he named me as a "target" of his investigation. This meant, essentially, that he was constructing a case against me—primarily, I felt, to try to force me to implicate the president.

Up until that point, former secretary of state and former attorney general Bill Rogers, the senior partner of the Washington law firm Rogers & Wells, where I was then practicing, had been informally advising me on legal matters related to the various Iran-contra investigations. Since I had nothing to hide and was on the right side of the issue, Bill Rogers met with prosecutors several times. He and I both thought I was a cooperating witness, so I was shocked, feeling that I had been misled by the government, when I received the "target letter." When I got the target letter, Bill recommended I hire a skilled criminal defense attorney. I had never had an attorney before; being one myself, and never having been personally involved in any legal matters greater than automobile insurance claims, I had no experience with finding outside legal help.

One name I remembered from an article about Washington attorneys was Robert Bennett, brother of Bill Bennett, who had been an excellent secretary of education in the Reagan administration. Bob Bennett, I knew, had a reputation of fighting for his clients rather than seeking plea bargains. Since I had not done anything to which I could plead guilty, I wanted a lawyer like Bob Bennett.

Bob was cordial and comforting over the telephone. He turned out to be a great attorney in every way, and he was well aware of the devastating effect of the charges, trumped up and false as they were. Bob reminded me of a holistic physician—he treated the whole patient, not just one particular problem. We worked well together, and he even accepted, with good grace, some of my suggestions, in a field in which I was no expert.

Bob and I both knew that we were about to embark on a long, miserable, all-consuming process. The grand jurors would have been given by the prosecutor a *general* impression of some wrongdoing, but without any argument or evidence to the contrary, because, of course, defense attorneys are not allowed to appear. The grand jury process reminded me of a story my father used to tell: A man saw an old friend on the street and said, "I haven't seen you in a long time. You were mixed up in that watch theft, weren't you?" The friend replied, "Yes. I was the man who had his watch stolen."

Bob Bennett and his partner Carl Rauh made valiant efforts to avert an indictment by informing the prosecutor at many meetings of the detailed strength of our defense. Bob also suggested that I take a lie-detector test, which I agreed to immediately. So one morning I rode out to a nondescript building in the Virginia countryside, and a retired specialist from the FBI attached all kinds of patches and wires to my arms, chest, and forehead. It was a chilling experience. The expert asked me five questions relevant to the Iran-contra matter and my notes, and then, after studying my reactions, he pronounced that I had passed with flying colors—no deception of any kind was shown. This was communicated immediately to the independent counsel's office, but it made not the slightest difference.

My good friend and one-time colleague in the Reagan administration, and at Rogers & Wells, Bill Clark, also joined in the fight. He made a special trip to Oklahoma for a meeting with Walsh, thinking that, since both of them had been judges, he might be able to persuade the independent counsel that the course he was pursuing was both absurd and terribly damaging. But after the meeting, Bill reported that Walsh was interested in only one thing: some kind of admission of guilt by me, preferably something—*anything*—that implicated President Reagan, or even Vice President Bush. If I would give that, the independent counsel's office could then arrange for no indictment and a light sentence. And, of course, I was to be "cooperative" with them as they pursued the president. This, I was told, was accompanied by a wink and a nudge. Bill pointed out to them that pleading guilty to something I had not done would be a lie—which was something I would not do—and that these "offers" by the independent counsel were improper, if not illegal, pressures.

As Paul Craig Roberts said so well in an editorial in the July 20, 1992, *Fair Comment*, this was "a good example of prosecutorial abuses employed to get witnesses not only to sing but also to compose."

Had we been dealing with any kind of reasonable prosecutor, the matter would have been dropped. But when Walsh and his team suddenly realized that the statute of limitations on one of the minor charges was to expire the next day, they rushed ahead and secured the grand jury's flaccid approval and issued their indictment on June 16.

I was scheduled to make a speech later that day in New York, but after Bob Bennett's call, my assistant, Kay Leisz, and I took the first shuttle back to Washington. The drive to LaGuardia and the hour-long flight seemed absolutely interminable. At Bennett's request, I went directly to his office and appeared at a press conference there. I made what would be my first and only public statement* until the whole ordeal was over:

> In order to avoid this indictment I was not willing to accept an offer by the Office of the Independent Counsel to plead to a misdemeanor offense of which I was not guilty, nor was I willing to give them statements which were not true about myself or others. I would not give false testimony nor would I enter a false plea. Because of this refusal, which to me is a matter of conscience, I have now been charged with multiple felonies.

The charges brought by Walsh and his staff were absolutely untrue. The major/lead count charged me with "obstructing" Congress by

---

* Bennett, quite rightly, advised that I not speak publicly about the case until after all of the legal proceedings had been concluded. It was unfortunate that the prosecutors did not follow these well-established rules.

purposely withholding my handwritten notes. In fact, these notes conclusively established my vigorous opposition to selling arms to Iran to free American hostages held in Lebanon. And had I realized they were relevant, I would have gladly provided them.

In late September 1992, U.S. District Judge Thomas F. Hogan recognized the wrongheadedness of this lead count and threw it out of court because it failed even to allege a criminal offense. Then Walsh tried to resurrect this claim by charging me with making a "false statement" to Congress about my notes in a subsequent one-count indictment. A little more than a month later, Judge Hogan dismissed this charge as well. In so doing, he criticized Walsh for seeking from the court "a license . . . to try another theory of prosecution when one theory fails."

Thus, Walsh's case had been reduced to the four subsidiary counts—all of which were based on twisted and untrue allegations cobbled together to look like "crimes." Three related to my testimony before the select congressional committees or their staff.

Two of these counts charged that I purposely lied before the select committees and their staff when I responded to certain questions about the Iran-contra mess by saying that I had "no memory" of a particular detail. My testimony was given more than two years after the events. General Colin Powell, my military assistant in 1985 and 1986, told Walsh in a sworn statement prior to my indictment that I do not have a particularly good memory for dates and details after events occur, let alone *years* afterward, especially given the vast flow of critical national security and other information through the office of the secretary of defense. I guess I should also add that in 1987, at age seventy, my memory, like that of many others, was not improving!

The actual language of these two charges demonstrates their misguided and reckless nature. Count II was based on the following question and answer that I gave in a deposition before the House Select Committee's staff on July 17, 1987:

Q: Do you recall learning at some point that the Saudis or some people connected with the Saudis provided funds for the contras?

A: No. *I don't have any memory* of any contra funding or anything connected with the Saudis *that I can remember now.*

Count IV was based on the following exchange with the counsel to the select committees during their hearing on July 31, 1987:

Q: And in addition, there are various documents which are in evidence before the Committee which refer to the Israeli desire and need for replenishment of weapons that the Israelis were sending. Did you know that replenishment was an issue?

A: No, *I have no memory of that.*

I did not lie to investigators about the state of my recollection, and Walsh had no evidence that I did.

Count III involved the claim that I had known in advance of the shipment of eighteen HAWK missiles to Iran by Israel in September 1985. This count was based on the following question and answer that I gave in an exchange with counsel to the select committees during the hearing on July 31, 1987:

Q: The Committee has also received testimony that on that weekend of November 23 and November 24, [1985] there was a shipment of 18 HAWK missiles from Israel to Iran. This [Exhibit 8] was a paper that was written immediately prior to that time. Let me just ask you: Did you have any knowledge that that transfer was to take place?

A: No, I did not.

I did not know about that shipment before the fact and was shocked when I learned about it. I had already made it clear to everyone, including President Reagan, that I vehemently opposed arms sales to Iran. Accordingly, no one was inclined to tell me about them, and the fact is that no one did. There was absolutely no evidence that I had advance knowledge of the shipment of eighteen HAWK missiles, and that is exactly how I testified.

The fifth and final count of the indictment was equally outrageous and untrue, and was part of a clever litigation strategy by Walsh and his team. Walsh charged me with lying to his assistant prosecutor about my notes in an October 1990 interview to which I voluntarily agreed. Then Walsh selected this same assistant prosecutor to be the lead trial prosecutor in order to bolster the credibility of the charge. Walsh did this even though it is unethical to use a lawyer who participated in the events on trial to seek unfair credibility advantages with a jury by having that lawyer be, in essence, an unsworn witness in the case. Fortunately, Bennett and his team crafted a compelling motion seeking to disqualify the prosecutor from the case. After the hearing on this motion, Judge Hogan in a strongly written opinion expressed grave concerns about the independent counsel's tactic. Seeing the handwriting on the wall, a few days later Walsh removed that prosecutor from the case and replaced him with another lawyer—a prominent San Francisco Democrat who had personally contributed to the Clinton-Gore campaign and whose law firm had donated over $20,000 to that campaign.

Moreover, there was no transcript of my voluntary interview in October 1990, and the FBI's description of the meeting was completely inaccurate. Furthermore, the idea that I had hidden notes from Walsh's team was preposterous. I never sought to hide them. Just before I left the Pentagon, I packed up my papers, including the little pads I used for my various jottings. I actually did this while being photographed in my office for archival purposes! Bob Bennett tracked down the photographer and obtained the photographs. This was forceful evidence of my innocence since Walsh claimed I had tried to conceal those notes. I then sent these papers to the Library of

Congress. When asked, I directed Walsh's investigators to my notes and other papers at the Library of Congress before, during, and after the October 1990 meeting mentioned in the indictment. Shortly after that meeting, I actually provided written authorization for the independent counsel to inspect and copy "such notes and documents related to the Iran-contra matter." At the Library of Congress, there was an index to my papers which specified they contained notes relating to Iran-contra. Apparently, for more than a year, Walsh's investigators were too sloppy to find the notes I authorized them to review.

So began, after the indictment, endless days of torment for me and my family. It was quite paralyzing at first. There was a tremendous desire to fight back, and the realization that you cannot; you have to go through the long, agonizing, excruciating procedure. There would be an exhaustive rehash of every sentence I had ever uttered and every action I had ever taken, which would drag on for several months even before the case reached court, and then the trial itself would probably take several more months.

Preparation for my trial was an emotionally exhausting exercise. I spent day after day either in Bennett's office or in a ratty old building on Connecticut Avenue, called a Secure Information Facility, where thousands of linear feet of the prosecutor's files, documents, and other materials were stored. There, Bob Bennett and I pored over papers and discussed many of the still-classified details of the whole unhappy saga. Bennett and I also attended numerous court hearings on motions and other matters pertaining to the handling of classified documents and things of that kind. Any time we entered or left the courthouse, we were pressed by dozens of news cameras and microphones.

The classified documents were particularly important to my case because certain secret intelligence reports about Iran actually showed I had not lied about my knowledge of events. Saul Pilchen and Ben Klubes of the Bennett/Rauh trial team spent two weeks in court explaining line-by-line the nature of the exculpatory reports to Judge

Hogan and fought Walsh's opposition to our use of them for my defense. In the end, I think the judge was inclined toward our view, but he did not rule before the pardon.

One of these hearings, on December 22, I believe, provided a bit of comic relief. As one of the technical points was being argued before Judge Hogan, a U.S. marshal handed Bennett a note. It read, "Please have Secretary Weinberger call Senator Dole immediately." With the pardon and other matters being then under discussion, we thought we should indeed make the call. Bob was granted a short recess and together we raced over to find a phone. The first bank of public phones was full and we continued our race down one of the courthouse's endless corridors. When we reached an empty phone and squeezed into the booth, I, panting hard, made the call. Bob tells me the color drained out of my face and that I stammered out, "Thank you very much, Senator, and to you, too." I hung up and Bob said, "Wha— wha—?" I said, "He wanted to wish us both a merry Christmas." We laughed all the way back to the courtroom but decided not to enlighten the court as to our secret cable.

Being inside the courtroom was extremely stressful. I could feel my heart beating rapidly and the heat of everyone staring at me, but I felt I had to remain outwardly impassive.

The whole thing was horribly debilitating. My wife, I am sure, felt much the same way, especially when she attended some of these hearings. Indeed, I knew that the overall strain on her was growing and that both my children and my grandchildren were being subjected to the inquiries and cruel gibes of friends and schoolmates.

My wife and I came down with shingles, an extremely painful disease that inflames the nerve endings. The health of our collie, my great friend, Kiltie, began to fail at this same time. Even lesser problems became difficult. Our Washington apartment flooded and the carpet had to be replaced—a normally minor project that under this stress seemed much larger.

Aside from these personal problems, prior commitments had to be honored and public appearances had to be made, mostly in connection with my work for *Forbes* magazine, which I had joined after leaving the Reagan administration. The first of these engagements was a talk at a Forbes conference in Bermuda, only a couple of days after the indictment. As part of the normal legal process, an order is issued that a defendant cannot leave the country, but Bennett was able to get this restriction lifted. When I went to the airport, however, I discovered that I had forgotten my passport, which meant a long and disconcerting delay. Eventually, I was allowed to board the plane. Making my speech there that night was particularly difficult because I was still in a state of shock and disbelief about my indictment. But the audience was very courteous—painfully so—and did an admirable job of acting as if nothing unusual were happening.

Fearing that I might be an embarrassment to the Forbes family, I offered, two or three times, to resign. I will always remember, with unbounded appreciation, the immediate and scornful dismissal of these suggestions by Steve Forbes and his three brothers, particularly Kip, with whom I work most closely. They said that they had complete faith in me and in all of the things I had done, and they expressed great admiration for my work at the Defense Department. They knew, too, how strongly I had opposed the whole Iranian initiative. Not only would they not hear of my resigning from *Forbes*, they insisted on my continuing with them, and their kindness reminded me of why I am so very glad that Malcolm Forbes Sr. urged me to join the magazine back in 1988.

I was, indeed, fortunate to have the unwavering support of many friends and colleagues, some of whom had themselves been subjected to harsh and unfair treatment before Walsh's grand jury.

A particularly disagreeable aspect of this whole affair was financial. Along with everything else, my legal bills seemed to be growing almost exponentially, amounting to several hundred thousand dollars a month, with no end in sight. It looked as if I would ultimately transfer the bulk of my estate not to my children but to my attorneys. I did not feel any resentment toward Bob Bennett. I knew it took a tremendous number of hours of legal work to go up against an independent counsel, who could draw as much money as he wanted out of the U.S. Treasury any time he wished. And I had a brilliant team of younger lawyers supporting Bob Bennett and Carl Rauh which included Saul Pilchen, Amy Sabin, Ben Klubes, Roberto Iraola, Bonnie Austin, Abby Raphael, and Stephen Vaughn.

My staggering legal bills were a source of double distress to me because, although Bennett assured me that he did not expect immediate payment, I have always made it a practice to pay every bill within a few days of receiving it. And, for years, I had not incurred any bills I could not pay for at the time.

Many people, aware of the problem, voluntarily sent contributions, and it occurred to a couple of friends, as well as Bennett's office, that it would be desirable to formalize this and establish some sort of fund to which contributions could be made. I reluctantly agreed—reluctantly because the idea of asking people for money runs counter to my self-sufficing, New England tendencies. Mike Burch, who had been assistant secretary of defense for public affairs when I was secretary, agreed to act as trustee, and three other volunteers, including Mrs. Frank Carlucci, ran the day-to-day operations of the legal defense fund. They sent out hundreds of letters of solicitation, and even more thank-you letters, to supporters all over the country, most of whom were kind, concerned citizens I had never even met.

In September 1992, the defense fund staff organized a fund-raising reception at the Mayflower Hotel in Washington. About one thousand people attended to show their support and urge contributions; a few even made speeches. Senator Alan Simpson's was one of the most memorable. In his usual blunt, straightforward style, he blasted the independent counsel and his treatment of me, using a stream of splendid expletives and jokes.

The event was a financial success, but for me personally, humiliating. It was embarrassing to be in such a position in the first place. My honesty or integrity had never been questioned before. I do not mean to give the impression that I did not appreciate everyone's most generous support—indeed I did, and always will. It was one of the most truly gratifying aspects of an otherwise very unhappy year.

Bob Bennett had requested a trial by judge, based on the belief that a judge would be much more likely to understand the issues of the case than an apathetic, perhaps even hostile, District of Columbia jury. But under law, the prosecutor must consent to a trial by judge, and, of course, he would not.

U.S. District Judge Thomas F. Hogan had been assigned to try our case, and he was the one handling the various motions both sides were putting forth. It was clear that he recognized the absurdity of the charge that I had obstructed Congress, and, as mentioned earlier, on September 29 he dismissed that count of the indictment.

But on October 30, days before the presidential election, the independent counsel returned a new indictment, which relied on many of the same factual allegations as the count that had been dismissed, just worded differently. Instead of obstructing Congress by withholding my notes, Walsh now said I had made false statements about my notes.

The timing of the reindictment was calculated to cause the maximum political damage to President Bush, which, of course, it did. The independent counsel included in the indictment, contrary to normal legal practice, some of the evidence on which he was going to rely. The piece he picked out to cite was a note that I was supposed to have written that allegedly indicated that Vice President Bush knew more about the "arms-for-hostages" plan, as it came to be called, than had previously been thought. It was scarcely a coincidence that this new indictment, with this particular citation, was issued only four days before the 1992 presidential election, in which President Bush was up for reelection. I have no doubt that this was another desperate attempt by the independent counsel to bring down as high an official as he could and support the Democratic candidate at the same time*—an effort undoubtedly tinged with revenge for my refusal to help him in this goal.

The Clinton campaign used the new indictment to maximum advantage. In fact, in its eagerness to use the indictment against President Bush, the Clinton team was a little sloppy, issuing a press release about it dated the day *before* the indictment was made public. Obviously, someone had leaked it to the Democratic campaign. This was simply more evidence of the blatant political vindictiveness of the prosecutor.

In early December, long after the election, this second indictment, consisting solely of Walsh's new lead charge, was also dismissed by the court, but the damage had been done. Indeed, inflicting that political damage was its only purpose. I believe it directly contributed to President Bush's defeat. (As did the presence in the race of Ross Perot, who, although he stood for nothing, managed to get about 19 percent of the vote. Perot's candidacy not only was devastating to President Bush, it also subjected our country to the Clinton presidency.)

That an independent counsel can have such a wide and powerful political reach—even going so far as to influence the outcome of a presidential election—underlines the fundamental error of the independent counsel law. The office of the independent counsel is a total anomaly in our system of government. An independent counsel is subject to absolutely no checks or balances. He has unlimited tenure.

---

* Walsh always made a big point of saying he was a registered Republican. This was supposed to give credibility to his baseless charges.

He has unlimited access to Treasury funds without the need to secure congressional consent. Indeed, he is not restricted by any requirements for approval—from Congress, the president, or the judicial branch—of any action he wishes to take. Theoretically, he is supposed to be under the eye of a three-judge federal court, but traditionally, this court has paid little attention to him.

Paul Craig Roberts best described the frightening power the office holds: "The office of special prosecutor is an amazing departure from American legal precedent. Unlike any other prosecutor, the special prosecutor has the power to bring the full weight and financial resources of the U.S. government to bear upon a single individual."[*] This runs counter to every tenet upon which a democracy is built.

Since its inception in 1978,[†] the independent counsel law has been renewed twice, but fortunately it was allowed to expire in June 1999.[‡] At the height of Walsh's assault on me there seemed no way to fight the power of his office, so when the idea of a presidential pardon was raised, I, after initial resistance, ultimately did not object.

Shortly after the 1992 election, several senators, particularly Bob Dole and Orrin Hatch, began calling for a presidential pardon as the best way to bring the whole sordid matter to an end and effectively put that independent counsel out of business. Some congressional Democrats also joined in this effort, as did some members of President Bush's

---

* "To Hold Prosecutorial Hounds at Bay," *Washington Times*, November 28, 1992.

† The Ethics in Government Act, which authorized the appointment of an independent counsel, was a result of the Watergate scandal. When President Nixon fired special prosecutor Archibald Cox (appointed by the attorney general) after Cox issued a subpoena for White House tapes, the public lost a great deal of trust in executive branch officials and their ability to investigate themselves. Consequently, Congress developed the idea of having an outside counsel, appointed by a special court, to investigate allegations of wrongdoing by top executive branch officials.

‡ Paradoxically, its most severe critics became the Democrats after Mr. and Mrs. Clintons' antics were subjected to investigation by an independent counsel.

administration—in particular, presidential counsel Boyden Gray and Vice President Dan Quayle. All of these people shared the recognition that the independent counsel was completely out of control.

Although I greatly appreciated this effort by so many friends, it had to be pointed out to me many times that the presidential power of clemency did not require any finding of guilt. I did not want any implication that I had done anything wrong. But equally weighty a consideration was how long the ordeal could drag on (predictions were for a three- to four-month trial) and how it would constantly be in the headlines. I agreed that a pardon would save me and my family an enormous amount of grief and strain and daily torture, and could end the whole thing once and for all, with no appeals. It would have been a nice, high-principled thing to have rejected any suggestion of a pardon, but the possibility that all of this pain could be alleviated by a single stroke of a presidential pen was the decisive factor for me.

On December 18, Bob Bennett prepared a formal request for a pardon, and on Christmas Eve morning, Boyden Gray called Bennett from Camp David to inform us that the president had granted a pardon to me and five others who had been snared in Walsh's net.* For the first time in nearly a year, I slept well and awoke happily. That Christmas was one of the best I can remember.

My family and I are eternally grateful to President Bush for sparing us the continuation of such a dreadful ordeal. I wrote him then, expressing our deep appreciation, and have done so every Christmas Eve since.

The president acted honorably in every way and had, quite properly, included in his pardon a number of others who had been subjected to the independent counsel's pressures, some for far longer than

---

* Robert McFarlane, Elliott Abrams, and CIA officials Clair George, Duane Clarridge, and Alan Fiers.

a year, and some of whom had indeed agreed to plea bargain since they did not have the financial resources to fight Walsh's overwhelming power. President Bush is a compassionate man who recognized the tremendous injustice being done by an overzealous independent counsel.

Walsh's reaction to the president's action could have been easily anticipated. He called a press conference to denounce the president furiously. He announced that President Bush himself was now a subject of his investigation. But Walsh's time was nearly out, and his frustration over failing to convict anyone else was left unrelieved.

The press was naturally clamoring for me to make appearances now. I was disinclined to continue the matter in any way, but during the closing weeks of the long ordeal, Larry King of CNN had been particularly kind and thoughtful in his remarks about the case, and so I agreed to be on his program. Besides, it afforded me a full hour to vent my feelings publicly about the injustices of Walsh's investigation—an exercise more therapeutic than I had expected, with many kind comments from Larry King's viewers.

Then there was the not-so-little matter of my remaining legal bills—a total of $2.3 million. The legal defense fund had raised about $600,000, which was a great help, but I did not want any more solicitations to be made. So, again with Bill Clark's most able assistance, we worked out with Bob Bennett an arrangement under which I would pay off the bills over the course of the next three years— almost as long as it had taken me to pay off my 1958 campaign debt after my bid for California attorney general. In fact, I mailed the check to Bennett for my last installment in 1995.

I was anxious to get back into a regular work schedule and some semblance of a normal life. After a year of these personal legal problems, it was hard for me to get even halfway interested in any further law practice, and the *Forbes* organization was kind enough to want me full-time. So I officially resigned my position at Rogers & Wells and devoted my full attention to *Forbes*. I enjoyed the work, the *Forbes* people, and the travel and writing my job entailed. The Forbes family had my eternal gratitude for their extraordinarily generous loyalty and support during that whole miserable year of 1992.

Indeed, I am most grateful to people from all around the country, even the world, who expressed their support—financially as well as with calls, letters, and prayers—to me and my family during that difficult time. No American should ever be subject to such an untrammeled prosecutorial assault. America needs to be as vigilant about its domestic rule of law and the rights of defendants as it is about its national defense—something the American people are better aware of than are some lawyers. Zealots should never be given an opportunity to abuse unlimited power, as the independent counsel did in the Iran-contra case. With the expiration of the independent counsel law—an expiration that former independent counsel Kenneth Starr fully supported—I hope this unfortunate period in American legal history is behind us.

CHAPTER 19

JOB STABILITY—AT LAST

*T*he "nightmare year" aside, the other aspects of my life since I left the Defense Department have been and continue to be quite fulfilling and enjoyable.

Left to myself, I would have finished out my term at Defense, but my wife's continued suffering with severe arthritis and osteoporosis dictated otherwise. There were many difficult and tiring demands on her as a cabinet wife, but she had stood by my side without complaint through my nearly seven-year tenure as secretary. I felt I should respect her wishes that I leave public office in 1987 after so much had been accomplished.

I expected to do some writing, so I wanted to stay near Washington and the relevant materials. Jane prefers our home in Maine, so I divide my time between there and our apartment in Washington.

The general practice at the Defense Department was for an outgoing secretary of defense to have a transition office at the Pentagon to handle transition correspondence and similar matters. At the time

I left, however, even the largest office building in the world had no extra rooms, and in any event I did not want my successor, Frank Carlucci, to feel that I was looking over his shoulder. So President Reagan generously offered me an office in the Old Executive Office Building, my old haunt from my OMB days.

I was in limbo for a few months, but frankly I rather enjoyed the break from heavy responsibilities. Still, it was hard not to react, almost automatically, like an old firehouse, to any new developments overseas. Then, in February 1988, I had a delightful, unexpected treat.

While I was attending a ceremony at the White House, the British ambassador to the United States, Sir Antony Acland, told me that Great Britain wanted to bestow on me an honorary knighthood, and he asked if I would accept. I was completely taken by surprise, but being an unabashed Anglophile, I answered with an immediate and enthusiastic yes. I assumed that Lady Thatcher had recommended me, as she had. I later learned that her foreign secretary, Sir Geoffrey Howe, also had quite a lot to do with it.

My guess that this award was in gratitude for the aid President Reagan and I had provided to England during the 1982 conflict in the Falkland Islands was confirmed by the words of Conservative member of Parliament Edward Leigh after my knighthood was announced: "Everybody knows that without private American help it wouldn't have been possible to have won the Falklands War." We did indeed help, but I do not entirely agree with Leigh's assessment; I think the decisive factor in Britain's victory was Mrs. Thatcher's firm and immediate decision to retake the islands, despite the impressive military and other advice she received that such an action could not succeed.

When, on April 2, 1982, the Argentine military dictatorship invaded the Falkland Islands, claiming that these territories—over which Britain had exercised full sovereignty for nearly 150 years— were owned by Argentina, they made a major miscalculation in assuming that Britain neither would nor could resist the junta in any effective way. As soon as Mrs. Thatcher ordered a full-scale counterinvasion, declaring that "the possibility of defeat simply does not exist," I vigorously expressed my view that it would be unthinkable for the United States to remain neutral when our oldest friend had been attacked in such a fashion. We could not condone, by silence or inaction, naked aggression anywhere, certainly not in our own hemisphere and not by a corrupt military dictatorship against one of our NATO allies. After some internal discussion, President Reagan agreed, and on April 30, he announced sanctions against Argentina and pledged that we would give the British material support.

I knew how vital speed would be for the extraordinarily difficult operation the British were about to undertake, so I had directed the Defense Department to expedite all existing requests from the United Kingdom for military equipment, and that all new British requests were to have first priority. Our material assistance was crucial, but it certainly would not have been if the British forces had not enjoyed Mrs. Thatcher's staunch leadership.

Mrs. Thatcher was a regular visitor to Washington during the Reagan years, and she was indefatigable in upholding Britain's national interests. She had a ready ear at the White House because President Reagan had known of her and admired her from reading her speeches even before she became prime minister. They spoke the same language. But that wasn't always enough to decide an issue. Once I had to tell Mrs. Thatcher that a British consortium, seeking a very large contract to supply NATO forces with mobile communications equipment, had come in with a bid more than a billion dollars higher than the bid of a French consortium, which was therefore going to win the contract. She looked steely regal and then said, "It is bad enough, Caspar, not to award the contract to us, but to give it to the Frrrrrench is quite unacceptable." I had never heard the word "French" said with five rolling r's—or with such ferocity.

I thought the Falklands War was her finest hour, when she disregarded the jeremiads of her military advisers and insisted on complete victory—a victory in which I was glad we were able to assist.

In any case, I never imagined that my actions in the conflict—to me, simply a matter of duty—would ever be recognized in such an extraordinary way as a knighthood. Still, as the old saying goes, the honors one enjoys the most are those one least expects and probably least deserves.

My wife and I flew to London the day before the ceremony and stayed at the American Embassy, which I had visited many times before as secretary of defense. Our embassy there is one of our finest homes—formerly the London residence of Barbara Hutton. It is located in a corner of Regent's Park and is a Georgian house with beautiful, large reception rooms and halls. The residence quarters are those of a supremely comfortable English country house. Our ambassador at the time, Charles Price, was a large, confident, affable, and cordial Missouri businessman—successful and at ease with British ways. His beautiful wife, Carol, was a most excellent hostess, and both were extremely popular and effective envoys.

That evening, a splendid dinner was held in my honor at 10 Downing Street; far too much praise was bestowed upon me. In attendance were about a hundred people, including the Duke of Edinburgh, the Prince of Wales and Princess Diana, various British cabinet members, and, of course, the prime minister and Denis Thatcher.

The next morning, I attended an investiture ceremony at Buckingham Palace, where the queen was presenting several awards to British subjects. The regular investiture procedure requires the honoree to kneel before the queen while she lightly taps him and dubs him "Sir Knight."

The press had been full of speculation over whether the only American to be honored and invested at this ceremony would kneel before the English sovereign. The queen most tactfully solved the problem by inviting Jane and me to a private audience with her after the formal investiture ceremony. Our small ceremony took place in her morning room, a lovely, golden room in the private quarters of the palace. Only the queen, Foreign Secretary Howe, my wife, and I were there. The queen was seated on a couch and invited us all to join her. We talked a while, and like everyone who has had that privilege, I noted mainly how extraordinarily well informed she was about everything going on in the world. She is small but has a most impressive presence, and at the same time she shows great informality and real friendliness.

At that private gathering, she had an insignia and badge of the Order of the British Empire, which she simply handed to me while we were all seated. She said, "We're very grateful to you for everything you have done for us, and we'd like you to have this."

It is a very handsome award, resting on silk—a red ribbon with the medal of the Order of the British Empire, and a separate silver star signifying the title "Knight Grand Cross," one of the highest orders of chivalry that can be bestowed on a foreigner. I learned that only fifty-five other Americans had been knighted and that only a handful were given this order.

Foreigners, of course, ordinarily do not use "Sir" before their names because the award is honorary. Also, our Constitution has some strict language about foreign titles. Nevertheless, the great honor of being given a knighthood was particularly gratifying for someone as steeped in English history as I.

When we returned home, I came down from that rather heady cloud, and my life resumed a more familiar tack.

Later in 1988, President Reagan appointed me to the National Economic Commission (NEC), a bipartisan commission established by Congress with the purported mandate to look for ways to reduce the federal budget deficit. But, much like Governor Brown's Commission on Government Reform in the late 1970s, the real purpose of the NEC, I felt, was to provide cover for tax increases.* The commission, primarily the brainchild of Senator Pat Moynihan, was supposed to say, "We can cut this, we can't cut that, but in the final analysis, we must have more revenue." Then Congress could raise taxes, saying the commission recommended it, and escape too much political opprobrium.

I accepted the appointment because the president asked me to, but from the start I argued against recommending tax hikes, which would have a contractive effect on the economy. I preferred to look for areas where the budget could be cut. I also spoke for tax *cuts* as the best way to encourage economic growth. This, of course, was totally unacceptable to the Democrats in Congress and on the commission—particularly Moynihan—who had sponsored the resolution to create the commission.

I also encountered much opposition when I defended continued substantial defense spending, but I believe strongly that the best social program is to keep people alive, safe, and healthy, which cannot be done without a commitment to effective national defense policies and adequate spending to support those policies.

After several months, the commission issued its recommendations. But—also like the Brown commission—the members were divided in their opinions, and two separate reports were submitted. I was a member of the commission majority, which believed that the deficit could be reduced by restraining federal spending—and

---

* The commission was made up of members from both the private sector (such as AFL-CIO president Lane Kirkland and Chrysler chairman Lee Iacocca) and the public sector (senators; congressmen; Don Rumsfeld, secretary of defense under President Ford; and myself).

without increasing taxes. In fact, we advocated a constitutional amendment that would require a balanced budget and limit the amount of revenue that could be raised. We also supported a line-item veto power for the president, and we believed that reform of the congressional budget process would be beneficial—particularly eliminating the duplication of separate Authorization and Appropriation Committees.

The minority report was considerably longer than ours, but it seemed quite ambiguous, and specific recommendations were difficult to discern. It basically just reiterated the problems and pointed out the difficulty of reaching a consensus about how to solve them. I think this was because the minority realized it could not persuade the majority to support a tax increase.

As nice as it had been to have a few months without any very heavy responsibilities, I needed to resume my income-tax-paying status. My longtime friend Bill Clark was a part-time senior consultant at the Washington law firm of Rogers & Wells, headed by former secretary of state William P. Rogers, an old friend who had served in President Nixon's first term. Bill recommended me to Rogers, who apparently felt I would be an asset to them, and he offered me a post with the firm. Although I had never had an overwhelming drive to be a lawyer, I accepted because I would be acting more in a consulting capacity, much as Bill Clark did. There were some interesting aspects; I advised their attorneys on banking and securities laws, worked on a case involving a World Bank grant to a new telecommunications company in the former Soviet republic of Georgia, and ran a seminar for the firm in Japan.

I was grateful to be with a reputable and successful firm, but as with every other time I had worked in a law office, I was not entirely satisfied. So I jumped at a most interesting, and surprising, opportunity that came my way in the fall of 1988.

When I was in New York for a Physical Fitness Awards Dinner,* the colorful publishing genius Malcolm Forbes, editor in chief of the venerable and much respected *Forbes* magazine, called and wanted to meet with me. I could not imagine why, but I agreed to see him just before the dinner that evening at the Waldorf-Astoria hotel.

We met in a room just off the banquet hall, and I was absolutely astounded when he asked me to become publisher of *Forbes* magazine. I was especially surprised in light of the fact that Malcolm himself had written some less-than-flattering editorials over the past years, criticizing defense spending and commenting on my stubbornness when I was at the Pentagon.†

---

* My own physique did not qualify me for an award; I was invited because when I was secretary of HEW, I had encouraged national physical fitness programs.

† There was one I remember, probably because he had paid me a nice compliment, though he then proceeded to illustrate it as a flaw:

"There are those who speculate that the mounting tempo and temper of criticism for Defense Secretary Weinberger's absolute refusal to consider removals from his overflowing budget platter might lead to his reassignment or resignation. They're whistling Dixie.

"We've contributed our critical mite, e.g., 'Cap the Butterknife,' etc. But we've never deluded ourselves that such might have much result.

"The defense secretary feels—rightly, I think—that any offer of his to reconsider or 'postpone' major projects, such as the MX missile or additional carrier groups, would be taken as a given by Capitol Hillers, and they'd promptly be in full cry for more. No one around the president enjoys his confidence more than Secretary Weinberger—and few for as long. Reagan's delighted with Cap's stubborn 'standup' to his critics.

"During this blazing Defense budget battle, people tend to overlook the fact that Cap Weinberger is one of the few genuinely and thoroughly nice guys in Washington. That's part of the problem. His convictions are genuine. He's not posturing for political power. That's more of a problem.

"If he were less nice, he wouldn't have been persuaded by all the Braid that everything they have asked for is essential. If he were more political, he would realize that Congress can't buy a deficit of a size that many of us feel would weaken America more than the proposed spending would strengthen it.

"If Cap were to recommend to the president that, considering the Whole Equation, perhaps it would be better to hold off on some of those Big Tickets, for sure Ronald Reagan would listen.

"Oh, would that Cap would."

Besides the general differences of opinion that Malcolm and I had, I was some years *older* than the retiring publisher, James Dunn. I really did not take the offer seriously at first (I was sure Malcolm was making one of his jokes). But as we talked, I realized he was quite serious, and I learned later that I was his first choice to succeed Dunn. Actually, the more I thought about it, the more attractive it sounded (Malcolm was enormously persuasive, whether talking to a potential new recruit or a potential new advertiser) because I had so enjoyed my previous minor experience in newspapers and publishing.

Apparently, Malcolm felt that I would not require much training, or "breaking in," and that a good portion of the magazine's readership would be interested in what I had to say about the world scene. Moreover, he knew that I was acquainted with a number of foreign government leaders and probably would be able to meet with them and record their views.

Also, I knew that *Forbes* had been a most respected and interesting business journal for decades. In fact, we are practically twins! *Forbes*'s first issue appeared about a week before I was born in 1917.

The Forbes family are great people, stemming from Scottish stock similar to my wife's. I had met Malcolm casually on a few previous occasions, mostly when I was invited aboard their glorious yacht, the *Highlander*, on its annual visits to Northeast Harbor, Maine.

I had known his oldest son, Malcolm Forbes Jr. (better known as Steve), when he was chairman of the Board for International Broadcasting and I was at Defense. He had come to my office a few times to talk about the great value of the Voice of America radio programs with respect to American interests abroad, essentially selling the virtues of democracy to those around the world who had not yet experienced it. I wholeheartedly agreed, and Steve did a fine job guiding the whole operation. He was as persuasive as his father.

Whatever the reason they wanted me, I accepted. Among other reasons, I thought that anyone who wanted to employ the aged should be encouraged. I then persuaded a rather reluctant Bill Rogers that I could do both Rogers & Wells assignments and the *Forbes* work.

I arrived at my second-story office in the magazine's Greenwich Village, New York, town house in September of 1988, and ever since I have thoroughly enjoyed every moment with *Forbes*.

When I am not traveling on *Forbes* trips, I typically spend about two days a week in New York, and more than that in my Washington *Forbes* office.

As I suspected, writing the column is a very satisfying part of the job. It gives me my own bully pulpit from which to inflict my biases on the large readership of *Forbes*. It is also a kind of forced discipline to keep up on world affairs. As promised, the content of my columns has never been restricted in any way (indeed, all *Forbes* columnists have free rein to express their views). The only requirements are that it fit one page and, of course, that it be done on time. The deadline comes along with terrible regularity, and I usually run too long, but with the skilled help of my executive assistant, Kay Leisz, and Merrill Vaughn, the column editor, my column always seems to make it on time and to fit into the allocated space.

Unlike traditional publishers, I did not directly solicit advertising, a task I was frankly glad not to have; I have never been comfortable with, or very good at, trying to sell things or asking people for money. But I did, as publisher (and continue to, as chairman), function as part of the "Forbes collection," whom potential advertisers might like to see and hear.

The so-called Cap-Kip Dinners began shortly after I joined the company. Every year, Christopher "Kip" Forbes (vice chairman of Forbes, Inc., and the third of four Forbes brothers)* and I host a

---

* Steve is the oldest brother. The second brother is Robert, president of *Forbes Global* and *Forbes FYI*, a leisure-oriented magazine supplement. Tim is the youngest Forbes brother and the company's chief operating officer.

series of these dinners in major cities around the country and invite business leaders, corporate CEOs, and other senior executives to attend. After dinner, I expound on world events while Kip Forbes sells, with great and understated skill, the magazine as the best place for these companies to invest their advertising dollars. In an unguarded moment, Kip once said, "People come to pick Cap's brains, and that gives me a chance to pick their pockets." One of our rivals, *BusinessWeek*, foolishly criticized Kip for his wit.

The Cap-Kip Dinners are of great benefit to me and, I hope, to the magazine. Talking with these executives gives me a wonderful window on the state of American business and its leaders' insights on issues like the economy, trade, and industry trends, all of which become potential fodder for my column.

Another feature of the Cap-Kip Dinners that I enjoy is dessert. Kip realized early on what a world-class chocoholic I am. As he confided recently to a friend, "When dessert was, say, strawberry mousse, Cap's remarks would be...fine. But serve 'death-by-chocolate,' and Cap is *on*!" I had never really noticed that chocolate affected my public speaking performance, but I do appreciate Kip's indulging my weakness.

The Forbes clan knows how to entertain in style. Besides the Cap-Kip Dinners, they also regularly host business executives on cruises in New York harbor on their lovely *Highlander*—a "capitalist tool" in every sense.* These excursions, which started about forty-five years ago, have much the same purpose as the other *Forbes* events. They provide a great "networking" opportunity and an excellent forum for the exchange of ideas. Many friendships have been formed there.

---

* "Capitalist Tool" is the magazine's motto and also was the name of the jet the company used to own. The motto came from an exasperated Khrushchev, who, after listening to Malcolm expound on the virtues of democracy, shouted angrily, "You're nothing but a capitalist tool."

Of course, it is certainly no hardship to sail on such an elegant vessel. Not long after I joined the company, Malcolm joked that "it's quite a comedown from admirals snapping to attention and the U.S. Navy as your fleet to merely the *Highlander* and a couple of speedboats, but Cap's adjusted very well."

She is indeed a beautiful ship, over 150 feet long, painted in Forbes green, and capable of sailing on oceans as well as smaller passages like the Amazon River and the Panama Canal. Much like the Forbes brothers themselves, the *Highlander* is elegant and relaxed at the same time; there is nothing ostentatious about it or them. The yacht is home to an eclectic art collection, six inviting guest staterooms, and several warm and comfortable lounges and seating areas, all of which afford expansive views of the passing shores and seas. And in addition to gracefully transporting happy guests, she carries a cigarette boat, two motorcycles, and the Forbes helicopter.

I feel most fortunate to be associated with this family and their many, many exciting ventures. My job is fun as well as stimulating— something that, I imagine, not many people are able to say. Everyone who works for the company is of the highest quality and each contributes to its success.

From the beginning, I have worked most closely with Kip Forbes, and I have treasured his friendship and his support over all these years. Kip is a man of many great skills and has a marvelous sense of humor. He is superb at his job. Just as admirable to me, he eschews strong-arm tactics in pursuit of advertising, instead promoting the magazine's virtues with genuine charm and a natural lack of pretension.

Kip is also an art historian of note, the founder and creator of the Forbes Collection of Victorian art and other splendid objects, including a dozen magnificent Fabergé Imperial eggs—a bigger collection than that of the Kremlin. He has written several books and articles about the collection.

Over the years, Kip and I have traveled not only to the Cap-Kip Dinners but literally all over the world. We normally do at least two Asian trips a year and one or two each to the Mideast, Europe, and Latin America, with stopovers in Africa and many other faraway points. We have probably racked up as many air miles as a pilot.*

One recent year, for example, my work for *Forbes* took me to the Philippines, Thailand, Portugal, Spain, Morocco, England, France, Saudi Arabia, Germany, Switzerland, Hong Kong, Taiwan, Poland, the Czech Republic, Hungary, Austria, Cyprus, Greece, Indonesia, Malaysia, and Mexico.

These trips allow me to meet the country's governmental and business leaders and observe its society firsthand. This gives me excellent material for my columns and enables me to make informal observations and judgments about that particular country's economic and political conditions and foreign policy. *Forbes* readers direct much of America's private overseas investment, and we write about the things they need to know.

There is also an advertising component to the trips. Most countries' business leaders are anxious to reach the people who own and manage America's businesses, and we are the magazine of choice for doing just that.

Essentially, as Kip says, we are "taking the Cap-Kip Show on the road." On these trips, he carries and completes huge bags full of correspondence and other paperwork covering every facet of the company's enterprises.

So, my usual travel companions are Kip Forbes and our very able advertising liaison, Christian Frost, a young man who, among other

---

* Typically, I am on an airplane three or four days a week. When I am in this country, two of those days are generally spent commuting from Washington or New York up to Maine and back. With only small commuter planes serving the area, that travel can be a bit frustrating, particularly in winter.

things, keeps everyone on schedule and organized. He is a skilled bicycle racer and, therefore, is quite resourceful and thinks well under pressure. I remember one occasion in Hong Kong when, after a luncheon with some of Hong Kong's business leaders, I was anxious to get back to the hotel for our next engagement. As it happened, the traffic leading to the tunnel we had to cross was extremely heavy and slow-moving. So we got out of the car, and Christian, who knew how to deal with traffic, even in Hong Kong, the most congested city in the world (next to Bangkok), took me on the subway and the Star Ferry, getting me to the hotel in ample time for the meeting.

These trips can often be quite exhausting. In a typical day's schedule, we arrive in the country after an overnight flight at, say, 6:30 A.M.; our first appointment is around 9 or 10 A.M.; there will be six or seven other appointments throughout the day, including lunches, dinners, and speeches; and we are lucky if we are through by 11 P.M. I have one major advantage, however: I do not seem to get jet lag, a trait that Kip calls "thoroughly obnoxious."

As tiring as the schedules might be, however, I do enjoy meeting new people (and seeing old friends) and learning how business is done, and public policy made, in other parts of the world. As Kip correctly concluded, if they were not scheduling all of this, I would probably be wanting to do it anyway. I do thrive on activity. Indeed, I am almost as busy as when I was secretary. The main difference is that the consequences of my mistakes are not as great now as then.

In early 1993, both *Forbes* and Rogers & Wells expressed interest in having me take on a greater role—in other words, choosing one or the other and no longer dividing my time between the two. I had become increasingly less interested in the law firm as Bill Rogers became less active. Bill Clark had already left. Accordingly, my decision took about ten seconds. *Forbes* was and is the right place for me.

In May 1993, the Forbes family made me chairman of the company, Forbes, Inc. My responsibilities did not change much; it is mostly an honorary title, and I am only the second person to fill the position. Malcolm Forbes had been the first, and it had been vacant since his death in 1990. So I feel honored indeed that his sons consider me a worthy successor.

I also feel very fortunate that they want to keep me on. As Kip frequently points out, I have now worked longer at *Forbes* than at any other job I have ever had. Never before have I appreciated the meaning of job stability!

Still, I am afraid that that has not prevented me from taking on new projects—even though I never go looking for any.

Several years ago, I met a man—on a plane, I believe—who recommended me to Thomas Clynes, a Florida television producer who was developing a new business talk show. Mr. Clynes soon proposed that I be the host of a new series called *World Business Review*.

The program would be aimed at business leaders, and the topics of discussion were to be heavily weighted toward the effects and changes that would be felt as new, ever changing technologies were applied to, and used by, business. As described in the show's promotional magazine, "Issues discussed ranged from deregulation of the utilities industry to Y2K solutions, from supply chain integration to banking and investment strategies, all in anticipation of the new millennium, and the exponential technological growth that it promises...." Many of the programs would be devoted to electronic commerce, including detailed and expert discussions of the Internet and the many new uses of e-commerce.

Technology is an area in which I have little knowledge or expertise,* but it sounded interesting and was clearly part of the immediate future. And I would have some help: the basic script would be written

---

* When my family gave me a laptop computer for Christmas a couple of years ago, my grandson had to teach me how to use it.

for me by staff and there would be full-scale television production and marketing specialists. On many programs, a technology or industry expert would serve as my cohost. After a brief introduction by me, a taped field report would give some background on the topic of that segment, and then we would guide an informal discussion of it with a panel of in-studio guests, whose companies were directly involved in either developing or using the technology under discussion.

I am always amazed at how many people it now takes to produce a television show, especially when I think back to my days of moderating *Profile: Bay Area*, where we had only three: the producer/director in the control room, one cameraman, and me. I actually preferred it that way, but there is no stopping the march of "progress."

I thought hosting *World Business Review* would be a perfect way for me to keep abreast of the phenomenal and rapid advances in modern technology (and might even provide good material for my *Forbes* columns), so I talked with the Forbes family about it. They seemed amused more than anything else and interposed no objections, so I accepted the job and began in the spring of 1996.

Since I had no spare time to speak of, the minimal time commitment required for *World Business Review* was ideal. I did three or four days of taping in Washington every other month, but what it lacked in frequency, it made up for in intensity and duration. The taping days were very long; we might tape as many as twenty-five or thirty 15-minute segments a day, starting at 7 A.M. and finishing after 8 P.M. (On the air, one show is half an hour long.)

World Business Review airs on cable and public television channels, reaching about fifty million households. It is also now shown in Europe, Asia, and the Middle East, which is only natural in today's global economy. I have even seen it occasionally on transcontinental or overseas flights; usually I don't even notice until fellow passengers ask if it is I on the screen.

I greatly enjoyed doing the program and meeting and working with the fine crew Tom Clynes assembled, and I learned a great deal. But my family felt that it was too tiring, so after many lengthy discussions I "compromised" and finally retired from the show in early January 2000, after nearly four years on the program. Interestingly, I was replaced by my Reagan administration colleague Al Haig, who has been doing a fine job. The show goes on.

Throughout my life, I seem to have alternated fairly consistently between public service and my more journalistic interests. In the mid-1990s, I had the opportunity to combine the two in a way that went beyond the magazine and newspaper editorials I had written over the years.

In 1995 I was approached by Peter Schweizer, a scholar at Stanford University's Hoover Institution on War, Revolution, and Peace, about collaborating on a book. He had recently written *Victory*, a compelling look at how President Reagan's very deliberate strategies brought an end to the Cold War. Indeed, Peter was the first responsible journalist/historian to assign due credit to President Reagan for winning that war. Peter was concerned—as was I—about the Clinton administration's virtual abdication of foreign policy leadership and its reckless reductions in our military capabilities. Peter and I felt that this needed to be exposed and reversed, and we decided that the most effective way was to write a novel about some of the problems our country might face if we continued on that course.

All of the scenarios we used were hypothetical but certainly not outside the realm of possibility: a North Korean invasion of South Korea, accompanied by a Chinese attack on Taiwan; aggression by Russia or Iraq; and terrorism. Some may argue that these events are quite improbable, but then, Pearl Harbor was improbable, too.

Peter carried by far the major burden of writing, and he skillfully interwove events, resulting in a fast-paced, taut novel, complete with unstable despots, geographical obstacles, time pressures, political intrigue, and friendly governments that turned into foes. Actually, what he described is similar to military war-gaming, in which all of these factors must be taken into consideration, in addition to military capabilities and intelligence reports. Although we, of course, did not use classified data or operational contingency plans, we did use current available assessments and estimates of our own and foreign military resources to make it as realistic as possible. Peter and I worked together very well, and my admiration for him and his work grew as time went on.

Our hope in writing *The Next War*, published by Regnery in the fall of 1996, was to try to persuade the people in the Clinton administration of the dangerous error of their ways. We hoped, too, to instruct future leaders in the importance of preparedness and peace through strength and to let the people know how vulnerable we had become since the end of the Cold War. Whether those lessons have been learned remains to be seen.

Those who know anything about me know that I believe that lasting peace can be achieved only by American power and the will to use that power. Rebuilding America's military—in both armed strength and essential morale—was the overriding goal for which I strove as secretary of defense. I tried to convey all of that in my 1990 memoir, *Fighting for Peace: Seven Critical Years in the Pentagon*. But everyone was anxious to speed that book to press as soon as possible after I left the Pentagon, and it did not have the impact I had hoped it would have.

A number of people have kindly suggested that because I was present at many interesting and crucial points in recent American history, I might have a unique perspective that I ought to share in a book of broader scope. So, despite the feeling that it is rather presumptuous to write an autobiography, I undertook to write this book, with more time and care and a broader purview. I hope I have conveyed a sense of what America was like during most of the last century and of some of the challenges we have faced and still confront.

For me, writing this autobiography has been a very fulfilling process, giving me reason to revisit memories and scenes and events I had not thought of in years. And it has reminded me of how fortunate I am to have had a long lifetime of interesting, varied, and satisfying experiences. I hope readers have enjoyed the journey as much as I have.

ACKNOWLEDGMENTS

ny list of people who have helped in the preparation of this book must certainly start with my wife and children, who have tolerated for so long and endured beyond measure the life of a husband and father whose many activities, vast travel, and frequent career changes probably failed to supply the stability most families need.

Arlin and Cap Jr. and their children have borne it all nobly and carved out their own careers with much promise, and of course much more to come. They have brought me great happiness and much satisfaction. I am deeply grateful to them.

And then there are so many others who have helped so much not only with the book but also with so many of the events that make up the story:

Thanks to all of the Forbes family, whose great support is chronicled in the story.

Bill and Joan Clark, Will and Julia Taft, Gordon and Bobbi Fornell, the many friends and colleagues from government days, Rich

Armitage, Colin Powell, Don Rumsfeld, Paul Wolfowitz, and Paul O'Neill are among the many I worked with who are serving again in government.

Kay Leisz has continued to overlook the eccentricities and other heavy requirements of serving as my executive assistant with the same skills noted in *Fighting for Peace,* and she manages my time and schedules and all the other things necessary to make it all possible with great efficiency and extraordinary talent.

And my colleague Gretchen Roberts has my great gratitude for all the years it took to produce this autobiography. She did much of the heavy lifting (sometimes literally) involved in searching the thousands of files and documents at the Library of Congress, the Hoover Institution, and wherever I left pieces of paper. Gretchen also traveled thousands of miles to interview people whose lives and mine intersected over the years.

Friends and teachers from my schooldays in San Francisco, college and law school, the army, state and federal government, and many other points along the road talked freely about their memories.

Thanks goes also to the many people who agreed to be interviewed and to those at the Library of Congress (David Wigdor and John Haynes, and the Manuscript Reading Room staff) and the presidential libraries, as well as the archivists at Harvard; Sacramento; Idaho Springs, Colorado (my father's boyhood home); and Grand Island, Nebraska (where my mother taught violin).

People like Bob Bennett and Carl Rauh have, with their highly skilled teams, represented me and also helped with the preparation of the book. All the kind friends who were good enough to comment on my manuscript, particularly the Buckleys, father and son, whose own books, and the pleasure of their company, have furnished me and countless others with the greatest of pleasure for so many years.

One of the most accomplished and gifted novelists and writers of our time, Jim Webb, deserves a special word. He gave unstintingly of his talents to help and encourage me, beginning in the Pentagon, and fortunately still continuing.

And, of course, there were and are many, many more—and some who may prefer not to be mentioned specifically but who know who they are and who know how deeply grateful I am to them, too.

As always, all that fine help does not involve or include responsibility for any errors. That is mine and mine alone.

INDEX